ENVIRONMENTAL AND FACILITIES PLANNING IN HOTEL INDUSTRY

D.K. Singh

NAMAN PUBLISHER & DISTRIBUTORS

NEW DELHI

Published by
Sangeeta Jain for Naman Publisher & Distributors
7360-B, Prem Nagar,
Gali No.1, Shakti Nagar,
Delhi-110007
PH: 23823642, MOB.: 09013478302
E-mail: rajivjain72@ymail.com

First Published – 2011

ISBN–978-81–920935–1-2

Published in an association with **HLDC**, Agra.

SOLE DISTRIBUTOR
JINDAL BOOK SERVICES
LG-4A, Ganpati Bhawan,
4675-B/21, Ansari Road,
Darya Ganj, Delhi - 110002

Jacket Designed by :
S.M. Graphics

Printed by:
Sachin Printers, Delhi, India

Preface

Environmental studies is the academic field which systematically studies human interaction with the environment. It is a broad interdisciplinary field of study that includes the natural environment, built environment, and the sets of relationships between them. While distinct from ecology and environmental science, the discipline encompasses study in the basic principles of those two fields of learning as well as the associated subjects, such as: policy, politics, law, economics, sociology and other social aspects, planning, pollution control, natural resources, and the interactions of human beings and nature.

The key to effective facility planning is to align the process and plan with your district's strategic plan. In a recent symposium on facility planning held by the U.S. Department of Education, experts and practitioners agreed on the need for careful and holistic planning before making major infrastructure investments. The group concurred that the plan should be: Flexible and open-ended enough to allow for growth, Attentive to the needs of all students and teachers, Affordable enough to start implementing in the near term. A key issue in facility planning is how to plan so that future obsolescence is minimized and delayed as long as possible.

Technology management structures the orderly, cost-effective, and educationally valid use of technology in the educational setting. Technology management responds to the instructional programme by selecting and using technology that will successfully supplement classroom and administrative activities, thus enhancing the educational process. As always, well-defined educational programme goals must come first. Technology supplements those goals efficiently and cost effectively.

The book contains chapters on various aspects, i.e. Effective Facility Planning, Indoor Air Quality, Hotel Interior Design, Designing of Food Service Facilities, Hotel Environmental Management, Waste Reduction in Hotels, Hotel Housekeeping and Sanitation, Eco-friendly Hospitality Business which are useful for those interested n this field. We hope this text book meets its intended purpose as a practical resource, and serve as a vehicle for promoting the professionalism of this important segment of the Hospitality Industry.

D.K. SINGH

HERITAGE

LEARNING & DEVELOPMENT CENTER

Heritage Learning and Development Centre (HLDC) is an extended arm of Heritage Institute of Hotel & Tourism (HIHT). Heritage Institute of Hotel & Tourism is an Institute of excellence of the upcoming chain of Management Institutes, founded by D. K. Singh, President. At HIHT, our endeavour is to take education to the higher domains of never ending success. Heritage Institute of Hotel & Tourism provides the best possible infrastructure for pursuing best quality Hotel Management Education. HIHT has three campuses Agra, Shimla and Goa and proposed campuses at Kolkata, Pune, and Singapore.

In the modern era, Hospitality Industry is a reality, fighting for extremely challenging phase and getting into a stability mode. There are SMILES everywhere and this is relatively controlled and guarded, a sign of maturing and learning of Hospitality, which is cyclic in nature. The Hospitality Industry reflects a bright future. Earlier days, hospitality was synonymous with only hotel industry, but today this industry holds its important place with tourism. Hospitality academic in India is still in its nascent stage when compared to the west.

HLDC has been developed through the inputs from the industry and experts from the academics. This panel of experts have gone through the book and made suggestions which were incorporated. Every attempt has been made to thoroughly cover the day to day problems faced in the profession. In this field, as in most any other, it is prudent to remember the old adage, actions speak louder than words. The information given in this book makes the students fit for the industry. It provides about technical skills, personality and soft skills and ability to think and make decision.

This book is designed and presented in an easy to read and easy to understand format. It will be beneficial to both aspiring professionals and those already in the industry.

We hope this text book meets its intended purpose as a practical resource, and serve as a vehicle for promoting the professionalism of this important segment of the Hospitality Industry.

Contents

1

Effective Facility Planning

The key to effective facility planning is to align the process and plan with your district's strategic plan. In a recent symposium on facility planning held by the U.S. Department of Education, experts and practitioners agreed on the need for careful and holistic planning before making major infrastructure investments. The group concurred that the plan should be:

— Flexible and open-ended enough to allow for growth,

— Attentive to the needs of all students and teachers,

— Affordable enough to start implementing in the near term.

They emphasized that versatility is an important feature in system design and that a plan that calls for multipurpose equipment is more likely to keep up with rapid changes in technology and applications than single-purpose purchases. Experts also suggested designing systems with the classroom, rather than a technology lab, as the basic unit. This has been shown to lead to better and more frequent use of the technologies, as well as more effective incorporation of the tools into the curriculum.

Finally, the group stressed that in addition to channels and hardware, technology design must consider another, less publicised kind of infrastructure - the web of "people that must craft the service that exists on the channels," said Chris Dede. "That infrastructure is getting little funding." According to the facility planning team of Noblesville Schools in Nobelsville, IN, it is important to know the following bfore you begin:

— How do you want people to function?

— How do you want students to interact with the technology?

— Computer labs - yes or no?

— How do you want teachers to interact with the technology?

— Should there be a computer on every teacher's desk?

— Should there be a telephone on every teacher's desk?

— Should there be an integrated voice mail system?

— Will teachers have the ability to project their computer's display onto a classroom screen?

— Video Network - Yes or No?

— Where is access needed?

— How will centralised storage and access to media sources be addressed?

Successful projects had a strategy for dealing with the challenge of rapid technological change. First, it is important to monitor technological change and assess what is critical for the project's service versus what is hyperbole or "nice to have". Second, caution is advised by many TIIAP project directors about the most advanced "leading edge" technologies, sometimes dubbed "bleeding edge" technologies. Many of the TIIAP projects have adopted technology that is slightly behind the most advanced in order to take advantage of lower costs, and the stability that is often associated with technology that has a track record. Third, it is recommended that a group try to assess the anticipated life cycle for a piece of equipment of software and ask if it is long enough to meet the project's needs.

One determining factor in deciding which level of technology may be appropriate was to ask a number of questions:

— What are the technical skills and resources of the organisations?

— Can the organisation manage the technology and repairs, or will they have to rely on a vendor?

Practical lessons learned:

— Seek out competent technical people who are able to speak in plain English to those who may lack technical expertise.

— Engineers at local telecommunications companies can be very helpful in teaching project groups the "tricks of the trade."

— Many state and local government agencies have significant database expertise and can be an important source of help.

— Watch out for so-called "technophiles" within your organisation or end-user organisations. They often want to simply play with expensive technological "toys" and cannot necessarily be counted upon the make wise recommendations.

— Be careful in dealing with beta products (that is, products that are still in a testing stage), or products that are not supported by a vendor.

— Leasing equipment may be an appropriate choice under some conditions, and can help an organisation from begin locked into an equipment purchase that might soon become obsolete.

— Although donated equipment can be very welcome, there may be a downside in terms of repairs.

— If possible, try to standardise terminal equipment within your organisation. Having to install new software or a new service on twenty-five personal computers, each from different equipment manufacturers and with a different configuration, can be frustrating, costly, and time-consuming.

— For many groups, it makes sense to out-source some technology-related work. This should be done locally.

Future-Proofing

A key issue in facility planning is how to plan so that future obsolescence is minimized and delayed as long as possible. Here is some advice from education practitioners:

> "Technology cannot simply be an add-on to existing educational facilities. Careful evaluation and planning are a must. Coupled with examination of effective learning strategies via technology, out educational programmes/facilities can move easily into the 21st century."

> "Planning for the technology of today without restricting our ability to respond to the potential of technology of the future is the real challenge!"

> "An area of frustration has been the great need for flexibility in facilities to provide for the changing wiring and cabling needs necessary to handle connections for networking equipment. A great deal of time is spend wiring and re-wiring when new equipment is added or changed and when changes are made to accommodate personnel changes. Quite often there is not provision of where to put the wiring. This can lead to an environment that is unsafe and unsightly".

> "Even in pre-wired situations, it is difficult to plan what wiring needs would come in the future. It might be a good idea to plan "channels" at the base of walls that would open easily to string new types of cabling when needed. Old obsolete wiring could also be removed easily or re-used for other purposes. The "channels" would have to be designed to fit well within the decor and function of the building. It should be possible to open the channel at any location to tap into the wiring system. This could accommodate wiring for phones, computer networks, cable TV, and any other technology that might require cabling. Connections should all be modular so installation could be done easily."

Retrofitting

"In communities across the country, overcrowding, or outdated facilities affect the quality of education available to all student. Many hotels need major repairs due to significant plumbing, heating, or lighting problems. Inadequate electrical wiring and telephone lines prevent hotel districts from using state-of-the-art educational technology."

FACILITY PLANNING SEQUENCE

Technology management structures the orderly, cost-effective, and educationally valid use of technology in the educational setting. Technology management responds to the instructional programme by selecting and using technology that will successfully supplement classroom and administrative activities, thus enhancing the educational process. As always, well-defined educational programme goals must come first. Technology supplements those goals efficiently and cost effectively.

If technology leads, the results can be a piecemeal and disjointed collection of gadgetry. It may look good in the local paper, but may not allow effective educational progress into the 21st century. Technology management examines classroom needs. It must also strategically examine technology in specialty areas such as the media center, administration/guidance, the arts, custodial equipment, energy management, and even building construction systems such as roofs.

Successful technology management ensures that each step toward technology use (as small as it may be) supports and educationally appropriate and definable goal. Only when educational goals are well defined and technology is selected to support those goals can a successful learning environment be planned and designed. If we believe that "form follows function" then the form of the learning environment must respond to the instructional programme and the technology that supports it. An outline of the planning process, including technology management and facility design.

Goals: Create well-defined goals statements for the entire hotel as well as each part, including instructional programmes, administrative functions, and support services.

Objectives: Define clearly and in measurable terms the outcomes to be accomplished by each part of the educational programme.

Technology Management: Evaluate which technology types can best meet the district's goals and objectives. Define precisely the type and extent of technology to be used. Look at the "big picture." Cluster common technology types where appropriate to improve efficiency and save money. Consider testing your proposed technology in an existing classroom or administration area before turning it over to the design team. Work out the "bugs" in advance. Visit existing applications in education or industry, and judge their successes carefully. Make sure it really works! Time well spent in the beginning can save money and improve design communications.

Technology Schematic Plan: Develop a specific schematic diagram that illustrates all networking requirement - within the individual classroom, between classrooms, between departments, between buildings, and with distant sources.

Define Facility Needs: Define the learning environments based on the instructional programme goals, activities, and technology applications. This is the role of educational specifications.

Evaluate Existing Buildings: Thoroughly evaluate existing buildings to determine their adequacy for accomplishing the district's educational goals and particularly the goals for technology. Understand clearly the conditions of each construction system and their future life-cycle costs for continued use.

Develop Facility Master Plans: Develop district-wide and building-level master plans that consider future enrollments, programmes, new construction/remodeling, budget, and schedule.

Project Design: Select your planning and design team carefully. Participate in the process.

Project Construction: Project construction must be monitored carefully.

Post-Occupancy Evaluations: After the building id built, test it. SIf imeets the programme and technology objectives. Document strengths and weaknesses so improvements can be made in future projects.

Personnel Facility Planning

Facility planning personnel today are getting cross-training in curriculum, instructional technology, architecture, engineering, and facility project management. Similarly, curriculum representatives to the planning process are learning more about instructional technology that applies to their subject areas. Together, they can plan how technology can help educators meet curriculum goals.

Facility planners must be able to give clear management and design direction to an increasingly sophisticated cadre of design professionals, particularly in the areas of engineering, information systems design, and energy management. They must also provide curriculum leadership for technology in many cases.

Unfortunately, many districts are too small to employ facilities management personnel on staff. As an alternative, programme management consulting firms are growing in popularity. This approach can save a district from frequent hiring and firing, since many construction programmes last only three t0 five years.

If your district decides to hire a programme management firm, ensure that a qualified educational facility planner is included on the firm's team or can be hired independently. As discussed earlier, this person should be experienced in educational curriculum, new instructional technology, and the facility management process.

If an architectural firm is selected to fulfil the programme management responsibility, likewise ensure that it has capable educational staff with appropriate continuing education course work in educational facilities planning and curriculum.

Staff Involvement

Staff involvement should not cease with the completion of educational specifications. Rather, the preparations of educational specifications should be just the first step of staff involvement in the planning and design process. With a well-developed educational specifications document as a guide, district staff and administration and community representatives can be meaningful involved in the architectural design review. This involvement should occur throughout the design process.

PRELIMINARY PLANNING

Scope refers to the size and complexity of a foodservice facility design project. The scope of the project influences the design approach taken by the owner or manager. If the project involves only the layout of a new hot-food production area for an existing restaurant, the approach used and the planning process will be fairly simple. If the project entails the construction of a new restaurant or the complete renovation of an existing facility, the planning process becomes more difficult. And if the project includes the construction of a new facility that is to serve as the prototype for a chain or franchise, the planning process is even more complex.

Scope can be divided into four levels of complexity, each of which requires the involvement of different individuals and different amounts of planning time. Determining the scope of the project is an important first step before the planning begins.

Projects of level I scope involve no more than the selection of a major piece of equipment or the replacement of a small area of a foodservice facility. Examples of level I projects include:

— Replacement of a dish machine and dish tables in a school cafeteria
— Replacement of the display refrigerator and service counter in a delicatessen
— Purchase and installation of an outdoor walk-in freezer in a nursing home
— Replacement of the range section in a country club

Projects of level I scope typically can be carried out under the leadership of the owner or manager, assuming that he or she is familiar with foodservice equipment and has a good grasp of the workings of the food facility. If the owner does not have a working knowledge of equipment, a food facilities design consultant may be needed. The owner also will require the assistance of the kitchen equipment dealer and/or manufacturer's representatives in selecting and installing the equipment. Figure 1 compares the professionals involved in projects with different levels of size and complexity.

	Level			
	I	*II*	*III*	*IV*
Owner	✓	✓	✓	✓
Foodservice Design Consultant	✓	✓	✓	✓
Architect		✓	✓	✓
Engineer	✓	✓	✓	✓
Interior Designer		✓	✓	✓
General Contractor		✓	✓	✓
Subcontractor		✓	✓	✓
Equipment Dealer	✓	✓	✓	✓
Manufacturer's Representative	✓			
Banker			✓	✓
Lawyer			✓	✓

Accountant	✓	✓
Realtor	✓	✓

Figure 1. Professionals involved in projects of different levels of scope.

Level I scope projects usually can be completed in a period of six to twelve weeks. Figure 1-2 compares the time requirements of typical projects at each of the four levels of scope.

Level II Scope

Level II scope projects involve the renovation of a significant portion of an existing foodservice facility. Examples of level II scope projects include:

— Renovation of the entire service area in a university foodservice facility

— Replacement of all of the walk-in coolers and freezers in a country club

— Replacement and relocation of the warewashing system in a hospital

— Addition of banquet rooms and serving kitchens in a hotel

The professionals likely to be involved in level II scope projects include the owner, an architect, mechanical and electrical engineers, a foodservice facility design consultant, and a kitchen equipment contractor. A full complement of professionals is necessary at level II because such projects are complex and require expertise in construction, engineering, and foodservice equipment layout and design.

Level II scope projects require a much longer time to complete than do level I projects. Figure 1-2 shows a typical time line for a level II renovation project.

Level III Scope

Level III scope projects involve the complete renovation of an existing foodservice facility or the design and construction of a new foodservice facility. Examples of level III scope projects include:

— Renovation of the dietary department of a hospital

— Construction of a new theme restaurant

— Renovation of the kitchen, service, and dining areas in a country club

— The development of foodservices for a new hotel.

Task	Level I	Level II	Level III	Level IV
Planning	1 week	4 weeks	6 weeks	3 months
Equipment Selection	1 week	2 weeks	1 month	2 months
Design and Engineering	1 week	4 weeks	2 months	4 months
Preparing Bid Documents	2 days	4 weeks	2 months	2 months
Equipment Delivery	4–6 weeks	2–3 months	4–6 months	4–6 months
Installation	3–5 days	2–6 weeks	1–3 months	1–3 months

Figure 2. Time lines for projects of different levels of scope.

The planning process for the renovation of a foodservice facility often is even more complex than designing a new facility because of the difficulty of dealing with existing walls, structural members, utilities, and space, and the demolition of parts of the existing structure. Moreover, in renovation projects decisions must be made about which pieces of existing equipment should or could be used in the newly renovated facility.

The professionals likely to be involved in level III scope projects include the owner, an architect, mechanical and electrical engineers, a foodservice facility design consultant, an interior designer, a general contractor, and a kitchen equipment contractor. Level III scope projects may take from one to three years from design to completion. Figure 1-2 shows a typical time line for a level III renovation project.

Level IV Scope

Level IV scope projects involve the development of a chain or franchise prototype. Chain or prototype foodservice facilities require intense planning and design efforts because they will be constructed in multiple locations. Inefficiencies in design or inadequacies in equipment could be repeated hundreds of times, and thus will be exceptionally expensive to correct. Such projects, in addition to the requirements of level III scope projects, involve a corporate strategy, a well-researched marketing plan, complex financial planning, and a strong management team. The food facility design at level IV must fit the needs of the menu, market, strategy, and financial package that is being developed by the corporation.

Professionals likely to be involved in level IV projects include investors and/or owners of the corporation, marketing consultants, financial planners, bankers, and corporate staff specialists as well as the design team, consisting of an architect, engineers, a foodservice design consultant, an interior designer, and contractors.

The time required for a level IV scope project is longer than for a level III project in the design phases but may be shorter in the construction phases. Figure 1-shows the typical amount of time required for level IV scope projects. Once the scope has been determined, the owner can move forward with the project. In level I and level II scope projects, moving forward means going directly to the design process. However, when the scope of the project involves the renovation of an existing facility or the development and construction of a new foodservice facility, the next step in the process is concept development.

Define Concept Development

The concept of a foodservice operation is the overall plan for how it will meet the needs and expectations of its intended market. A foodservice operation's concept is expressed in many ways, including its menu, decor, form of service, pricing, and location. Concept development means developing a plan for the success of the operation in its market in advance of actually designing —let alone building—the facility.

It is not unusual for a person to consider a new restaurant or, in fact, to open a new restaurant without knowing what type of food facility will have the best chance of succeeding. The potential entrepreneur may have some investment money, a location or a theme in mind, and a great amount of enthusiasm for the food business, but has not really thought through the total concept of the operation. Unfortunately, enthusiasm and great food products are only half of the success equation. The other half of the equation is the market.

Concept development precedes the actual design of a foodservice facility because the foodservice design team must know what the menu, demand, hours of operation, and mode of service will be.

The client who most frequently comes to the food facilities design consultant for help with concept development is the individual restaurant owner. The restaurant owner typically organises a corporation comprised of a small number of local businesspeople and then begins to develop a concept that will eventually become a freestanding restaurant. The success or failure of the venture often depends on how well the concept was planned and how well the plan was followed. Numerous concepts are possible for single-unit restaurants. Commonly found concepts often are described in terms of the following general categories:

— *Fine-dining restaurants.* Fine-dining restaurants are distinguished by fine cuisine prepared by celebrity chefs, attentive service, stylish decor, and high prices.

— *Theme restaurants.* Theme restaurants offer a dining experience that evokes special times, places, or events, such as English pubs, restaurants owned by sports celebrities, and re-creations of diners from the 1950s.

— *Casual dinner houses.* Casual dinner houses emphasize a comfortable and contemporary decor, as well as high value. Well-known casual dinner houses are not single-unit restaurants, but chains such as Bennigan's, T.G.I. Friday's, and Max & Erma's.

— *Ethnic restaurants.* Ethnic restaurants are closely tied to the cultures or foodways from which they originated. They include Mexican, Italian, French, German, Thai, and Indian restaurants, to name but a few.. Family restaurants. Family restaurants specialise in relatively inexpensive fare and are kid-friendly.

— *Quick-service restaurants.* Quick-service restaurants specialise in convenience and fast service and include fast-food operations as well as delis, bagel shops, and sandwich shops.

Each of these categories of foodservice concept involves differences in menu, decor, mode of service, and price. However, not all of these factors are equally important within a given concept. Price is a critical factor in the success of quick-service, family, and casual dinner restaurants, where customers are value-conscious. However, price may not be as important in finedining restaurants, where customers expect to pay top dollar. Similarly, location is crucial for quick-service restaurants because their clientele depend upon convenient access. But for some fine-dining and theme restaurants, location is not critical. Concept development for a single-unit restaurant is thus a complex process.

When Dave Thomas, the late chairman of the board of Wendy's, traveled around the country with Colonel Sanders in the mid-1950s trying to promote a chicken franchise, he learned many of the dos and don'ts of food franchise marketing. Thomas certainly picked up good ideas about concept development for chain restaurants and franchises, as the success of Kentucky Fried Chicken (known as "KFC") and then Wendy's demonstrates. The basic objectives he developed, which led to the formation of Wendy's, were the following:

— Produce a "Cadillac" hamburger with a large number of available condiments.

— Limit the menu to the smallest number of items possible, as most restaurants can prepare only a few food items extremely well.

— Create an image different from major competitors. In the case of Wendy's, distinctive features included an old-fashioned, nostalgic theme, carpet on the floor, marketing directed at adults, and a larger hamburger than the competition's.

Concept development for Wendy's was more comprehensive than that for a single-unit restaurant. The franchise strategy was carefully thought out to create a balance between company-owned stores and franchised stores. In 1970, only two stores were open, both of them owned and operated by the company. By 1975, 83 company-owned stores and 169 franchised stores were in operation. A ratio of 30 to 40 percent company-owned stores to 60 to 70 percent franchised stores permitted a balance of control and greater financial return. The strategy entailed rapid expansion of the franchise and heavy promotion of the Wendy's name through national advertising. Wendy's now has over 5,400 stores worldwide.

Multiunit casual dinner houses and theme restaurants, such as Chili's, Bennigan's, and the Olive Garden, follow a similar pattern in concept development. Their emphasis is on identifying the key characteristics of their target markets and then locating restaurants where there is a high concentration of individuals who have those characteristics. Key characteristics may include income, age, education, and home ownership.

What gives multiunit restaurants a competitive advantage over singleunit restaurants is the opportunity to learn from experience with multiple examples of the same concept. When a chain restaurant firm has five hundred virtually identical restaurants, it can analyse the factors that differentiate its high-performing restaurants from its low-performing restaurants, and make changes as necessary before opening additional units.

Multitheme Restaurant Concepts

A particular form of multiunit restaurant for which concept development is critical to success is the restaurant organisation that opens and operates restaurants whose concepts are not identical but different. The Levi Organisation and Lettuce Entertain You are two examples of successful restaurant chains that have developed multitheme restaurant concepts. These two companies each use several different themes, and each restaurant is promoted with its theme rather than by using the corporate name. Lettuce Entertain You, for example, operates Papagus (a Greek concept), Maggiano's (an Italian concept), Ben Pao (an Asian concept), Cafe Ba-Ba-Reeba! (a tapas bar), and the Corner Bakery. The development of these restaurant concepts through excellent marketing, well-planned menus, and good design comes about through the efforts of a very sophisticated management team.

Development of foodservice concepts

The development of foodservice concepts for hotels has evolved in recent years from the traditional view that considered the food and beverage department as a necessary evil to the modern idea that the food and beverage department is an important profit center. Some large hotels have food and beverage sales of over $35 million per year, an amount that exceeds room sales and creates in management a high expectation of profit from these two departments.

The Hilton Hotel in Atlanta, Georgia, has developed a concept for its first-class rooftop restaurant that goes beyond the idea of a foodservice facility as a profit center. The restaurant, called Nikolai's Roof, was conceived as a luxury dining room and is marketed to the city of Atlanta as well as to hotel guests. The decor is exquisite, the food is served with flair and showmanship, and the entire theme captures the imagination of the city's residents. The concept was developed with such success that the hotel's own guests had great difficulty getting reservations to dine. A hotel restaurant so overcrowded that it could not serve the guests of the hotel would have been unthinkable in earlier days of hotel keeping in the United States. Nikolai's Roof is an excellent example of the execution of a hotel dining concept that complements the hotel itself as well as drawing a significant number of guests from the community.

Hotel managers have known for many years that hotel restaurants must have certain desirable features if they are to be successful. These features include:

— Availability of parking
— Unique theme or decor (differing from the decor of the hotel itself)
— Strong promotion to the community
— A menu and a method of service that are distinctive

The developers of hotel properties, and in some cases hotel chains, have used outside foodservice facilities and interior design consultants to create unique specialty restaurants that can be successfully marketed to both hotel guests and the community.

Institutional foodservice is usually conceived as a service to an organisation, and most often has a not-for-profit philosophy. Most institutional food operations are expected to break even, and all are expected to budget and operate within well-defined ranges of costs so that they do not become a financial burden on the organisation they serve. In some cases, the institutional food operation is expected to make a profit and to pay for all of its direct and indirect operational costs.

The development of an operational concept for the institution is often ignored, and this is usually a serious mistake. The institution must accurately interpret its market and must "sell" its products, even when the food is indirectly paid for by the customer. For instance, in hospital foodservice, an unattractive meal presentation will cause dissatisfaction and complaining on the part of the patient and possibly adverse health effects as well if he or she does not eat a meal and thus does not get sufficient nourishment. In a college or university dining hall, a comprehensive concept of service and decor can greatly influence financial success. Attractive food court service or a scramble design, for example, can increase the popularity of a college foodservice operation and generate additional profit. A dining facility operated by a corporation for its employees should also have a well-planned concept and decor. The ability of corporate foodservice operations to attract employees may influence the degree of subsidy that a company is willing to contribute to the operation.

Five M'S Of Concept Development

The successful foodservice operation combines the following elements of concept development: market, menu, money, management, and method of execution.

The importance of conducting market studies before proceeding with the construction of a food facility cannot be too heavily stressed. The basic marketing questions that must be answered are:

— To whom is the food operation being marketed?

— Is the market large enough to generate sales and produce a profit?

— How will the market be identified?

— What method will be used to communicate to this market?

— Will the potential customer want or need the food product?

— Will a quality assurance plan be developed that will encourage the customer to return because of superior service and/or product quality?
— Will internal marketing successfully sell the customer additional services or products after he or she arrives at the food facility?

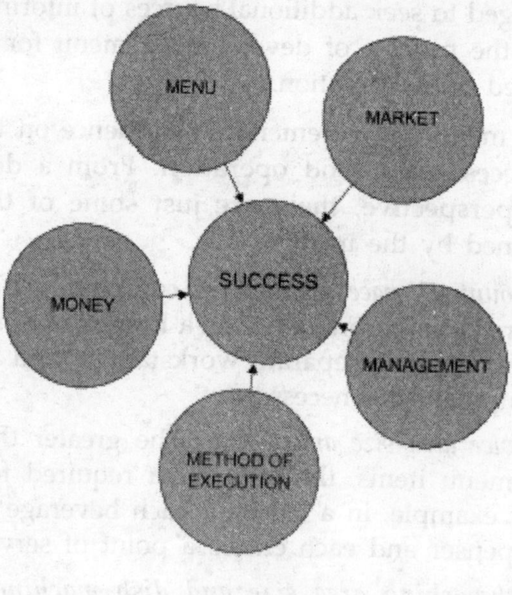

Figure 3. The five M's of concept development.

A classic mistake made by both large corporations and individual restaurant operators is to conduct the market analysis and then fail to act on the basis of the information obtained. There are several cases in which extensive marketing feasibility studies were conducted by outside market-ing firms, but the owners and managers made their decisions on gut feelings rather than from the hard data derived from the study.

Even owners (or potential owners) of food operations who have no marketing background can conduct their own market research, with a small amount of guidance and a large amount of energy and common sense.

The importance of the menu to the design of the food facility cannot be overemphasised. The subject of menu writing is too broad to be addressed adequately in a book on foodservice facilities design. The owner or manager is encouraged to seek additional sources of information as a part of the process of developing a menu for a new or renovated food operation.

The menu has a tremendous influence on the design and success of a food operation. From a design and layout perspective, these are just some of the factors determined by the menu:

— *Amount of space required.* A complex menu requires more space to prepare than a limited or simple menu does, because separate workstations and additional equipment are necessary.

— *Service area size and design.* The greater the number of menu items, the more area required for service. For example, in a cafeteria each beverage requires a dispenser and each entree a point of service.

— *Dishwashing area size and dish machine capacity.* Complex menus often require multiple plates, dishes, and utensils, and so the dishwashing area and machine capacity will need to be greater than in the case of simple menus.

— *Types of cooking equipment.* Complex menus require multiple types of equipment, especially in the final preparation area, where it may be necessary to steam, fry, bake, broil, and sauté.

— *Equipment capacity.* Limited menus may require

relatively few pieces of equipment but need large capacities of each. Complex menus may require many different types of equipment with relatively small capacities.

— *Size of dry and refrigerated storage areas.* Complex menus may require larger storage areas to maintain the par stocks necessary to meet demand.

— *Number of employees.* Simple menus require fewer employees than do complex menus.

— *Amount of investment required.* When large or complex menus require more equipment, space, and employees, costs rise.

Money

Successful capitalisation of a food facility includes funds for:

— Planning costs

— Building construction or renovation

— Equipment (fixed)

— China, glassware, utensils

— Furniture and fixtures

— Decor

— Operating costs

These funds must be identified and committed before serious planning can begin. Yet, in concept development, the commitments may not be made in the early planning stage because the costs are not yet known. Therefore, planning for capital funds is a two-step process: First the financial needs are estimated and sources of financial support are contacted to determine the possibility of obtaining investment funds; then, after concept development has taken place, preliminary designs and construction estimates have been made, and market research is completed, financial commitments are made by lenders and investors.

Quality of management

The quality of the management of the foodservice operation will be the most important element in achieving success. Following are typical questions to be addressed by the owners:

— Who will operate the foodservice facility?

— What kind of food experience and educational background must this person have?

— Who will assist this person in covering the long hours that are usually required to operate a foodservice facility?

— What level of pay will this person receive?

— Will this person be rewarded in some way for excellent sales and profit results?

— How will the owners set operational policies and communicate these to the management staff?

The answers to these questions will determine the organisational structure and the kind of management team that will be used to operate the food facility. The successful restaurant often is owned and operated by one individual whose personality becomes a part of the guests' dining experience. On the other hand, the management of the food and beverage department of a hotel may be under the control of more than one person and usually is part of a more complex organisational team.

In this case, the policies and procedures of the food

facility should be described in an operations manual to ensure consistent implementation of management policy. From the point of view of the investor or the institutional administration, the management of a food facility must follow traditional management principles of good communication, strong controls, and sound personnel relations regardless of the number of people operating the facility. The operational philosophy and specific management guidelines to be used in foodservice operations must be carefully considered by the investors in a foodservice facility. Failure to develop management guidelines will very likely lead to the financial failure of the operation.

Execution method

The last step in concept development involves operational matters. Although the opening date might seem to be in the distant future to the person planning a food facility, decisions about operating methods must be made during the concept development phase on matters such as production methods, control systems, and personnel.

Will convenience foods or traditional "from scratch" cookery be used? This decision will have a great influence on the size of refrigerated and dry storage areas and on the size of the kitchen. Production methods will also determine the number of employees in the kitchen and the skill level of these employees.

Control Systems

Food and beverage controls involve many different parts of the facility, and planning for these controls before the project is under construction is strongly recommended. The following areas of control should be carefully considered:

— Cash control
— Sales analysis
— Guest check control
— Food production forecasting
— Storeroom and refrigeration control
— Back door security
— Labor control
— Purchasing and receiving control
— Quality control
— Portion control

The development of financial feasibility studies cannot begin until the amount of labor required is known. The employee schedules, hours of operation, staffing patterns, staff benefits, skill levels, and level of supervision of employees must all be determined before serious development of the food facility begins. As part of its concept development, the fast-food industry based its low labor costs on the use of hourly unskilled labor, scheduled to work short periods of time. When the food operation is busy, part-time employees are scheduled to work. The traditional eight-hour day is seldom used in the fast-food industry, except for supervisors and managers. The use of part-time employees in fast-food restaurants has also significantly reduced the cost of benefits. The use of part-time employees was an important part of concept development in the fast-food industry.

Feasibility

Many terms are commonly used in the hospitality industry to describe the process of determining whether or not a food facility is likely to return a profit to its owners. The following is a partial list of these terms:

— Market or marketability study
— Market segmentation analysis
— Market and operations analysis
— Appraisal report
— Economic study
— Time-share feasibility study
— Feasibility study, report, or analysis
— Financial feasibility study
— ROI (return on investment) analysis
— Sales/performance study

Although each term has a slightly different meaning or involves a slightly different approach, they all share the goal of determining the potential of a facility to generate sales and a profit. In the case of the financial feasibility or ROI (return on investment) analysis, the emphasis is on financial matters such as capital needs, operating funds, cash flow, and return on investment. However, even financial feasibility reports have as their primary focus the determination of whether or not a facility under good management can give investors or owners a return on their investment. For purposes of explaining the feasibility studies and of guiding the owner, manager, or student into a commonsense approach to these studies, they are classified here into two general categories: those that deal with market feasibility and those that attempt to determine financial feasibility.

The two forms of feasibility study can be understood in relation to the financial statements for the operation. The market feasibility study focuses on the income statement and is conducted to determine whether revenues are sufficient to generate a profit. The financial feasibility study focuses on the balance sheet and is conducted to determine whether retained earnings (derived from net income) will be sufficient to satisfy the owners' expectations for a return on their investment.

Market Feasibility Study

The primary question addressed in the market feasibility study is: What level of sales revenues can the operation be expected to generate? The answer to this question really cannot be known until the operation has opened; however, building a new restaurant only to find that the sales are insufficient to generate a profit is an expensive lesson. The market feasibility study attempts to project the sales level for the operation before the investors have committed their funds to purchase property, construct a building, and hire a team of employees.

The sales revenue for a foodservice facility is a function of two factors over an appropriate period of time: the number of customers and the price they paid.

$$\text{Sales} = \text{Price} \times \text{Quantity}$$

Market feasibility studies thus have to formulate sales estimates from two separate projections: How many customers will there be? How much will each customer spend? These two estimates are interrelated through the simple economic principle that demand (quantity sold) is more or less a function of price.

Market feasibility studies can be conducted either to test the feasibility of an established foodservice concept or to develop new foodservice concepts that would be appropriate for a given market. Chain restaurant organizations interested in expansion usually want to determine whether, or where, in a given market area their concept would enjoy the greatest opportunity for success. Independent restaurateurs, as well as chain restaurant organisations, who are interested in developing a new restaurant use the market feasibility study to develop and refine the concept.

Because the market feasibility process is complex and time-consuming, it is often conducted by specialised consultants. Independent restaurateurs may find that the cost of engaging a market feasibility consultant is prohibitive. However, it is possible—and certainly advisable—for entrepreneurs to conduct an abbreviated market feasibility study. Resources and guidelines for conducting a restaurant feasibility study are available from the National Restaurant Association.

Market feasibility studies generally follow the process presented—in simplified and shortened form—in Figure 4. Demographic data and economic factors for the community are analysed to determine the potential market for the restaurant. Traffic counts and proximity to demand generators are used to assess the viability of possible sites for the restaurant. A competitive analysis is performed to determine whether the market can sustain another restaurant at each potential site. Based on these analyses, sales projections are formulated.

Demographic data include information about the population near the proposed location of the restaurant, including age, income, gender, occupation, number of children at home, home ownership, the use of automobiles, and similar information. These data about individuals are relevant because target market segments for restaurants are often described in terms of the same factors. Demographics thus are known to predict restaurant behavior. For example, the developers of a casual dinner house may believe that their concept will attract young, single professionals between the ages of twentysix and thirty-four who have incomes in the \$35,000–\$50,000 range and who pay monthly rents between \$1,000 and \$1,600.

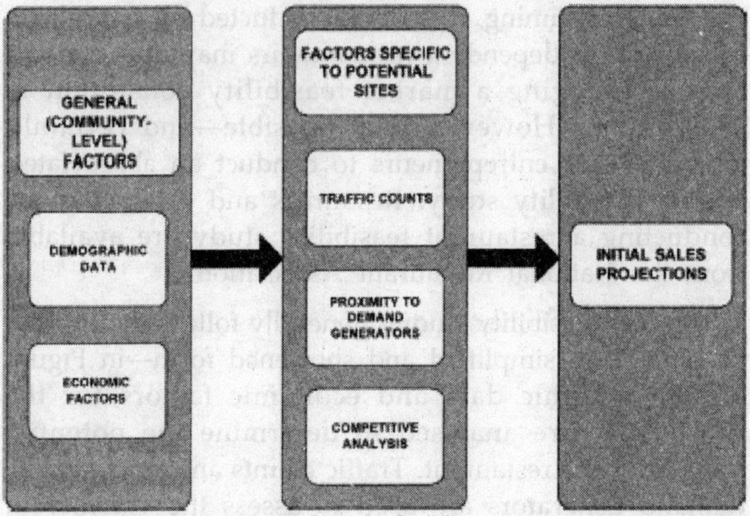

Figure 4. The market feasibility process.

Obviously, the dinner house should be located where there is a high concentration of individuals who fit the profile of the target market. Gathering demographic data enables the developers to detect the presence of the proposed restaurant's target market segment.

The most comprehensive demographic data are gathered in the decennial U.S. Census. Until recently, using census data involved either extensive library research or access to a mainframe computer. Now, however, detailed census data are available to the public on CD-ROM at a reasonable cost. Also, in the interest of promoting economic growth, many local municipalities have developed extensive databases combining demographic data with information about businesses, organised on detailed maps of the area. This kind of database, called a GIS (geographic information system), gives restaurant developers immediate access to information about the market and the competition.* GS software and databases also are increasingly available for desktop computers and so bring the resources of high-priced market consultants to the fingertips of entrepreneurs.

Economic Factors

The prevailing economic climate in a community has a significant impact on the market feasibility of a foodservice operation. The health of the restaurant industry in a local area is closely related to the disposable income of its residents. Generally, when disposable income rises in boom times, restaurants prosper. In bust times, disposable income falls and restaurants suffer. However, the effects of economic prosperity and depression affect various restaurant concepts differently. Concepts that offer a high degree of perceived value for the price will suffer less than restaurants with high prices. Also, restaurants that draw customers from a particular industry or from a few large, nearby firms may be protected from broader economic fluctuations if the industry or the large firms prosper during down times. Economic projections for a local area often are available from the chamber of commerce or the local economic development council.

New housing developments are an important indicator of economic growth, especially when they are located on the fringes of existing communities. New restaurants often follow new housing developments. County planning commissions usually are quite willing to share information about planned housing developments, new roads, and zoning issues.

Restaurants are usually developed along major thoroughfares. Determining market feasibility requires an estimate of the number of cars that pass by each potential location, which is used in determining which site is optimal. Traffic counts can usually be obtained free of charge from the local chamber of commerce, highway department, mayor's office, tourism agency, or other municipal offices.

Some fast-food chains have developed very exact specifications for locating a good site for the foodservice facilities. For instance, one of the guidelines for placement of a Kentucky Fried Chicken (KFC) outlet is that it be located on the "going-home side of the street," for obvious reasons. Other chains have minimum community size, minimum traffic count, and minimum average income standards that must be met before consideration will be given to building or franchising on a particular site.

Demand generators are destinations that draw extensive traffic, such as shopping malls, recreation and sports facilities, and public facilities such as museums, zoos, and parks. Restaurants located near demand generators benefit from the traffic they produce—as, for example, when shoppers have lunch after visiting the local mall.

For some foodservice concepts, proximity to other restaurants enhances rather than hurts market feasibility. Fast-food concepts, for example, often locate in clusters along interstate highway interchanges. Similarly, cities and suburbs often have a "restaurant row" in commercial areas.

A competitive analysis is crucial to the market feasibility study because the local market potential for a given concept must be shared among all of the competitors. If demographic research identifies an area that has a sales potential of $6 million to $8 million for casual dinner houses, it is important to know how many already are in operation. Moreover, when the restaurateur identifies an area that appears to be ripe for development, he or she should assume that the competition will soon arrive. Most chain restaurant organisations have access to GIS market data, and many of them use those data extensively to identify prime development opportunities.

An independent restaurant entrepreneur who is conducting a market feasibility analysis should identify all the similar concepts within the geographic area, compare menus and prices, and count seats. More importantly, he or she should count customers at various times during the week at the restaurants that would be the closest competition. If patrons arc lined up outside the doors to get a seat on Monday or Tuesday night, that is good news. However, if there is no waiting at the competition on Friday or Saturday night, the independent restaurateur should look elsewhere. It is also important to take seasonal factors into account. Counting cars and customers at the competition during the summer months will bias estimates upward, just as counts taken during the winter when two feet (610 millimeters) of snow are on the ground may bias estimates downward.

Sales projections are informed by the information gathered about demographics, economic factors, traffic patterns, demand generators, and competitive analysis. Recall that sales projections are composed of estimates about quantity (number of customers) and price. Demographic data indicate the relative size of the local population and thus are useful in projecting the number of customers (quantity). Income information may also be found in demographic data and may thus assist in estimating the price range that people are willing to accept. Economic factors are especially important in projecting price. Entrepreneurs often make the mistake of basing their sales estimates on data gathered during boom times and thus find themselves suffering during bust times. Traffic pattern data are crucial in estimating customer counts, as is the presence of demand generators. Competitive analysis helps the entrepreneur determine his or her share of the customer market and predict price points against the competition.

The weakness in many market feasibility studies can be found within the sales projection section. This part of the feasibility report is often the first place that a banker will look to determine the accuracy of the financial forecast. Bankers always appreciate conservative sales projections that reflect the restaurateur's planning for sales fluctuations during difficult periods. Restaurant entrepreneurs also often overestimate the dining patterns and price sensitivities of the local market. Sometimes this is the result of wishful thinking, but other times it is the result of insufficient planning and preparation. A valuable way for the entrepreneur to check his or her assumptions about the market is to develop a questionnaire and distribute it to those who reside or work in the area. A questionnaire is helpful in determining such things as:

— Detailed demographic data about age, income, and family size

— Eating-out patterns (frequency, meal preferences)
— Price sensitivity and the average price paid for lunch and dinner at competing establishments
— Favorite eating places for various occasions

For a hotel, the sales pattern would be influenced by the house count (number of persons who occupy the guest rooms). The calculation, therefore, should be based on the projected occupancy. Data on hotel occupancy levels are available from leading hospitality industry accounting firms. Price Waterhouse Coopers, Smith Travel Research, and Pannell, Kerr, Foster, for example, regularly publish hotel operations data from all parts of the country and different segments of the hotel field (resorts, transient hotels, and motels). By utilising these resources, one should be able to make accurate sales projections that will be credible to the lending institution or investor.

Projections for hospitals and nursing homes are based on patient room occupancy data, but in the health care field a feasibility study usually does not include any data on sales. Foodservice in hospitals and other health care institutions is a service and support arm of the facility, with the primary management and financial considerations focused on the quality of the service and cost containment of the operation.

Once relevant market data have been gathered, a complete sales forecast should be prepared. The lending institution, investor, owner, and manager will all want to know the financial projections for the planned new or renovated food facility. Each of these persons will, of course, have a different set of reasons for seeking the projections, and each will want data from the projections presented in a different manner. For instance, the banker will be looking in part for the ratio of invested capital to borrowed capital. The banker may also want to know the amount of operating cash and the cash flow from sales that will be involved in the operation. The manager needs to know what his or her budget is and what the expectation of the owner is concerning profit and loss.

The manager and the banker probably will not be using the same financial reports and projections, but they certainly will be getting their information from the same original source, which will probably be the financial feasibility study. Usually in the financial feasibility study two basic documents —the projected balance sheet and the pro forma profit-and-loss statement—are prepared, along with other supporting reports and schedules. A good outline of the kind of information that must be projected can be made by examining the line items on each of these documents.

The balance sheet is a simplification of the projected comparative balance sheet that should be developed under the guidance of the firm's accountant. Note that the balance sheet shows a projected comparison between the assets, liabilities, and capital for a twelve-month period. The balance sheet illustrates a number of projections that must be made by the person or firm preparing the financial feasibility study. On the asset side of the balance sheet:

— The amount of cash needed as operating funds
— The amount of cash tied up in food inventory
— The investment in land and building
— The cash needed for a down payment on land and building
— The cost of furniture, fixtures, equipment, and utensils
— The cost of parking lots, driveways, lighting, and

other improvements to the property On the liabilities and equity side of the balance sheet:

— Necessary short-term funds that must be borrowed. The amount of payables
— The amount of long-term mortgages on building and land
— The amount of funds that will represent the owner's equity (capitalisation)

Decisions regarding the type of business organisation (proprietorship, partnership, corporation, and so forth) and control of ownership (closely held, limited number of investors, the sale of common stock, and so forth) are made prior to preparing the projected balance sheet.

The pro forma profit-and-loss (P&L) statement should be prepared by the owner, manager, or other persons who will be involved in the management of the food facility. This statement projects the income and expense for a particular period of time. For the financial feasibility study, a three-to-fiveyear projection would be considered sufficient. The format for the P&L should follow the Uniform System of Accounts developed for hotels and restaurants for income and expense categories that fit the needs of the food operation. An example of a pro forma P&L is found in Figure 1-7.

Several supporting schedules are prepared to supplement the P&L statement. Because food and labor costs combined typically run between 60 and 80 percent of sales revenue, schedules providing detailed information on how the cost of food sales and the cost of personnel and related expenses were calculated are often provided.

Cost of Sales : A schedule detailing how the amount shown on the cost-ofsales line of the P&L statement was calculated is often prepared. Because the cost of sales for the menu equals the selling price minus the cost of the ingredients used in preparation, two closely related steps are involved in preparing the schedule: determining the portion cost for each menu item and estimating the price for each menu item.

The portion cost for each menu item is determined by examining the recipe and costs for each ingredient. Figure 1-8 illustrates the costing process for a menu item. The form provides the following information:

— A list of all food ingredients

— The portion size of each ingredient

— The cost of each ingredient

— The total portion cost

If the menu price includes the meat, vegetable, dessert, and beverage, then the above example would necessarily include a complete list of all foods that are a part of this meal. A small amount ($.05) might be added to cover the cost of seasonings and other condiments.

The two traditional methods for determining the selling price for menu items are (a) to divide the portion cost by a set percentage (the desired food cost percentage for the operation), and (b) to add a set dollar amount to the cost. Using the first pricing approach, a manager who seeks to have a 32 percent food cost percentage would divide the food cost of a menu item by the desired percentage. For example, a food cost for a ham sandwich of $.72 would be divided by.32, and the selling price would be $2.25. Using the second approach, the manager would add a fixed amount to the cost of each menu item. Adding $2 to the cost of the ham sandwich would result in a selling price of $2.72.

A third approach to setting prices involves looking not at each item but at the menu and menu mix (the quantity sold of each menu item) as a whole. The goal of this approach is to set prices so that the contribution margin (the amount of revenue remaining when the cost of sales has been subtracted from revenue) is sufficient to pay all expected fixed expenses and satisfy the owner's expectations for a return on investment.

A spreadsheet like that shown in Figure 1-9 can be used to estimate the overall cost of sales by building from the cost of each menu item. It shows columns for the projected price, the portion cost, the contribution margin (price minus cost), the menu item cost percentage (cost divided by price), the projected quantity sold (the menu mix), the total sales (price multiplied by quantity), the total cost (portion cost multiplied by quantity), the total cost (cost multiplied by quantity), and the total contribution (contribution multiplied by quantity) for each menu item. The total cost, $4,871.45, when divided into $13,648.25, the total sales, gives an overall cost percentage of 35.69 percent given the projected prices, costs, and menu mix.

Using a spreadsheet like that shown in Figure 1-9 allows the owner to evaluate the effects of different pricing strategies on the overall food cost percentage for the operation. The advantage of the spreadsheet approach over traditional strategies to pricing, such as simply marking up the cost by a given percentage or dollar amount, is that prices can be set to generate the maximum contribution margin. In foodservice, profits come not from minimizing the food cost percentage but from maximizing the contribution margin. However, for the purposes of preparing the pro forma profit-andloss statement, the overall food cost percentage derived from the spreadsheet can be used to estimate the cost of sales.

Finally, it is essential to check the competition in setting prices for each menu item, because an operation that is not competitively priced will suffer.

Once the menu pricing and preferred menu mix have been established, the calculation of the cost of food sales is simple: The projected sales revenue is multiplied by the overall food cost factor, and the result is shown on the pro forma P&L statement. In Figure 1-9, the cost factor is 40 percent of food sales. For the years shown, the cost of food sales is estimated to be 40 percent of the sales revenue.

Cost of Personnel and Related Expenses: The method of projecting the total labor costs for the pro forma P&L statement is to decide on the number of persons needed in each job category and then prepare an employee sched-ule. Salary and wage levels should be estimated, and the annual cost of labor computed. A small amount, perhaps 10 to 12 percent, should be added for overtime. The labor schedule might appear as shown in Figure 1-10.

The examples illustrated are very simple to construct and take a commonsense approach to providing the backup data that are often required for a financial feasibility study. Other major costs, such as utilities and taxes, should be obtained from local utility and government agencies, to be sure of accurate projections. After completing the market and financial feasibility studies and presenting these to bankers and potential investors, the owners can make a good judgment as to the potential success of the food facility project. Further contacts with zoning boards, liquor license agencies, and other municipal groups will bring the project to a point of decision. The accumulation of the data contained in the feasibility studies together with encouragement or discouragement from lenders, investors, and municipal agencies will lead the owner to the first go/no-go decision. In other words, if the project looks financially sound, the market is identified, a need for the foodservice exists, and the capital is obtainable, the decision to go ahead can be made. If one or more elements of the go/no-go decision are uncertain, there are three alternative courses to explore. The first is to correct the problem area that has been identified. Is the facility too large? Are the labor costs too high? Is the menu wrong for the market? Is the competition too strong in the immediate trading area?

The second option is to abandon the project and look for another place to invest the funds. The third alternative is to delay the decision until the final go/no-go decision point. This alternative is financially risky, because to progress from this point means incurring costs for foodservice facilities design consultants, architects, lawyers, accountants, and other professionals.

E. M. Statler's famous quote, "The three most important things for the success of a hotel are location, location, and location," is certainly true for many foodservice facilities. A poorly located restaurant will certainly experience a low level of sales, and a coffee shop in a hotel may miss a significant amount of business unless it has easy access both to the hotel guests and to street traffic. On a college campus, students will typically select convenience as the primary reason for eating in a particular food facility. Avoiding high rent by selecting a location that is inconvenient or out of the mainstream of foot or automobile traffic is usually a bad decision. The location of a food facility on the immediate left or right of an entrance to a shopping mall is often considered a poor location, because the typical mall customer needs first to enter the mall and then look around for interesting places to shop and/or eat. Other considerations for site selection are:

— *Visual recognition.* Can the food facility be easily seen by potential customers? Will the appearance of the outside of the facility communicate the character and concept of the dining experience inside?

— *Convenience.* The developers of a destination restaurant, in which the customer has previously made a decision to dine, must consider parking, an attractive entrance, valet parking, and safe surroundings as important site selection criteria. Coffee shop, deli, and fast-food entrepreneurs must depend on impulse buying as the primary market, and therefore site selection must focus on signage, ease of entry, and drive-in windows and/or take-out service.

— *Code restrictions.* Site selection may involve local code requirements for setback from the street, parking capacity, street access, or the acceptability of a food facility in a particular neighborhood. Usually these code requirements are available from the engineering or city planning office of the municipality where the food facility will be located.

— *Environmental issues.* In suburban areas, the development of an attractive site for a foodservice facility may encroach upon wetlands or adversely affect water runoff in nearby neighborhoods. In older, urban areas, sites may have previously been used for industrial and manufacturing processes that left dangerous materials in the ground. Environmental factors such as these are increasingly important to the site selection process because they present additional costs.

The approval process for a new or renovated foodservice facility is typically long and complicated, involving many different agencies. Developers often experience the approval process—and the inevitable delays that occur—as frustrating because they are eager to get the facility open and operating so that it can generate a positive cash flow. In defense of those agencies and departments who must be satisfied before proceeding, it is worthwhile to recall that the project needs to be controlled so that it does not create an unsanitary, unsafe, or unattractive addition to the community. Each municipality has a different group of agencies who must approve the food facility, and each has a definite sequence in which the approvals are given. For example, a health department may require preliminary approval of the equipment layout before construction begins and a final inspection after the facility is built and the equipment is in place.

The way to obtain necessary approvals for a complex project (new construction or major renovation) is to develop a comprehensive checklist, in which each member of the planning team (architect, engineers, foodservice consultant, financial advisors, lawyers, etc.) submits a list of necessary agencies and deadlines. After dates are recorded, one person (usually the architect) serves as the coordinator of the approval process.

Typical approval agencies involved in foodservice projects include:

— Zoning board
— Health department
— Municipal engineers (water, sewer, gas, and electrical)
— City planner
— Fire marshal

— Liquor control board
— Telephone company
— State or federal agencies (on state or federal projects)

Effective Facilities Planning Layour Optimisation then Simulation,

Facility layout is the arrangement of activities, features and spaces in consideration of the relationship that exists between them. It belongs to the class of spatial allocation problems that have been studied in various contexts, including architecture space planning, manufacturing layout, offices layout and VLSI Layout. Facility or plant layout is a part of facilities design, which includes more global issues such as plant location, building design, material handling, etc. In general, plant layout analysis includes a study of the production line process flow charts, material flow diagrams, product routings, processing times, development of from-to charts, relationship diagrams between different departments in the facility and the cost of material movement.

In its most basic form, a facility layout problem (FLP) is analytically formulated according to the Quadratic Assignment Problem (QAP), a classical model in discrete optimisation optimisation which works by enumerating different layout configurations until the best arrangement is obtained. Although mathematically elegant, QAP is an NP-hard problem, which implies it is computationally impractical for problems involving over fifteen departments (Partovi,and Burton 1992). Due to the combinatorial aspects of optimally solving the FLP, analysts have developed various heuristics to substitute for blind search methods. These are categorised as either construction or improvement-type routines:

— *Construction-type layout routines:* This type of routine generates a block layout based on the relationship between different departments. Among the most popular routines within this category are CORELAP (computerised relationship layout planning), ALDEP (Automated layout design) and PLANET (Plant layout analysis and evaluation techniques).

— Improvement-type layout routines: This type of routine requires an input of a feasible block layout and aim to reduce movement cost by attempting simultaneous pair-wise (or more) position exchanging among the departments. Among the most popular improvement-type routines are CRAFT (computerised relative allocation of facilities technique) and COFAD (Computerised facilities design).

Although computationally efficient, FLP heuristics are still far from meeting the constraints commonly found in daily layout tasks. Simulation has been requisitely used to incorporate many of these requirements into the facility layout study.

According to Grajo, layout optimisation and simulation are two tasks that are crucial to any facility planning and layout study. According to Burgess et al., simulation is the only methodology robust enough to systematically examine the role and impact of product complexity and other key variables on factory performance.

This is especially true because simulation models can capture many of the requirements and attributes of real life problems that are difficult to consider using analytical models for the layout optimisation problems. Typically, a simulation study is used in layout studies to estimate system parameters associated with the following tasks:

— Develop a series of improved layouts that has been

generated using traditional facility layout routines or algorithms.

— Contrast different layout configurations in terms of operational parameters, such as utilisation, flow-time and buffer sizes.

— Evaluate various strategies for the operation of the facility or justify the embracement of manufacturing concepts such as Group technology and flexible manufacturing systems.

— Identify potential problems and bottlenecks in proposed layout structures prior to implementation.

— Compress or expand time to study the layout in steady state or under specific short-term scenarios such as product mix changes, breakdowns or emergencies.

— Incorporate stochastic behavior and uncertainty of demand.

— Use simulation model to generate random flow volumes to be subsequently supplied to traditional facility layout routines.

Despite the wide application of simulation modeling in facility layout studies, the organisation of these two tasks has been informally addressed and applied.

Specifically, the question of whether a layout study should precede simulation modeling or vice versa to obtain effective layouts has been a point of debate. It seems that two schools of thought exist in this regard. The first school suggests that layout optimisation should be conducted prior to a simulation study, while the second one advises that the contrary will result in better layout efficiency.

Advocates of the "layout then simulate" paradigm characterise simulation analysis as local and operational, while posting layout optimisation as global and strategic. Grajo indicate that starting with a layout process with a simulation study will result in around 10%-15% improvement, while missing a much larger opportunity for improvement, had it been the case that layout optimisation had been conducted first. Layout studies that embrace this paradigm start by generating a block layout using facility layout routines and deterministic flow volumes; then, improve the operational characteristics based on the results of a simulation study.

Applications of this approach typically assume that overall production strategies and manufacturing technologies are predetermined, where the objectives involve comparing, testing, adjusting and validating different layout configurations. In addition, stochastic demand or complex production rules are not significant enough to be incorporated early in the process while the layout optimisation is taking place.

While this approach may save time, it runs the risk of inheriting the shortcomings of the preliminary block layout. That is, the window of improvement available to the simulation study is restrained within the primitive block layout generated.

Contrary to the previous paradigm, advocates from this school of thought claim that a simulation study needs to be conducted prior to layout optimisation. That is, an optimised process that delivered the desired levels of throughput, WIP, and utilisation, will result in a more efficient layout.

In fact, Sly states that skipping simulation prior to layout optimisation will result in layouts that fail to reduce inventory levels and throughput times and will result in only a little more than rearranging furniture within the plant. Applications within this paradigm include justifying operational parameters and adjusting production levels before attempting to optimise the layout.

This has the advantage of supplying more accurate volume and flow data to the layout optimisation study, especially when significant stochastic intricacies impede the accurate estimation of production levels using analytical models. In addition, this paradigm has been embraced when simulation is needed to generate random flow volumes to be subsequently used as input for a layout optimisation routine. For instance, Altinkilinc has first simulated the system to improve its parameters and then supplied the results to the CRAFT method to optimise the layout.

Moreover, Pandey et al. have optimised the dynamic system parameters using simulation then adapted the layout accordingly. However, as far as development pace, layout studies based on this paradigm are relatively more time consuming, due to the experimental and statistical analysis involved in simulation studies.

Objectives of the Layout Study

Facility layout studies can contain several contradicting objectives. Minimising distances while minimising travel congestion is a case in point. The prioritisation of the facility layout objectives largely determine the best approach to pursue. For instance, in a facility layout study, where higher priority is given to reducing the typical traveled distance or improving adjacency score, then the "layout then simulation" paradigm fits better.

On the other hand, if the objectives of the study are to produce layouts that improve shop-floor performance measures, such as minimising congestion, then the "simulate then layout" is expected to outperform the former paradigm. In addition, the second paradigm is better used when the objective is to justify the benefits of implementing general production principles such as Group Technology (GT), switching to flexible manufacturing systems (FMS), introduction of robotics or AGVs.

2

Indoor Air Quality

Indoor Air Quality (IAQ) deals with the content of interior air that could affect health and comfort of building occupants. The IAQ may be compromised by microbial contaminants (mold, bacteria), chemicals (such as carbon monoxide, radon), allergens, or any mass or energy stressor that can induce health effects.

Recent findings have demonstrated that indoor air is often more polluted than outdoor air (albeit with different pollutants) although this has not changed the common understanding of air pollution. In fact, indoor air is often a greater health hazard than the corresponding outdoor setting. Using ventilation to dilute contaminants, filtration, and source control are the primary methods for improving indoor air quality in most buildings.

Techniques for analysing IAQ include collection of air samples, collection of samples on building surfaces and computer modelling of air flow inside buildings. The resulting samples can be analysed for mold, bacteria, chemicals or other stressors. These investigations can lead to an understanding of the sources of the contaminants and ultimately to strategies for removing the unwanted elements from the air.

Risk Assessment

Radon

Radon is the invisible, radioactive atomic gas that results from radioactive decay of some forms of uranium that may be found in rock formations beneath buildings or in certain building materials themselves. Radon is probably the most pervasive serious hazard for indoor air in the United States and Europe, probably responsible for tens of thousands of lung cancer deaths per annum. There are relatively simple tests for radon gas, but these tests are not commonly done, even in areas of known systematic hazards.

Radon is a very heavy gas and thus will tend to accumulate at the floor level. Building materials can actually be a significant source of radon, but very little testing is done for stone, rock or tile products brought into building sites. The half life for radon is 3.8 days indicating that once the source is removed, the hazard will be greatly reduced within a few weeks.

Mold Health Issues

These biological agents can arise from a host of means, but there are two common classes:

— moisture induced growth of mold colonies and

— natural substances released into the air such as animal dander and plant pollen.

Moisture buildup inside buildings may arise from water penetrating compromised areas of the building envelope or skin, from plumbing leaks, from condensation due to improper ventilation, or from ground moisture penetrating a building slab. In areas where cellulosic materials (paper and wood, including drywall) become moist and fail to dry within 48 hours, mold colonies can propagate and release allergenic spores into the air.

In many cases, if materials have failed to dry out several days after the suspected water event, mold growth is suspected within wall cavities even if it is not immediately visible. Through a mold investigation, which may include destructive inspection, one should be able to determine the presence or absence of mold. In a situation where there is visible mold and the indoor air quality may have been compromised, a mold remediation may be needed. Indoors, mold growth can be inhibited by keeping humidity levels below fifty percent and by eliminating leaks or moisture condensation and accumulation.

There are some varieties of mold that contain toxic compounds (mycotoxins). However, exposure to hazardous levels of mycotoxin via inhalation is not possible in most cases, as toxins are produced by the fungal body and are not at significant levels in the released spores. The primary hazard of mold growth, as it relates to indoor air quality, comes from the allergenic properties of the spore cell wall. More serious than most allergenic properties is the ability of mold to trigger episodes in persons that already have asthma, a serious respiratory disease.

Carbon Monoxide (CO)

One of the most acutely toxic indoor air contaminants is carbon monoxide (CO), a colourless, odourless gas that is a byproduct of incomplete combustion of fossil fuels. Common sources of carbon monoxide are tobacco smoke, space heaters using fossil fuels, defective central heating furnaces and automobile exhaust. Improvements in indoor levels of CO are systematically improving from increasing numbers of smoke-free restaurants and other legislated non-smoking buildings. By depriving the brain of oxygen, high levels of carbon monoxide can lead to nausea, unconsciousness and death.

Legionnaire's Disease

Legionellosis or Legionnaire's Disease is caused by a waterborne bacterium that grows best in slow moving or still warm water. The primary route of exposure is aerosolisation, most commonly from evaporative cooling towers or showerheads. A common source of Legionella in commercial buildings is from poorly placed or maintained evaporative cooling towers, which often release aerosolised water that may enter nearby ventilation intakes. Outbreaks in medical facilities and nursing homes, where patients are immuno-suppressed and immuno-weak, are the most commonly reported cases of Legionellosis. More than one case has involved outdoor fountains in public attractions. The presence of Legionella in commercial building water supplies is highly under-reported, as healthy people require heavy exposure to acquire infection.

Legionella testing typically involves collecting water samples and surface swabs from evaporative cooling basins, shower heads, faucets, and other locations where warm water collects. The samples are then cultured and colony forming units (cfu) of Legionella are quantified as cfu/Liter.

Legionella is a parasite of protazoans such as amoeba, and thus requires conditions suitable for both organisms. The bacterium forms a biofilm which is resistant to chemical and antimicrobial treatments, including chlorine. Remediation for Legionella outbreaks in commercial buildings vary, but often include very hot water flushes (160°F), sterilisation of standing water in evaporative cooling basins, replacement of shower heads, and in some cases flushes of heavy metal salts. Preventative measures include adjusting normal hot water levels to allow for 120°F at the tap, evaluating facility design layout, removing faucet aerators, and periodic testing in suspect areas.

Asbestos Fibers

The U.S.Federal Government and some States have set standards for acceptable levels of asbestos fibers in indoor air. Many common building materials used before 1975 contain asbestos, such as some floor tiles, ceiling tiles, taping muds, pipe wrap, mastics and other insulation materials. Normally significant releases of asbestos fiber do not occur unless the building materials are disturbed, such as by cutting, sanding, drilling or building remodelling. Inhalation of asbestos fibers over long exposure times is associated with increased incidence of lung cancer.

While smokers have a greater risk of lung cancer than asbestos workers that do not smoke, smokers that are exposed to high levels of asbestos over many years have a much greater risk of developing lung cancer than either smokers that have not been exposed to asbestos, or persons that have been exposed to high levels of asbestos that do not smoke.

Carbon Dioxide

Carbon dioxide is a surrogate for indoor pollutants emitted by humans and correlates with human metabolic activity. Carbon dioxide at levels that are unusually high indoors may cause occupants to grow drowsy, get headaches, or function at lower activity levels. Humans are the main indoor source of carbon dioxide. Indoor levels are an indicator of the adequacy of outdoor air ventilation relative to indoor occupant density and metabolic activity. To eliminate most Indoor Air Quality complaints, total indoor carbon dioxide should be reduced to below 600 ppm above outdoor levels. NIOSH considers that indoor air concentrations of carbon dioxide that exceed 1,000 ppm are a marker suggesting inadequate ventilation (1,000 ppm equals 0.1%). ASHRAE recommends that carbon dioxide levels not exceed 700 ppm above outdoor ambient levels.

Definition of Indoor Air Quality in HVAC Design

There is a movement in the commercial and residential HVAC industry to pay more attention to the issue of indoor air quality (IAQ) throughout the design and construction stages of a buildings life. The "Green Design" movement also places emphasis on IAQ. Indoor air quality must be understood in order to discuss ventilation as a method of maintaining high IAQ, and ways to introduce demand controlled ventilation (DCV).

For the past several years, there have been many debates among indoor air quality specialists about the proper definition of indoor air quality and specifically what constitutes "acceptable" indoor air quality. Consequently, it is probably best to reference the currently accepted definition shown in the American Society of Heating, Refrigerating and Air-Conditioning Engineers (ASHRAE) ventilation standard.

HVAC Engineering Issues

A basic way of maintaining the health of indoor air is by the frequency of effective turnover of interior air by replacement with outside air. In the UK, for example, classrooms are required to have 2.5 outdoor air changes per hour. In halls, gym, dining, and physiotherapy spaces, the ventilation should be sufficient to limit carbon dioxide to 1,500 ppm. In the USA, and according to ASHRAE Standards, ventilation in classrooms is based on the amount of outdoor air per occupant, not air changes per hour. Since Carbon dioxide indoors comes from occupants and outdoor air, the adequacy of ventilation per occupant is indicated by the concentration indoors minus the concentration outdoors.

The value of 650 ppm above the outdoor concentration indicates approximately 15 cubic feet per minute of outdoor air per adult occupant doing sedentary office work. In classrooms, the requirements in the ASHRAE standard 62.1, Ventilation for Acceptable Indoor Air Quality, would typically result in about 3 air changes per hour, depending on the occupant density. Of course the occupants aren't the only source of pollutants, so outdoor air ventilation may need to be higher when unusual or strong sources of pollution exist indoors.

The use of air filters can trap some of the air pollutants. The Department of Energy's Energy Efficiency and Renewable Energy section wrote "[Air] Filtration should have a Minimum Efficiency Reporting Value (MERV) of 13 as determined by ASHRAE 52.2-1999." Air filters are used to reduce the amount of dust that reaches the wet coils. Dust can serve as food to grow molds on the wet coils and ducts and can reduce the efficiency of the coils.

Moisture management and humidity control requires operating HVAC systems as designed. Moisture management and humidity control may conflict with efforts to try to optimise the operation to conserve energy. For example, Moisture management and humidity control requires systems to be set to supply Make Up Air at lower temperatures (design levels), instead of the higher temperatures sometimes used to conserve energy in cooling-dominated climate conditions. However, for most of the US and many parts of Europe and Japan, during the majority of hours of the year, outdoor air temperatures are cool enough that the air does not need further cooling to provide thermal comfort indoors. However, high humidity outdoors creates the need for careful attention to humidity levels indoors. High humidities give rise to mold growth and moisture indoors is associated with a higher prevalence of occupant respiratory problems.

The "dew point temperature" is an absolute measure of the moisture in air. Some facilities are being designed with the design dew points in the lower 50's °F, and some in the upper and lower 40's °F. Some facilities are being designed using desiccant wheels with gas fired heater to dry out the wheel enough to get the required dew points. On those systems, after the moisture is removed from the make up air, a cooling coil is used to lower the temperature to the desired level.

Commercial buildings, and sometimes residential, are often kept under slightly-positive air pressure relative to the outdoors to reduce infiltration. Limiting infiltration helps with moisture management and humidity control. Dilution of indoor pollutants with outdoor air is effective to the extent that outdoor air is free of harmful pollutants. Ozone in outdoor air occurs indoors at reduced concentrations because ozone is highly reactive with many chemicals found indoors. The products of the reactions between ozone and many common indoor pollutants include organic compounds that may be more odorous, irritating, or toxic than those from which they are formed. These products of ozone chemistry include formaldehyde, higher molecular weight aldehydes, acidic aerosols, and fine and ultrafine particles, among others.

The higher the outdoor ventilation rate, the higher the indoor ozone concentration and the more likely the reactions will occur, but even at low levels, the reactions will take place. This suggests that ozone should be removed from ventilation air, especially in areas where outdoor ozone levels are frequently high. Recent research has shown that mortality and morbidity increase in the general population during periods of higher outdoor ozone and that the threshold for this effect is around 20 parts per billion (ppb).

Institutional Roles

The topic of IAQ has become popular due to the greater awareness of health problems caused by mold and triggers to asthma and allergies. Awareness has also been increased by the involvement of the United States Environmental Protection Agency.

A variety of scientists work in the field of indoor air quality including chemists, physicists, mechanical engineers, biologists, bacteriologists and computer scientists. Some of these professionals are certified by organisations such as the American Industrial Hygiene Association and the American Indoor Air Quality Council. AIHA and A2LA both offer laboratory accreditation programmes that relate to indoor air quality.

On the international level, the International Society of Indoor Air Quality and Climate (ISIAQ), formed in 1991, organises two major conferences, the Indoor Air and the Healthy Buildings series. The next conference, Indoor Air 2008, will take place in Copenhagen, Denmark so go to it you A might learn something new you never know.

Healthy Buildings 2009 will be held in Syracuse, New York. ISIAQ's journal Indoor Air is published 6 times a year and contains peer-reviewed scientific papers with an emphasis on interdisciplinary studies including exposure measurements, modelling, and health outcomes.

Development of Indoor Air Quality

According to the National Safety Council, Americans spend about 90 percent of their time indoors, and 65 percent of that time at home. Thus poor indoor air quality can have a significant impact on people's lives, especially those who are most vulnerable: infants and children, pregnant women, the elderly, and those who have chronic illnesses.

Steps can be taken to help improve indoor air quality at home, the workplace, and in other indoor environments. Some of those steps include the following:

— *Understand the role of Green Cleaning*. Many "green" cleaning products contain chemicals that react with ozone to form toxic and irritating chemicals, as described above, through indoor air chemical reactions. The result is air that may contain more hazardous chemicals than were present before the green cleaning products were used. In particular, citrus based solvents and pine-based solvents have been shown to react with ozone and form formaldehyde, higher molecular weight aldehydes, acidic aerosols, and fine and ultrafine particles. Ozone can be removed from outdoor air by filtration with carbon, but large amounts of carbon are required to remove a high fraction of the ozone present in most urban and many ex-urban areas.

— *Install an air purifier, or an air purification system.* Caution is advised. Ozone-based air cleaners are not advised and both the U.S. EPA and the California Air Resources Board have issued advisories on the use of ozone air cleaners. California is currently proposing to regulate ozone air cleaners.

— *Introducing plants to reduce the levels of indoor air pollution is only minimally effective.* Many advocates of plants have advised introducing "toxin-consuming plants" to your home, office, and other indoor environments. Certain plants, including: philodendron, spider plants, golden pothos, peace lilies, bamboo palms, mums, and english ivy remove dangerous toxins (e.g., formaldehyde, carbon monoxide, benzene, and others) from the air, but at extremely low rates. Even minimal ventilation with outdoor air removes them more quickly. In fact, the plants themselves do not play a major role in the removal of pollutants whereas the soil or other medium in which they are planted have been shown to play the removal role. The amount of pollutants removed by plants is actually minuscule compared to the removal that occurs even with very low rates of outdoor air ventilation. There is also a risk of increasing indoor humidity levels and of promoting mold growth when indoor plants are not properly maintained.

— Use natural household cleaning products and reduce exposure to potentially toxic airborne substances. Be wary of so-called "green" cleaning products if outdoor ozone concentrations are above 50 ppb.

— Use natural pest control techniques indoors whenever possible. Banish pesticides from your garden and lawn as well, as these toxins can easily be transported into the house on shoes and clothing and by air.

— Keep your plumbing traps filled with water to help prevent sewer gas from entering the building.

— Regularly clean the vents in your kitchen, bathroom, and dryer, and make sure they operate properly.

— Do not smoke or allow smoking in your home, and avoid indoor areas where smoking takes place.

— Avoid or reduce biological contaminants by maintaining humidifiers, dehumidifiers, and air conditioners; emptying water trays in dehumidifiers, air conditioners, and refrigerators frequently; drying or removing any water-damaged carpets or furniture; and routinely cleaning bedding and items used by pets.

— Prevent carbon monoxide exposure by keeping gas appliances properly serviced, having your central heating system inspected and cleaned yearly, and never idling your car inside an attached garage. Install an automatic door closer on the door connecting the garage to the house.

— Change filters on central cooling and heating systems and air cleaners according to the manufacturer's directions.

— Test your home for radon. Radon can seep into the house from contaminated earth and rock under the home, or from well water and/or building materials. Easy, do-it-yourself kits can be purchased at hardware and other retail outlets.

— Ensure good ventilation.

— Have any air-contioning systems inspected regularly to verify that there is no internal contamination build up contributing to poor indoor air quality.

Effect of Indoor Air Pollution

It refers to the physical, chemical, and biological characteristics of air in the indoor environment within a home, building, or an institution or commercial facility.

Indoor air pollution is a concern in the developed countries, where energy efficiency improvements sometimes make houses relatively airtight, reducing ventilation and raising pollutant levels. Indoor air problems can be subtle and do not always produce easily recognised impacts on health. Different conditions are responsible for indoor air pollution in the rural areas and the urban areas.

In the developing countries, it is the rural areas that face the greatest threat from indoor pollution, where some 3.5 billion people continue to rely on traditional fuels such as firewood, charcoal, and cowdung for cooking and heating. Concentrations of indoor pollutants in households that burn traditional fuels are alarming. Burning such fuels produces large amount of smoke and other air pollutants in the confined space of the home, resulting in high exposure. Women and children are the groups most vulnerable as they spend more time indoors and are exposed to the smoke.

In 1992, the World Bank designated indoor air pollution in the developing countries as one of the four most critical global environmental problems. Daily averages of pollutant level emitted indoors often exceed current WHO guidelines and acceptable levels. Although many hundreds of separate chemical agents have been identified in the smoke from biofuels, the four most serious pollutants are particulates, carbon monoxide, polycyclic organic matter, and formaldehyde. Unfortunately, little monitoring has been done in rural and poor urban indoor environments in a manner that is statistically rigorous.

In urban areas, exposure to indoor air pollution has increased due to a variety of reasons, including the construction of more tightly sealed buildings, reduced ventilation, the use of synthetic materials for building and furnishing and the use of chemical products, pesticides, and household care products. Indoor air pollution can begin within the building or be drawn in from outdoors. Other than nitrogen dioxide, carbon monoxide, and lead, there are a number of other pollutants that affect the air quality in an enclosed space.

Volatile organic compounds originate mainly from solvents and chemicals. The main indoor sources are perfumes, hair sprays, furniture polish, glues, air fresheners, moth repellents, wood preservatives, and many other products used in the house. The main health effect is the imitation of the eye, nose and throat. In more severe cases there may be headaches, nausea and loss of coordination. In the long term, some of the pollutants are suspected to damage to the liver and other parts of the body.

Tobacco smoke generates a wide range of harmful chemicals and is known to cause cancer. It is well known that passive smoking causes a wide range of problems to the passive smoker (the person who is in the same room with a smoker and is not himself/herself a smoker) ranging from burning eyes, nose, and throat irritation to cancer, bronchitis, severe asthma, and a decrease in lung function.

Pesticides, if used carefully and the manufacturers, instructions followed carefully they do not cause too much harm to the indoor air. Biological pollutants include pollen from plants, mite, hair from pets, fungi, parasites, and some bacteria. Most of them are allergens and can cause asthma, hay fever, and other allergic diseases. Formaldehyde is a gas that comes mainly from carpets, particle boards, and insulation foam. It causes irritation to the eyes and nose and may cause allergies in some people.

Asbestos is mainly a concern because it is suspected to cause cancer. Radon is a gas that is emitted naturally by the soil. Due to modern houses having poor ventilation, it is confined inside the house causing harm to the dwellers.

All of us face a variety of risks to our health as we go about our day-to-day lives. Driving in cars, flying in planes, engaging in recreational activities, and being exposed to environmental pollutants all pose varying degrees of risk. Some risks are simply unavoidable. Some we choose to accept because to do otherwise would restrict our ability to lead our lives the way we want. And some are risks we might decide to avoid if we had the opportunity to make informed choices. Indoor air pollution is one risk that you can do something about.

In the last several years, a growing body of scientific evidence has indicated that the air within homes and other buildings can be more seriously polluted than the outdoor air in even the largest and most industrialised cities. Other research indicates that people spend approximately 90 percent of their time indoors. Thus, for many people, the risks to health may be greater due to exposure to air pollution indoors than outdoors.

While pollutant levels from individual sources may not pose a significant health risk by themselves, most homes have more than one source that contributes to indoor air pollution. There can be a serious risk from the cumulative effects of these sources. Fortunately, there are steps that most people can take both to reduce the risk from existing sources and to prevent new problems from occurring. This booklet was prepared by the U.S. Environmental Protection Agency (EPA) and the U.S.

Consumer Product Safety Commission (CPSC) to help you decide whether to take actions that can reduce the level of indoor air pollution in your own home.

Causes Indoor Air Problems

Indoor pollution sources that release gases or particles into the air are the primary cause of indoor air quality problems in homes. Inadequate ventilation can increase indoor pollutant levels by not bringing in enough outdoor air to dilute emissions from indoor sources and by not carrying indoor air pollutants out of the home. High temperature and humidity levels can also increase concentrations of some pollutants.

There are many sources of indoor air pollution in any home. These include combustion sources such as oil, gas, kerosene, coal, wood, and tobacco products; building materials and furnishings as diverse as deteriorated, asbestos-containing insulation, wet or damp carpet, and cabinetry or furniture made of certain pressed wood products; products for household cleaning and maintenance, personal care, or hobbies; central heating and cooling systems and humidification devices; and outdoor sources such as radon, pesticides, and outdoor air pollution.

The relative importance of any single source depends on how much of a given pollutant it emits and how hazardous those emissions are. In some cases, factors such as how old the source is and whether it is properly maintained are significant. For example, an improperly adjusted gas stove can emit significantly more carbon monoxide than one that is properly adjusted.

Some sources, such as building materials, furnishings, and household products like air fresheners, release pollutants more or less continuously. Other sources, related to activities carried out in the home, release pollutants intermittently. These include smoking, the use of unvented or malfunctioning stoves, furnaces, or space heaters, the use of solvents in cleaning and hobby activities, the use of paint strippers in redecorating activities, and the use of cleaning products and pesticides in housekeeping. High pollutant concentrations can remain in the air for long periods after some of these activities.

If too little outdoor air enters a home, pollutants can accumulate to levels that can pose health and comfort problems. Unless they are built with special mechanical means of ventilation, homes that are designed and constructed to minimize the amount of outdoor air that can "leak" into and out of the home may have higher pollutant levels than other homes. However, because some weather conditions can drastically reduce the amount of outdoor air that enters a home, pollutants can build up even in homes that are normally considered "leaky."

Infiltration Process

Outdoor air enters and leaves a house by: infiltration, natural ventilation, and mechanical ventilation. In a process known as infiltration, outdoor air flows into the house through openings, joints, and cracks in walls, floors, and ceilings, and around windows and doors. In natural ventilation, air moves through opened windows and doors. Air movement associated with infiltration and natural ventilation is caused by air temperature differences between indoors and outdoors and by wind. Finally, there are a number of mechanical ventilation devices, from outdoor-vented fans that intermittently remove air from a single room, such as bathrooms and kitchen, to air handling systems that use fans and duct work to continuously remove indoor air and distribute filtered and conditioned outdoor air to strategic points throughout the house. The rate at which outdoor air replaces indoor air is described as the air exchange rate. When there is little infiltration, natural ventilation, or mechanical ventilation, the air exchange rate is low and pollutant levels can increase.

Apartments can have the same indoor air problems as single-family homes because many of the pollution sources, such as the interior building materials, furnishings, and household products, are similar. Indoor air problems similar to those in offices are caused by such sources as contaminated ventilation systems, improperly placed outdoor air intakes, or maintenance activities.

Solutions to air quality problems in apartments, as in homes and offices, involve such actions as: eliminating or controlling the sources of pollution, increasing ventilation, and installing air cleaning devices. Often a resident can take the appropriate action to improve the indoor air quality by removing a source, altering an activity, unblocking an air supply vent, or opening a window to temporarily increase the ventilation; in other cases, however, only the building owner or manager is in a position to remedy the problem. You can encourage building management to follow guidance in EPA's IAQ Building Education and Assessment Model (I-BEAM).

I-BEAM updates and expands EPA's existing Building Air Quality guidance and is designed to be comprehensive state-of-the-art guidance for managing IAQ in commercial buildings. This guidance was designed to be used by building professionals and others interested in indoor air quality in commercial buildings. I-BEAM contains text, animation/visual, and interactive/calculation components that can be used to perform a number of diverse tasks. You can also encourage building management to follow guidance in EPA and NIOSH's Building Air Quality: A Guide for Building Owners and Facility Managers.

Indoor Air and Health

Health effects from indoor air pollutants may be experienced soon after exposure or, possibly, years later. Immediate effects may show up after a single exposure or repeated exposures. These include irritation of the eyes, nose, and throat, headaches, dizziness, and fatigue. Such immediate effects are usually short-term and treatable. Sometimes the treatment is simply eliminating the person's exposure to the source of the pollution, if it can be identified. Symptoms of some diseases, including asthma, hypersensitivity pneumonitis, and humidifier fever, may also show up soon after exposure to some indoor air pollutants.

The likelihood of immediate reactions to indoor air pollutants depends on several factors. Age and preexisting medical conditions are two important influences. In other cases, whether a person reacts to a pollutant depends on individual sensitivity, which varies tremendously from person to person. Some people can become sensitised to biological pollutants after repeated exposures, and it appears that some people can become sensitised to chemical pollutants as well.

Certain immediate effects are similar to those from colds or other viral diseases, so it is often difficult to determine if the symptoms are a result of exposure to indoor air pollution. For this reason, it is important to pay attention to the time and place the symptoms occur. If the symptoms fade or go away when a person is away from the home and return when the person returns, an effort should be made to identify indoor air sources that may be possible causes. Some effects may be made worse by an inadequate supply of outdoor air or from the heating, cooling, or humidity conditions prevalent in the home.

Other health effects may show up either years after exposure has occurred or only after long or repeated periods of exposure. These effects, which include some respiratory diseases, heart disease, and cancer, can be severely debilitating or fatal. It is prudent to try to improve the indoor air quality in your home even if symptoms are not noticeable.

While pollutants commonly found in indoor air are responsible for many harmful effects, there is considerable uncertainty about what concentrations or periods of exposure are necessary to produce specific health problems. People also react very differently to exposure to indoor air pollutants. Further research is needed to better understand which health effects occur after exposure to the average pollutant concentrations found in homes and which occur from the higher concentrations that occur for short periods of time.

Identifying Air Quality Problems

Some health effects can be useful indicators of an indoor air quality problem, especially if they appear after a person moves to a new residence, remodels or refurnishes a home, or treats a home with pesticides. If you think that you have symptoms that may be related to your home environment, discuss them with your doctor or your local health department to see if they could be caused by indoor air pollution. You may also want to consult a board-certified allergist or an occupational medicine specialist for answers to your questions.

Another way to judge whether your home has or could develop indoor air problems is to identify potential sources of indoor air pollution. Although the presence of such sources does not necessarily mean that you have an indoor air quality problem, being aware of the type and number of potential sources is an important step toward assessing the air quality in your home.

A third way to decide whether your home may have poor indoor air quality is to look at your lifestyle and activities. Human activities can be significant sources of indoor air pollution. Finally, look for signs of problems with the ventilation in your home. Signs that can indicate your home may not have enough ventilation include moisture condensation on windows or walls, smelly or stuffy air, dirty central heating and air cooling equipment, and areas where books, shoes, or other items become moldy. To detect odours in your home, step outside for a few minutes, and then upon reentering your home, note whether odours are noticeable.

Measuring Pollutant Levels

The federal government recommends that you measure the level of radon in your home. Without measurements there is no way to tell whether radon is present because it is a colourless, odourless, radioactive gas. Inexpensive devices are available for measuring radon. EPA provides guidance as to risks associated with different levels of exposure and when the public should consider corrective action. There are specific mitigation techniques that have proven effective in reducing levels of radon in the home.

For pollutants other than radon, measurements are most appropriate when there are either health symptoms or signs of poor ventilation and specific sources or pollutants have been identified as possible causes of indoor air quality problems. Testing for many pollutants can be expensive. Before monitoring your home for pollutants besides radon, consult your state or local health department or professionals who have experience in solving indoor air quality problems in non-industrial buildings.

Weatherisation

The federal government recommends that homes be weatherised in order to reduce the amount of energy needed for heating and cooling. While weatherisation is underway, however, steps should also be taken to minimize pollution from sources inside the home. In addition, residents should be alert to the emergence of signs of inadequate ventilation, such as stuffy air, moisture condensation on cold surfaces, or mold and mildew growth. Additional weatherisation measures should not be undertaken until these problems have been corrected.

Weatherisation generally does not cause indoor air problems by adding new pollutants to the air. However, measures such as installing storm windows, weather stripping, caulking, and blown-in wall insulation can reduce the amount of outdoor air infiltrating into a home. Consequently, after weatherisation, concentrations of indoor air pollutants from sources inside the home can increase.

Three Basic Strategies

Source Control

Usually the most effective way to improve indoor air quality is to eliminate individual sources of pollution or to reduce their emissions. Some sources, like those that contain asbestos, can be sealed or enclosed; others, like gas stoves, can be adjusted to decrease the amount of emissions. In many cases, source control is also a more cost-efficient approach to protecting indoor air quality than increasing ventilation because increasing ventilation can increase energy costs.

Another approach to lowering the concentrations of indoor air pollutants in your home is to increase the amount of outdoor air coming indoors. Most home heating and cooling systems, including forced air heating systems, do not mechanically bring fresh air into the house. Opening windows and doors, operating window or attic fans, when the weather permits, or running a window air conditioner with the vent control open increases the outdoor ventilation rate. Local bathroom or kitchen fans that exhaust outdoors remove contaminants directly from the room where the fan is located and also increase the outdoor air ventilation rate.

It is particularly important to take as many of these steps as possible while you are involved in short-term activities that can generate high levels of pollutants—for example, painting, paint stripping, heating with kerosene heaters, cooking, or engaging in maintenance and hobby activities such as welding, soldering, or sanding. You might also choose to do some of these activities outdoors, if you can and if weather permits. Advanced designs of new homes are starting to feature mechanical systems that bring outdoor air into the home. Some of these designs include energy-efficient heat recovery ventilators (also known as air-to-air heat exchangers).

Role of Air Cleaners

There are many types and sizes of air cleaners on the market, ranging from relatively inexpensive table-top models to sophisticated and expensive whole-house systems. Some air cleaners are highly effective at particle removal, while others, including most table-top models, are much less so. Air cleaners are generally not designed to remove gaseous pollutants.

The effectiveness of an air cleaner depends on how well it collects pollutants from indoor air (expressed as a percentage efficiency rate) and how much air it draws through the cleaning or filtering element (expressed in cubic feet per minute). A very efficient collector with a low air-circulation rate will not be effective, nor will a cleaner with a high air-circulation rate but a less efficient collector. The long-term performance of any air cleaner depends on maintaining it according to the manufacturer's directions.

Another important factor in determining the effectiveness of an air cleaner is the strength of the pollutant source. Table-top air cleaners, in particular, may not remove satisfactory amounts of pollutants from strong nearby sources. People with a sensitivity to particular sources may find that air cleaners are helpful only in conjunction with concerted efforts to remove the source.

Over the past few years, there has been some publicity suggesting that houseplants have been shown to reduce levels of some chemicals in laboratory experiments. There is currently no evidence, however, that a reasonable number of houseplants remove significant quantities of pollutants in homes and offices. Indoor houseplants should not be over-watered because overlay damp soil may promote the growth of microorganisms which can affect allergic individuals.

At present, EPA does not recommend using air cleaners to reduce levels of radon and its decay products. The effectiveness of these devices is uncertain because they only partially remove the radon decay products and do not diminish the amount of radon entering the home. EPA plans to do additional research on whether air cleaners are, or could become, a reliable means of reducing the health risk from radon. EPA's booklet, Residential Air-Cleaning Devices, provides further information on air-cleaning devices to reduce indoor air pollutants.

For most indoor air quality problems in the home, source control is the most effective solution. Source-by-source look at the most common indoor air pollutants, their potential health effects, and ways to reduce levels in the home.

— Ozone generators that are sold as air cleaners was prepared by EPA to provide accurate information regarding the use of ozone-generating devices in indoor occupied spaces. This information is based on the most credible scientific evidence currently available.

— "Should you have the air ducts in your home cleaned?" was prepared by EPA to assist consumers in answering this often confusing question. The document explains what air duct cleaning is, provides guidance to help consumers decide whether to have the service performed in their home, and provides helpful information for choosing a duct cleaner, determining if duct cleaning was done properly, and how to prevent contamination of air ducts.

Source-Specific Controls

The most common source of indoor radon is uranium in the soil or rock on which homes are built. As uranium naturally breaks down, it releases radon gas which is a colourless, odourless, radioactive gas. Radon gas enters homes through dirt floors, cracks in concrete walls and floors, floor drains, and sumps. When radon becomes trapped in buildings and concentrations build up indoors, exposure to radon becomes a concern. Any home may have a radon problem. This means new and old homes, well-sealed and drafty homes, and homes with or without basements. Sometimes radon enters the home through well water. In a small number of homes, the building materials can give off radon, too. However, building materials rarely cause radon problems by themselves.

Health effects of radon

The predominant health effect associated with exposure to elevated levels of radon is lung cancer. Research suggests that swallowing water with high radon levels may pose risks, too, although these are believed to be much lower than those from breathing air containing radon. Major health organisations (like the Centers for Disease Control and Prevention, the American Lung Association (ALA), and the American Medical Association) agree with estimates that radon causes thousands of preventable lung cancer deaths each year. EPA estimates that radon causes about 14,000 deaths per year in the United States—however, this number could range from 7,000 to 30,000 deaths per year. If you smoke and your home has high radon levels, your risk of lung cancer is especially high.

Reducing Exposure to Radon in Homes

You can't see radon, but it's not hard to find out if you have a radon problem in your home. Testing is easy and should only take a little of your time. There are many kinds of inexpensive, do-it-yourself radon test kits you can get through the mail and in hardware stores and other retail outlets. EPA recommends that consumers use test kits that are state-certified or have met the requirements of some national radon proficiency programme. If you prefer, or if you are buying or selling a home, you can hire a trained contractor to do the testing for you. You should call your state radon office to obtain a list of qualified contractors in your area. You can also contact either the National Environmental Health Association's (NEHA) National Radon Proficiency Programme (NRPP) www.neha-nrpp.org or the National Radon Safety Board (NRSB)—www.nrsb.org for a list of proficient radon measurement and/or mitigation contractors.

Radon reduction methods.

— Ways to reduce radon in your home are discussed in EPA's Consumer's Guide to Radon Reduction. There are simple solutions to radon problems in homes. Thousands of homeowners have already fixed radon problems. Lowering high radon levels requires technical knowledge and special skills. You should use a contractor who is trained to fix radon problems.

— A trained radon reduction contractor can study the problem in your home and help you pick the correct treatment method. Check with your state radon office for names of qualified or state-certified radon-reduction contractors in your area.

Scientific evidence indicates that smoking combined with radon is an especially serious health risk. Stop smoking and lower your radon level to reduce lung cancer risk.

While radon in water is not a problem in homes served by most public water supplies, it has been found in well water. If you've tested the air in your home and found a radon problem, and you have a well, contact a lab certified to measure radiation in water to have your water tested. Radon problems in water can be readily fixed.

Environmental Tobacco Smoke (ETS)

Environmental tobacco smoke (ETS) is the mixture of smoke that comes from the burning end of a cigarette, pipe, or cigar, and smoke exhaled by the smoker. It is a complex mixture of over 4,000 compounds, more than 40 of which are known to cause cancer in humans or animals and many of which are strong irritants. ETS is often referred to as "secondhand smoke" and exposure to ETS is often called "passive smoking."

Health Effects of Environmental Tobacco Smoke

In 1992, EPA completed a major assessment of the respiratory health risks of ETS. The report concludes that exposure to ETS is responsible for approximately 3,000 lung cancer deaths each year in nonsmoking adults and impairs the respiratory health of hundreds of thousands of children.

Infants and young children whose parents smoke in their presence are at increased risk of lower respiratory tract infections (pneumonia and bronchitis) and are more likely to have symptoms of respiratory irritation like cough, excess phlegm, and wheeze. EPA estimates that passive smoking annually causes between 150,000 and 300,000 lower respiratory tract infections in infants and children under 18 months of age, resulting in between 7,500 and 15,000 hospitalisations each year. These children may also have a build-up of fluid in the middle ear, which can lead to ear infections. Older children who have been exposed to secondhand smoke may have slightly reduced lung function.

Asthmatic children are especially at risk. EPA estimates that exposure to secondhand smoke increases the number of episodes and severity of symptoms in hundreds of thousands of asthmatic children, and may cause thousands of non-asthmatic children to develop the disease each year. EPA estimates that between 200,000 and 1,000,000 asthmatic children have their condition made worse by exposure to secondhand smoke each year. Exposure to secondhand smoke causes eye, nose, and throat irritation. It may affect the cardiovascular system and some studies have linked exposure to secondhand smoke with the onset of chest pain.

Reducing Exposure to Environmental Tobacco Smoke

The 1986 Surgeon General's report concluded that physical separation of smokers and nonsmokers in a common air space, such as different rooms within the same house, may reduce—but will not eliminate—nonsmokers' exposure to environmental tobacco smoke.

Open windows or use exhaust fans. Ventilation, a common method of reducing exposure to indoor air pollutants, also will reduce but not eliminate exposure to environmental tobacco smoke. Because smoking produces such large amounts of pollutants, natural or mechanical ventilation techniques do not remove them from the air in your home as quickly as they build up. In addition, the large increases in ventilation it takes to significantly reduce exposure to environmental tobacco smoke can also increase energy costs substantially. Consequently, the most effective way to reduce exposure to environmental tobacco smoke in the home is to eliminate smoking there.

Biological Contaminants

Biological contaminants include bacteria, molds, mildew, viruses, animal dander and cat saliva, house dust mites, cockroaches, and pollen. There are many sources of these pollutants. Pollens originate from plants; viruses are transmitted by people and animals; bacteria are carried by people, animals, and soil and plant debris; and household pets are sources of saliva and animal dander. The protein in urine from rats and mice is a potent allergen. When it dries, it can become airborne. Contaminated central air handling systems can become breeding grounds for mold, mildew, and other sources of biological contaminants and can then distribute these contaminants through the home.

By controlling the relative humidity level in a home, the growth of some sources of biologicals can be minimized. A relative humidity of 30-50 percent is generally recommended for homes. Standing water, water-damaged materials, or wet surfaces also serve as a breeding ground for molds, mildews, bacteria, and insects. House dust mites, the source of one of the most powerful biological allergens, grow in damp, warm environments.

Some biological contaminants trigger allergic reactions, including hypersensitivity pneumonitis, allergic rhinitis, and some types of asthma. Infectious illnesses, such as influenza, measles, and chicken pox are transmitted through the air. Molds and mildews release disease-causing toxins. Symptoms of health problems caused by biological pollutants include sneezing, watery eyes, coughing, shortness of breath, dizziness, lethargy, fever, and digestive problems.

Allergic reactions occur only after repeated exposure to a specific biological allergen. However, that reaction may occur immediately upon re-exposure or after multiple exposures over time. As a result, people who have noticed only mild allergic reactions, or no reactions at all, may suddenly find themselves very sensitive to particular allergens.

Some diseases, like humidifier fever, are associated with exposure to toxins from microorganisms that can grow in large building ventilation systems. However, these diseases can also be traced to microorganisms that grow in home heating and cooling systems and humidifiers. Children, elderly people, and people with breathing problems, allergies, and lung diseases are particularly susceptible to disease-causing biological agents in the indoor air.

Reducing Exposure to Biological Contaminants

These actions can eliminate much of the moisture that builds up from everyday activities. There are exhaust fans on the market that produce little noise, an important consideration for some people. Another benefit to using kitchen and bathroom exhaust fans is that they can reduce levels of organic pollutants that vaporize from hot water used in showers and dishwashers. Keeping humidity levels in these areas below 50 percent can prevent water condensation on building materials.

If using cool mist or ultrasonic humidifiers, clean appliances according to manufacturer's instructions and refill with fresh water daily. Because these humidifiers can become breeding grounds for biological contaminants, they have the potential for causing diseases such as hypersensitivity pneumonitis and humidifier fever. Evaporation trays in air conditioners, dehumidifiers, and refrigerators should also be cleaned frequently.

Thoroughly clean and dry water-damaged carpets and building materials (within 24 hours if possible) or consider removal and replacement. Water-damaged carpets and building materials can harbour mold and bacteria. It is very difficult to completely rid such materials of biological contaminants.

Keep the house clean. House dust mites, pollens, animal dander, and other allergy-causing agents can be reduced, although not eliminated, through regular cleaning. People who are allergic to these pollutants should use allergen-proof mattress encasements, wash bedding in hot (130° F) water, and avoid room furnishings that accumulate dust, especially if they cannot be washed in hot water. Allergic individuals should also leave the house while it is being vacuumed because vacuuming can actually increase airborne levels of mite allergens and other biological contaminants. Using central vacuum systems that are vented to the outdoors or vacuums with high efficiency filters may also be of help.

Minimize biological pollutants in basements

Clean and disinfect the basement floor drain regularly. Do not finish a basement below ground level unless all water leaks are patched and outdoor ventilation and adequate heat to prevent condensation are provided. Operate a dehumidifier in the basement if needed to keep relative humidity levels between 30-50 percent. To learn more about biological pollutants, read Biological Pollutants in Your Home issued by the U.S. Consumer Product Safety Commission and the American Lung Association.

Stoves, Heaters, Fireplaces, and Chimneys

In addition to environmental tobacco smoke, other sources of combustion products are unvented kerosene and gas space heaters, woodstoves, fireplaces, and gas stoves. The major pollutants released are carbon monoxide, nitrogen dioxide, and particles. Unvented kerosene heaters may also generate acid aerosols. Combustion gases and particles also come from chimneys and flues that are improperly installed or maintained and cracked furnace heat exchangers. Pollutants from fireplaces and woodstoves with no dedicated outdoor air supply can be "back-drafted" from the chimney into the living space, particularly in weatherised homes.

Health effects of combustion products

Carbon monoxide (CO) is a colourless, odourless gas that interferes with the delivery of oxygen throughout the body. At high concentrations it can cause unconsciousness and death. Lower concentrations can cause a range of symptoms from headaches, dizziness, weakness, nausea, confusion, and disorientation, to fatigue in healthy people and episodes of increased chest pain in people with chronic heart disease. The symptoms of carbon monoxide poisoning are sometimes confused with the flu or food poisoning. Fetuses, infants, elderly people, and people with anemia or with a history of heart or respiratory disease can be especially sensitive to carbon monoxide exposures.

Nitrogen dioxide (NO_2) is a colourless, odourless gas that irritates the mucous membranes in the eye, nose, and throat and causes shortness of breath after exposure to high concentrations. There is evidence that high concentrations or continued exposure to low levels of nitrogen dioxide increases the risk of respiratory infection; there is also evidence from animal studies that repeated exposures to elevated nitrogen dioxide levels may lead, or contribute, to the development of lung disease such as emphysema. People at particular risk from exposure to nitrogen dioxide include children and individuals with asthma and other respiratory diseases.

Particles, released when fuels are incompletely burned, can lodge in the lungs and irritate or damage lung tissue. A number of pollutants, including radon and benzo(a)pyrene, both of which can cause cancer, attach to small particles that are inhaled and then carried deep into the lung.

Reducing Exposure to Combustion Products in Homes

Consider potential effects of indoor air pollution if you use an unvented kerosene or gas space heater. Follow the manufacturer's directions, especially instructions on the proper fuel and keeping the heater properly adjusted. A persistent yellow-tipped flame is generally an indicator of maladjustment and increased pollutant emissions. While a space heater is in use, open a door from the room where the heater is located to the rest of the house and open a window slightly.

Using a stove hood with a fan vented to the outdoors greatly reduces exposure to pollutants during cooking. Improper adjustment, often indicated by a persistent yellow-tipped flame, causes increased pollutant emissions. Ask your gas company to adjust the burner so that the flame tip is blue. If you purchase a new gas stove or range, consider buying one with pilotless ignition because it does not have a pilot light that burns continuously. Never use a gas stove to heat your home. Always make certain the flue in your gas fireplace is open when the fireplace is in use.

Make certain that doors in old woodstoves are tight-fitting. Use aged or cured (dried) wood only and follow the manufacturer's directions for starting, stoking, and putting out the fire in woodstoves. Chemicals are used to pressure-treat wood; such wood should never be burned indoors.

Blocked, leaking, or damaged chimneys or flues release harmful combustion gases and particles and even fatal concentrations of carbon monoxide. Strictly follow all service and maintenance procedures recommended by the manufacturer, including those that tell you how frequently to change the filter. If manufacturer's instructions are not readily available, change filters once every month or two during periods of use. Proper maintenance is important even for new furnaces because they can also corrode and leak combustion gases, including carbon monoxide.

Household Products

Organic chemicals are widely used as ingredients in household products. Paints, varnishes, and wax all contain organic solvents, as do many cleaning, disinfecting, cosmetic, degreasing, and hobby products. Fuels are made up of organic chemicals. All of thesse products can release organic compounds while you are using them, and, to some degree, when they are stored.

EPA's Total Exposure Assessment Methodology (TEAM) studies found levels of about a dozen common organic pollutants to be 2 to 5 times higher inside homes than outside, regardless of whether the homes were located in rural or highly industrial areas. Additional TEAM studies indicate that while people are using products containing organic chemicals, they can expose themselves and others to very high pollutant levels, and elevated concentrations can persist in the air long after the activity is completed.

Health Effects of Household Chemicals

The ability of organic chemicals to cause health effects varies greatly, from those that are highly toxic, to those with no known health effect. As with other pollutants, the extent and nature of the health effect will depend on many factors including level of exposure and length of time exposed. Eye and respiratory tract irritation, headaches, dizziness, visual disorders, and memory impairment are among the immediate symptoms that some people have experienced soon after exposure to some organics. At present, not much is known about what health effects occur from the levels of organics usually found in homes. Many organic compounds are known to cause cancer in animals; some are suspected of causing, or are known to cause, cancer in humans.

Reducing Exposure to Household Chemicals

Potentially hazardous products often have warnings aimed at reducing exposure of the user. For example, if a label says to use the product in a well-ventilated area, go outdoors or in areas equipped with an exhaust fan to use it. Otherwise, open up windows to provide the maximum amount of outdoor air possible.

Throw away partially full containers of old or unneeded chemicals safely. Because gases can leak even from closed containers, this single step could help lower concentrations of organic chemicals in your home. (Be sure that materials you decide to keep are stored not only in a well-ventilated area but are also safely out of reach of children.) Do not simply toss these unwanted products in the garbage can. Find out if your local government or any organisation in your community sponsors special days for the collection of toxic household wastes. If such days are available, use them to dispose of the unwanted containers safely. If no such collection days are available, think about organising one.

Consumer products that contain methylene chloride include paint strippers, adhesive removers, and aerosol spray paints. Methylene chloride is known to cause cancer in animals. Also, methylene chloride is converted to carbon monoxide in the body and can cause symptoms associated with exposure to carbon monoxide. Carefully read the labels containing health hazard information and cautions on the proper use of these products. Use products that contain methylene chloride outdoors when possible; use indoors only if the area is well ventilated.

Benzene is a known human carcinogen. The main indoor sources of this chemical are environmental tobacco smoke, stored fuels and paint supplies, and automobile emissions in attached garages. Actions that will reduce benzene exposure include eliminating smoking within the home, providing for maximum ventilation during painting, and discarding paint supplies and special fuels that will not be used immediately.

Perchloroethylene is the chemical most widely used in dry cleaning. In laboratory studies, it has been shown to cause cancer in animals. Recent studies indicate that people breathe low levels of this chemical both in homes where dry-cleaned goods are stored and as they wear dry-cleaned clothing. Dry cleaners recapture the perchloroethylene during the dry-cleaning process so they can save money by re-using it, and they remove more of the chemical during the pressing and finishing processes. Some dry cleaners, however, do not remove as much perchloroethylene as possible all of the time. Taking steps to minimize your exposure to this chemical is prudent. If dry-cleaned goods have a strong chemical odor when you pick them up, do not accept them until they have been properly dried. If goods with a chemical odor are returned to you on subsequent visits, try a different dry cleaner.

Formaldehyde is an important chemical used widely by industry to manufacture building materials and numerous household products. It is also a by-product of combustion and certain other natural processes. Thus, it may be present in substantial concentrations both indoors and outdoors.

Sources of formaldehyde in the home include building materials, smoking, household products, and the use of unvented, fuel-burning appliances, like gas stoves or kerosene space heaters. Formaldehyde, by itself or in combination with other chemicals, serves a number of purposes in manufactured products. For example, it is used to add permanent-press qualities to clothing and draperies, as a component of glues and adhesives, and as a preservative in some paints and coating products.

In homes, the most significant sources of formaldehyde are likely to be pressed wood products made using adhesives that contain urea-formaldehyde (UF) resins. Pressed wood products made for indoor use include: particleboard (used as subflooring and shelving and in cabinetry and furniture); hardwood plywood paneling (used for decorative wall covering and used in cabinets and furniture); and medium density fiberboard (used for drawer fronts, cabinets, and furniture tops). Medium density fiberboard contains a higher resin-to-wood ratio than any other UF pressed wood product and is generally recognised as being the highest formaldehyde-emitting pressed wood product.

Other pressed wood products, such as softwood plywood and flake or oriented strandboard, are produced for exterior construction use and contain the dark, or red/black-colored phenol-formaldehyde (PF) resin. Although formaldehyde is present in both types of resins, pressed woods that contain PF resin generally emit formaldehyde at considerably lower rates than those containing UF resin.

Since 1985, the Department of Housing and Urban Development (HUD) has permitted only the use of plywood and particleboard that conform to specified formaldehyde emission limits in the construction of prefabricated and mobile homes. In the past, some of these homes had elevated levels of formaldehyde because of the large amount of high-emitting pressed wood products used in their construction and because of their relatively small interior space. The rate at which products like pressed wood or textiles release formaldehyde can change. Formaldehyde emissions will generally decrease as products age. When the products are new, high indoor temperatures or humidity can cause increased release of formaldehyde from these products.

During the 1970s, many homeowners had urea-formaldehyde foam insulation (UFFI) installed in the wall cavities of their homes as an energy conservation measure. However, many of these homes were found to have relatively high indoor concentrations of formaldehyde soon after the UFFI installation. Few homes are now being insulated with this product. Studies show that formaldehyde emissions from UFFI decline with time; therefore, homes in which UFFI was installed many years ago are unlikely to have high levels of formaldehyde now.

Formaldehyde, a colourless, pungent-smelling gas, can cause watery eyes, burning sensations in the eyes and throat, nausea, and difficulty in breathing in some humans exposed at elevated levels (above 0.1 parts per million). High concentrations may trigger attacks in people with asthma. There is evidence that some people can develop a sensitivity to formaldehyde. It has also been shown to cause cancer in animals and may cause cancer in humans.

3

Hotel Interior Design

Commercial interior design was once referred to as contract design. In fact, many interior designers still use this term, which developed from interior designers' use of a contract to outline services, fees, and responsibilities related to the project. Until approximately 30 years ago, contracts of this type were used primarily by interior designers working on business facilities. Today, most residential interior designers also use contracts, so the designation is less applicable.

One could argue that commercial interior design began when the first trade and food stalls opened somewhere in Mesopotamia or another ancient country. Certainly buildings that housed many commercial transactions or that would be considered commercial facilities today have existed since early human history. For example, business was conducted in the great rooms of the Egyptian pharaohs and the palaces of kings; administrative spaces existed within great cathedrals, and in portions of residences of craftsmen and tradesmen.

The lodging industry dates back many centuries, beginning with simple inns and taverns. Historically, hospitals were first associated with religious groups. During the Crusades of the Middle Ages, the hospitia, which provided food, lodging, and medical care to the ill, were located adjacent to monasteries. In earlier centuries, interior spaces created for the wealthy and powerful were designed by architects.

Business places such as inns and shops for the lower classes were most likely "designed" by tradesmen and craftsmen or whoever owned them. Craftsmen and tradesmen influenced early interior design as they created the furniture and architectural treatments of the palaces and other great structures, as well as the dwelliings and other facilities for the lower classes.

As commerce grew, buildings specific to business enterprises such as stores, restaurants, inns, and offices were gradually created or became more common. Consider the monasteries of the 12th century, as well as the mosques and temples of the Middle East and the Orient; the amphitheaters of ancient Greece and Rome; and the Globe Theatre in London built in the 16th century. From the 17th century on, the design of commercial building interiors became increasingly important.

For example, offices began to move from the home to a separate location in a business area in the 17th century, numerous bank buildings were constructed in the 18th century, and hotels began taking on their grand size and opulence in the 19th century. Furniture items and business machines such as typewriters and telephones, as well as other specialised items, were also being designed in the 19th century.

In the 20th century, reinforced concrete, modular construction technologies, and numerous advances in the building industry changed the appearance of commercial facilities. The early commercial buildings of architects such as Frank Lloyd Wright, Bauhaus architects such as Walter Gropius, and International Style architects such as

Le Corbusier, to name just a few, advanced commercial architecture and interior design with contemporary aesthetics. Technology also changed the interior finishing of structures.

New products such as bent tubular steel for furniture designed by Mies van der Rohe and Marcel Breuer, molded plywood used by Alvar Aalto and Charles Eames, and the fiberglass designs of Eero Saarinen also changed the interior design of commercial facilities. These are only a few of the achievements and advances in furniture design and interior design made in the early 20th century.

The sweeping open spaces of the Johnson Wax Building in Racine, Wisconsin, designed by Frank Lloyd Wright, were precursors of the open plan designs that emerged in office spaces. Open planning or open landscape, began in 1958 in Germany. That planning concept gradually gained acceptance and caused major rethinking of office planning. New furniture items focusing on the use of panels and individualised components were introduced in the late 1960s, changing office planning and design dramatically. Commercial interiors changed for many reasons in the second half of the 20th century.

Technological changes in construction and mechanical systems, code requirements for safety, and electronic business equipment of every kind have impacted the way business is conducted throughout the world. Consumers of business and institutional services expect and demand better environments as part of the experience of visiting stores, hotels, restaurants, doctors' offices, and schools—everywhere they go to shop or conduct business. Interior design and architecture must keep up with these changes and demands. This is one of the key reasons that an interior designer must be educated in a wide range of subjects and understand the business operations of clients.

The interior design profession also grew in stature in the 20th century with the development of professional associations, professional education, and competency testing. The decorators' clubs that existed in major cities in the 1920s and 1930s were the precursors of the two largest interior design professional associations in the United States. The American Society of Interior Designers (ASID) has over 38,000 members involved in residential and commercial interior design.

In professional education and testing, the most significant advances occurred in the second half of the 20th century. Many schools have had interior design programs with varying content and quality since the early 20th century. In 1963 the Interior Design Educators Council (IDEC) was organised to advance education in interior design and meet the needs of faculty members in interior design programs. The growth of the profession encouraged many other programs, and in 1970 the Foundation for Interior Design Education Research (FIDER) was incorporated to serve as the primary academic accrediting agency for interior design education.

In 2005, the Foundation changed the name of the organisation to the Council for Interior Design Accreditation. The National Council for Interior Design Qualification (NCIDQ) was incorporated in 1974 to meet the need for an independent organisation to test for competency in the profession.

Client's Business

The design of a commercial interior begins with an

understanding of the business of the business, which refers to understanding the goals and purposes of a business. In fact, it is important to understand the business specialty even before seeking projects in that specialty. When the interior designer and team understand the client's business in general and the client's goals for the project from a business point of view as well as from a design standpoint, solutions are more functional for the client and lead to more creative design concepts.

For example, space planning and product specifications are different for a pediatrician's suite than for the offices of a cardiologist. Planning decisions are different for a small gift shop in a strip shopping center than for one in a resort hotel. Understanding this from the onset is critical for the design firm.

An obvious advantage of understanding the client's business is that the interior design will be more functional. Businesses seek interior design firms that are not "learning on the job" with the client's project. Of course, creative solutions that are aesthetically pleasing are important to many clients. However, a creative and attractive office that does not work or is not safe is not helpful to the client. Creativity alone does not mean success in commercial interior design.

One issue that influences the interior design of a commercial space is the type of facility: is it a doctor's office suite with exam rooms or a hospital acute care unit? Is it a coffee shop or a high-end, full-service restaurant? Is the project an elementary school or the business college at a university? Is it a bed and breakfast or a convention hotel? Each type of facility has many different requirements. Space planning, furniture specification, materials that can be used, codes that must be adhered to, and the functions and goals of the business are just some of the many factors that influence the interior design based on the type of facility.

Location is another issue. Is the project in a small town or an urban area? Will the accounting office be located in a strip shopping center or an office building? Is the restaurant in a stand-alone building or incorporated into a hotel? The impact of the location of the business will relate to the client base the business wants to attract. The dollars spent on the interior may very well be different based on the project's location. Customer expectations will be greater when the business is located in a high-end area.

Another issue is the expected customers of the business. Different design decisions will be made if a restaurant's customers are neighbourhood residents, tourists, or business executives. Obvious differences in design and amenities will be made for a hotel along an interstate highway than for a resort hotel in the mountains. Retail stores catering to Generation will have different detailing and colour choices from stores located in retirement communities.

The type of work conducted in a business also varies with the nature of the business. The work done in a coffee shop that only sells coffee products and bakery goods is very different from that of a full-service, high-end restaurant. The display fixtures and ambiance of a jewelry store are significantly different from those of a sporting goods store. Acceptable accommodations for a traveller at a motel along the highway are entirely different from those of the individual who has travelled across the country to attend a professional conference.

Your client is another influencing factor. He or she may be the owner of an accounting office or the neighbourhoods restaurant or bed and breakfast, or developer, creating office space for anyone or any type of office function. Then again, the owner might be the board of directors and the facility manager for a major corporation's new headquarters or the local jurisdictional governing body, retaining an interior designer for the design of a new county courthouse. Maybe your client is a charitable foundation adding a new wing to a museum. Each client has different goals for the business, and the interior designer is challenged to satisfy all their unique demands.

Obviously, understanding the business of the business and its characteristics is important to understanding how to go about designing the interior. The more you know about the hospitality industry, for example, the more effective your solutions will be for a lodging or food service facility. Gaining experience and knowledge about retailing will be an advantage for you in designing any kind of retail space. In fact, the more you know about any of the specialty areas of commercial interior design, the greater your success in working with those clients.

Working in Interior Design

The design of commercial interiors is complex and challenging. It requires attention to detail, comfort with working effectively as part of a team, and the ability to work with numerous stakeholders—individuals who have a vested interest in the project, such as members of the design team, the client, the architect, and vendors. Often the interior designer works with employees of the business rather than the owner. However, design decisions must also please the owner.

Regulations must be met that can influence certain decisions and choices about the interior design. The architect, interior designer, contractor, and other stakeholders involved in the design, construction, and installation of products must be sure that the design decisions meet the aesthetic goals of the client and adhere to building, life safety, and accessibility standards and codes that apply to the particular type of facility.

Commercial interior design projects must follow all phases of the design process closely. Missing steps or halfheartedly doing any of the tasks in programming, schematic design, or design development; incomplete preparation of construction documentation; or faulty contract administration can be disastrous. Thus, interior designers working in one of the commercial specialties must be very detail oriented to ensure that all tasks are performed completely and correctly.

Margins for error are often nonexistent, as many projects are fast-tracked, where design plans for one phase of the project are created as construction is proceeding on another phase to ensure early occupancy. It is far easier to take care of the details as they arise than to solve problems later on. Programming is of particular importance and the information obtained at the beginning of the project must be carefully gathered. Information about the client's space and aesthetic preferences is only the beginning. Of course, it is important to understand what codes or other standards may apply to the project.

Regardless of the type of facility, the client's business goals and plans are very important in the successful functional design of the interior. Knowing where the business wants to go is as important to the designer as where it is on the day that programming information is obtained. Many large interior design firms offer assistance with strategic planning for businesses that do not already engage in this type of planning. Teamwork is also a vital part of commercial projects. Since the projects can be very large, it is difficult for one or two people to handle all the work.

Project managers and senior design staff will be in charge of several interior designers and support personnel. Entry-level and junior members of the staff are often delegated smaller, targeted tasks. However, all the tasks needed to complete these projects are important. Willingness to be part of the team, effectively doing one's job, and offering to be involved are not only important in completing the project but bode well for advancement in the firm.

A critical skill for commercial interior designers is effective communication. Whether one is referring to verbal, written, or design graphics, communicating the designer's concepts and justifications for design ideas is critical. General correspondence and notes that must be forwarded to the client and peers, as well as accurate specifications of the products, are a few examples of written communications that must be accomplished in a professional manner.

Interior designers must make numerous verbal presentations to clients, team members, clients, supervisors, and others. Making such presentations effectively and professionally is a crucial skill for interior designers to master. Of course, graphic communications have become easier with the computer. As long as the correct information is inputted, the drawings will be accurate. Skill in computer-aided drafting (CAD) is mandatory in commercial interior design.

Accuracy is important to meet codes and regulations. The interior designer must satisfy several users of the interiors. First is the owner of the property itself. This might be a developer building an office building on spec with no particular tenant in mind. The owner of the property might be a corporation building a new corporate headquarters or branch facility or a hotel chain building or remodelling a property. For publicly owned buildings like government offices and schools, the first user to be satisfied is the jurisdictional governmental agency that will actually own the property.

A second group of users of a commercial facility is the employees working for the tenants or businesses. Study after study has shown that productivity in offices is related to the design of the office itself. Research shows that if the facility has been designed with a pleasing and safe atmosphere as well as a functional environment, the employees will work more effectively. An exciting interior for a restaurant that brings in large crowds willing to spend on food and drink will bring better-quality wait staff to serve the customers. Unfortunately, the employees don't usually get to "vote" on the design decisions, but they may vote unofficially through their willingness to stay with the company and serve its clients effectively.

A third user is the customer who comes to the facility. In some instances, the ambiance of a restaurant or the beauty of the setting of a resort influences whether a customer returns. In other circumstances, ambiance plays a minimal role in this decision. The relationship of a doctor to a patient is more important than the doctor's exquisitely designed office. If your local city government offices had marble on the walls and floors and gold faucets in the restrooms, as a citizen, you might think that your tax dollars had been overspent. Designing for these various users is challenging, to say the least. Adherence to building, life safety, and accessibility codes is another critical part of the work of commercial interior designers.

The health, life safety, and welfare of the client and the various users of the facility affects many design decisions, including space planning, architectural materials, lighting, furniture and fabric specification, and even the colour palette in some situations. There can be no margin for error or fudging of the codes in a commercial project. The user of the facility trusts that the design and specification of the facility are safe in all the ways the jurisdiction requires.

Finally, as mentioned before, the interior designer should know something about the client's business before seeking a commercial interiors project. Understanding the business of the business is crucial to solving the problems and achieving the functional and aesthetic goals of the client. No designer can solve the client's problems without understanding the problems as thoroughly as possible.

Commercial interior design is a very challenging way to work in the design profession. It is exciting to be part of a team that is responsible for the interior design of any kind of commercial facility. Being involved in the project from its inception and seeing it come together as it is constructed and the various components are installed can be thrilling. Like any career it is also hard work, sometimes involving long hours, certainly working effectively with team members, and perhaps dealing with irate clients. However, few interior designers who have worked in commercial interior design for many years would do anything else.

There are important issues to consider when working in commercial interior design whether you are a student considering entering this part of the profession or a professional considering moving from residential to commercial interior design. All but the smallest commercial interior design projects require a team of designers and related professionals. An independent interior designer can design the interior of a medical office suite or a bed and breakfast, a small retail store or other smaller-scale projects.

Large projects like building a resort hotel, remodelling a high school, or designing a new county government building require teamwork. In some respects, every project, regardless of its size, is accomplished by the efforts of a team. Led by a project manager and a senior project designer, the project team may include interior designers at many skill and experience levels. The team may involve architects, lighting designers, engineers, and consultants—perhaps a commercial kitchen designer for a restaurant, for example.

Entry-level and mid-level interior designers will assist more senior members of the team in drafting, product and materials research, codes research, and other tasks. Let us not forget the client and his or her team of decision makers. The project manager and team members must be able to work with the client to reach decisions about many issues as the project moves through its design phases. The project may have several layers of client decision makers. For example, for a hotel, the facility manager, housekeeping manager, security office, banquet manager, food and beverage group, hotel general manager, and the owners or developers will all have a say in the design decisions.

The interior designer and client are only part of the design team. A general contractor and many subcontractors will be hired to do the actual construction work. Vendors who will supply the furniture, fixtures, and equipment (FF&E) and materials are selected through competitive bidding. The design project manager must be prepared to work with these various stakeholders to ensure that the project is completed as designed and specified, on time and on budget.

Exactly what your role will be in the team will depend on what kind of firm you decide to work for. Whether you choose to work for a small interior design firm or seek employment in a large multifaceted firm or an office furnishings dealership is up to you. Each has positives and negatives.

A small firm gives entry-level and less experienced interior designers an opportunity to become involved in projects sooner. Perhaps inventorying existing furniture to be used in the remodelling of a law office doesn't seem like design, but it is a way for the entry-level interior designer to gain an understanding of the design considerations for that professional office and become closely involved in the reality of office furniture and equipment.

Small firms rarely have the opportunity to work on glamorous projects like casinos, large resort hotels, flashy new restaurants, or corporate headquarters. The experience gained in the small firm, however, provides the entry-level interior designer with valuable training and skills that can be taken to the firm that gets the glamorous projects—assuming that is a goal.

Another consideration in working for a small firm is that it is healthy and strong as long as the owner keeps up the efforts to market the firms services and obtain new clients. Small firm owners are constantly changing hats from project manager to marketing director, general manager, and interior designer. If new projects stop coming because the owner is busy with design work, then the less experienced professional staff may need to look for other jobs.

Constant marketing for new work is a reality of any firm. Even a large firm can lose its focus or be caught in an economic downturn. If you wish to work for a larger firm, you will definitely need to work well with others and willingly take orders and directions from more senior interior designers. You may also find yourself spending time doing what may seem to be drudge work—taking care of the library, endlessly drafting small project details, and keeping files organised. This is part of the apprenticeship common in larger firms.

Working for a larger firm may bring prestige and more opportunity for internal mentoring. Project managers in larger firms are expected to do more supervision and training of newer staff than the owner of a small firm. This is a great opportunity to learn skills and techniques in such areas as how to deal with clients and other stakeholders, shortcuts in developing schematic and construction drawings, and many other aspects of the profession. Larger firms may also be more responsive to your involvement in a professional association and professional educational updating.

For most entry-level designers, the greatest disadvantage of working for a large firm is that they will not be given their own clients for some time. The firm must know what you can do and feel confident about your capabilities in working with clients before you are allowed to manage your own projects. Unless you have worked somewhere else, it may take you two or three years to move up to project responsibility in a large multifaceted interior design or architecture firm.

A third place to work in commercial interior design is an office furnishings dealership. Companies that specialise in offices and feature systems furniture are great places to begin and maintain a career in commercial interior design. The interior designers in such companies focus on large corporate and many kinds of professional offices. The learning and training received here prepare many interior designers to move to an interior design firm that might specialise in hospitality, healthcare, or government facilities.

Critical Issues

Sustainable design

A very important issue facing commercial interior designers in the 21st century is sustainable, environmentally safe design, also commonly called green design. According to the World Commission on Environment and Development, sustainable design seeks to "meet the needs of the present without compromising the ability of future generations to meet their needs." It involves finding a balance between meeting users' immediate needs in constructing a building and finishing its interior while creating as little harm as possible to the environment for future generations. Being sure that the veneer you choose for a desk or cabinet comes from a certifiably sustainable source is a way of utilising green design.

Sustainable design means finding methods and processes of design that consume fewer nonrenewable resources and are more energy efficient. The designer chooses to use materials and products for the interior that are also less damaging to the environment in both their manufacture and their use as finished products.

Constructing buildings and completing their interiors consumes vast quantities of materials —only some of which are renewable. According to the U.S. Department of Energy in 2003, all buildings in the United States consume 40 percent of raw materials and generate more than one-third of municipal solid waste. Other sources report that construction waste accounts for 40 percent of what goes into landfills.

In addition, the Environmental Protection Agency (EPA) reports that indoor air quality is on average 2 to 10 times more polluted than outside air. Volatile organic compounds (VOCs) are toxic fumes emitted from carpeting, paints, the glues used to make the composite woods in furniture, and many other common materials and products used in commercial and residential interiors. Some are carcinogens; all can cause irritation and allergic reactions in many people. The sealed environment of many office buildings and other types of commercial spaces with poor ventilation means that indoor air can be very harmful due to the products that are specified.

Increased demand on resources by the economies of emerging countries and wasteful practices make sustainability and thinking green critical issues for those in the built environment industry and for consumers. As responsible professionals, we need to think beyond recycling plastics and paper in the office. Sustainable building design became a prominent part of the architecture and interior design professions in the 1970s. The oil embargo of 1973 forced everyone in the built environment industry and consumers to consider energy usage and efficiency in the design of their projects.

Designers began examining solar energy potential in earnest as one way to cut down on our dependency on fossil fuels. In 1977 a cabinet-level Department of Energy was created to deal with energy conservation and usage in the United States. The 1970s also saw the beginning of recycling efforts as a way to deal with overfilled landfills. Earth Day programs help to bring additional attention to the need for sustainable design and energy and resource conservation in many ways.

Environmental concerns continued to impact the attention of those in the built environment industry. In the 1980s, it became more widely known and reported that our buildings were making us sick, so more attention was paid to the interior environment and the products used there. The 1980s and 1990s saw continued and growing research and conferences on environmental issues. The United Nations World Commission on Environment and Development defined sustainable development and provided a major boost to the growing concern for sustainable buildings and green design.

Sustainable building and design have continued to grow through the efforts and support of the architecture and interior design professional associations and the government, along with business and industry. One of the most successful nonprofit organisations is the U.S. Green Building Council (USGBC). Founded in 1993, this organisation brings together professionals in architecture and construction, real estate developers, interior designers, product manufacturers, government agencies, and others in or interested in the design-build industry. Today the USGBC works to "promote buildings that are environmentally responsible, profitable and healthy places to live and work."

A very important part of the work of the USGBC is the LEED® Certification program. LEED—Leadership in Energy and Environmental Design—is a voluntary green rating system that helps define buildings that are healthy, profitable, and environmentally responsible. LEED Certification validates a building owner's efforts to create a green building. LEED Certification can be obtained for New Construction, Existing Buildings, and Commercial

Interiors. LEED Certification will also include certification of Homes, Neighbourhoods Developments, and Core and Shell projects. From a business standpoint, the designer may wish to point out the following points from the USGBC to a client related to pursuing LEED-CI ratings:

— "Reduces operating and maintenance costs

— Improves property value

— Enhances occupant health and productivity

— May reduce liabilities related to air quality and other indoor environmental issues"

When a project is reviewed for LEED Certification, it must meet all prerequisites and is awarded points based on five categories of achievement: Sustainable Sites, Water Efficiency, Energy and Atmosphere, Materials and Resources, and Indoor Environmental Quality, with additional points awarded for Innovation and Design Process. Let us look at these categories as they relate to a generic commercial structure, with emphasis on the interior.

The categories of Sustainable Sites, Water Efficiency, and Energy and Atmosphere are not areas of responsibility for most interior design firms. But a few words related to these areas are warranted. The category of Sustainable Sites looks at where the building is built. For example, points are awarded if tenants select a building located in developed areas with existing infrastructure, such as an urban area, rather than farmland or undisturbed greenfields. Points are also awarded if the building site provides priority parking for car pools or van pools, alternate fuel vehicles, or underground parking rather than on-grade parking lots.

In the category of Water Efficiency, points are awarded for highly efficient fixtures and equipment such as low-flow faucets and toilets. And in the category of Energy and Atmosphere, the building owner or tenant must meet specific and stringent code requirements related to refrigerants for HVAC systems. These are only a few examples of the ways tenants can be awarded points toward LEED-CI Certification levels. Of more concern to the interior designer is the rating category Materials and Resources. It is important to use materials that are salvaged, refurbished, or reused. Examples include wood for flooring that might come from a demolished building or using existing furniture moved from a previous location.

The project receives points when the design maintains interior nonstructural components such as walls, flooring, and ceiling systems that help to conserve resources and reduce waste. Projects also receive points for diverting construction waste from landfills using strategies such as recycling. As much as possible, interior designers should specify carpets, wall finish materials, and ceiling treatments that are made from low-toxicity or nontoxic materials. The specification of materials that contain recycled content, such as carpet made from recycled plastic bottles, is another way to receive LEED points.

Specifying products made from rapidly renewable material such as wool carpet will also earn LEED points. All these things and many others are examples of what can be done in the specification of interior products to help keep a space green. Indoor Environmental Quality is another important category that is reviewed for LEED Certification. The interior designer can have a significant impact on the space and ensure a healthy, productive environment for the tenant. As much as possible, the designer should specify carpets, wall finish materials, and ceiling treatments that are made from low-emitting materials. Low-VOC paints compliant with LEED standards should be used for painted surfaces. In addition, the interior designer should look for low-toxicity fabrics and foams for upholstered goods.

If smoking is not prohibited, the smoking area must be designed in such a way that the smoke is vented out of the building, not circulated into nonsmoking areas. Rooms within a building designated as smoking areas should be enclosed with impermeable full-height walls and doors, not just with a partition that is open at the top, and operated at negative pressure compared to surrounding areas. Here are a few more important ways for the project to earn LEED points.

The interior designer can make sure that sealants and adhesives for the installation of carpeting and wall treatments do not exceed VOC limits. The designer can also avoid specification of furniture items that have used formaldehyde in adhesives. Providing occupants with control over lighting, temperature, and ventilation contributes to LEED points. To varying degrees, this can be done with raised floor systems. Designers who maximise occupants' access to daylight will achieve more points for the project. The last category is Innovation and Design Process.

A project obtains a point for utilising the services of a LEED Accredited Professional. Projects are also awarded points if the project implements a new technology or strategy that is not covered in the rating system. Obviously, when the interior designer is involved from the beginning of the project, incorporating LEED guidelines is easier. The designer understands the goals of the project and makes specification and space-planning decisions that are in line with certification guidelines. Ideally, the architect and interior designer are LEED Accredited Professionals.

Another factor in designing and selling green buildings to clients is economics. Most complaints from clients who do not want to go green focus on this issue. They have heard about the extra expense of using low-VOC paint or building a section of the restaurant for smoking with a separate ventilation system and move away from green design. However, recent projects have proven that green design and sustainable building do not have to be more expensive. While some projects have a slight increase in up-front costs, green buildings provide significant cost savings in the long term due to increased energy and water efficiency and improved employee performance.

Efficient and thoughtful design from the very beginning of a project can guide the design team to many cost-effective decisions that add to LEED Certification. One economic technique that can be incorporated into planning for a green or sustainable project is life cycle assessment (LCA), which analyses materials, finished products, and buildings to evaluate their environmental and health impacts over their life. This environmental assessment can begin at the time raw materials for a specific product are obtained and continue through its manufacture into a final product, its installation in a building, and its eventual disposal. For a client who is committed to having a truly green facility, LCA of the products and materials is critical.

LCA measures overall "environmental performance of a product over its full life cycle, often referred to as 'cradle-to-grave' or 'cradle-to-cradle analysis.'" Products that can be reused or recycled or that will decompose when sent to a landfill are considered cradle-to-cradle products. An example would be solid wood flooring that can be reused in another project, packaging used to ship recycled goods, and any kind of material that is completely biodegradable.

A product that is used and is not reused, recycled, or otherwise discarded before its useful life is complete is considered a cradle-to-grave product in green design terms. Carpeting that is removed because of an aesthetic change to the interior and is taken to the landfill is a common example. Another example is the shipping cardboard that goes to a landfill rather than a recycling plant. Clearly, cradle-to-cradle products are considered greener than cradle-to-grave products.

Another economic technique that is used in relation to sustainable design is life cycle costing (LCC), which combines the actual cost of the product with the cost of its maintenance, periodic replacement, and residual value. Everything, of course, has an initial cost. If carpet tiles are specified rather than broadloom carpet, for example, damaged tiles can easily be replaced. By contrast, if broadloom carpet is damaged, the entire room might have to be recarpeted. Of course, the economic benefits of LCC will affect long-term owners of the building rather than tenants.

According to green design experts, a project that has utilised sustainable design methodologies and products can also be more valuable to an owner. Maintenance costs will be lower; safer indoor air quality will result in fewer employee absences; and the natural quality of many products used in a green building is often more pleasing and attractive, creating an environment that both employees and guests will appreciate. Energy conservation impacts the work of the interior designer, regardless of the type of commercial space that is being designed.

According to the Department of Energy, buildings consume 68 percent of all electricity. One of the largest energy users in commercial spaces is lighting. Many states have mandated low-watt lamps and lighting specification with maximum watts per square foot to help reduce electrical energy use. A few considerations in lighting design that can be applied to many types of commercial spaces are offered here. Low-watt, high-output fluorescent lamps used in place of incandescent lamps also produce energy savings. A larger portion of the energy used by incandescent lamps is released as heat, adding to the burden of the HVAC system.

Designs that utilise as much daylighting as possible reduce the amount of energy consumed by artificial lighting. Of course, in some areas, extensive use of windows for daylighting can cause energy loss due to heat gain through the windows. In those cases, the design team should specify low-E, high-performance window glazing. In many commercial projects, sensors that turn lights on and off when someone enters or exits a space such as a conference room or classroom can help reduce energy consumption.

Designs that combine ambient and task lighting can also enhance energy efficiency, regardless of the use of most spaces. "By providing a variety of independent task lights in interiors, the designer can achieve the most important goal: good illumination where it is needed and no waste of energy where it is unnecessary." The interior designer can also increase energy efficiency by specifying energy-efficient equipment. Appliances like refrigerators and stoves in employee cafeterias and electronic equipment like computers and printers that have received the Energy Star designation save energy. Low-flow faucets in showers and toilet rooms in hotels save energy by reducing the hot water used.

These are just a few ways that the interior designer can help to bring energy efficiency to commercial interiors. As part of the design team, the interior designer should encourage the architect and client to utilise as many energy-efficient and sustainable design products and construction methods as possible.

As the reader can see, sustainable design can be incorporated into all types of commercial projects using thoughtful space planning and careful specification of products. Consider these examples: the odor of new carpet does not exist in the new medical office suite; wood table tops in a restaurant substitute for the off-gassing of plastic laminates and composite wood tops; offices move full-height walls to the center of the space, allowing daylight to penetrate into the office footprint; and low-water-usage water closets are specified in sports arenas.

Security and Safety Issues

Owners, developers, and tenants of every type of commercial facility are concerned about the security and safety of their employees, clients, and visitors. The tragic events of September 11, 2001, heightened the importance and awareness of making buildings safe. Stories about workplace shootings, harm to customers and employees in retail settings, school violence, and theft of personal information are regularly reported. Customers and employees expect to be safe in public and business environments.

Clients are asking design teams to plan for better security and safety in all types of commercial facilities.

Common security and safety issues include protection of employees and customers, life safety, burglary, employee pilferage, vandalism, theft of company records, and protection of company property such as intellectual property. The threats can come from many sources, and the issues vary with the type of business.

In a retail store, theft of merchandise is a big security issue. In hospitals and medical office suites, theft of controlled substances creates design challenges. In offices, unauthorised visitors can cause a variety of security problems. Guests at hotels want to feel safe in their rooms and while walking the grounds. Individuals want to feel safe exiting auditoriums and theaters. Many professional offices have huge amounts of personal customer information stored on computers, the theft of which can cause enormous harm for the business and customers. Government buildings face threats of terrorism.

The easiest way for interior designers to meet their responsibilities related to security and safety in the commercial projects they design is to adhere strictly to applicable building and life safety codes. Model building codes, notably the International Building Code (IBC) in the United States and the National Building Code (NBC) in Canada standardise construction standards and provide limited mechanical systems, accessibility, and interior finishing standards. In addition to the building codes are the Life Safety Code published by the National Fire Protection Association (NFPA), which provides standards for fire and life safety but not building construction.

Separate mechanical codes such as the National Electrical Code and the National Plumbing Code provide regulations for these systems. The local jurisdiction may have additional regulations. For example, some jurisdictions have stronger design standards for earthquake protection in all types of facilities. Food service facilities and hospitals, to name just two, have various health department regulations that can impact the interior design of a facility. However, there is no model code for security planning and design.

Issues of security can be found in building codes and local jurisdictional codes. Yet, most security plans and solutions are derived from discussions with the business owner, security experts, and vendors who supply products like card-access entry locks, security cameras, and blastproof glass. When it comes to safety issues for the protection of those whom S. C. Reznikoff calls the "captive consumer" —workers and users of a commercial facility—planning and specification decisions based on strict adherence to building and life safety and fire safety codes are critical.

Arrangement of exits, sizes of exit access corridors, planning for places of refuge, specifying architectural materials with low smoke propagation or flame resistance, and many other life safety issues are mandatory design fundamentals. Interior designers must become aware of security options for their clients' facilities. "Good security involves physical as well as electronic barriers. The physical layout and construction of a space can have a profound effect on fundamental security as well as on how easy or difficult it is to plan and install monitoring and access devices."

Many businesses want a security system that protects but is not visible but transparent. Visible layers of security can create unnecessary anxiety in employees, customers, or other users of the facilities. Security can be transparent by providing clear sight lines to entrances from reception counters or other areas in lobbies and waiting rooms. Bullet-resistant glass in windows in some types of medical facilities and financial institutions is another way to add subtle but effective security in design. When the project is more complex, requiring an extensive security program, the interior designer will work with the architect and a security consulting firm along with the client to make security plans.

Security issues need to be addressed in programming so that the interior designer knows what level of security is needed for the facility and can make necessary adjustments in space planning and specifications to address security needs. Many projects will need solutions such as card access to hotel rooms, electronic security devices at entrances to retail stores, and buzzer access from a doctor's waiting room to the exam rooms, to mention a few.

Security cameras are used to monitor not only the entrances of many buildings, but also stores, banks, schools, and many other facilities that may be considered high risk. Lighting is a major way to increase occupants' feelings of security and safety. Appropriate lighting design eliminates dark or hazardous areas in interiors. Good lighting means that occupants feel safe since they can see where they are and where they are going—as well as who might also be in the area.

Accessibility

By now the reader is no doubt familiar with the Americans with Disabilities Act (ADA) and the guidelines that were established in the 1990s to make public buildings more easily accessible for individuals with many disabilities. As of this writing, revised guidelines are being reviewed by various agencies and enforcement is expected to begin—well, whenever numerous government agencies have completed their review and the new guidelines find their way into state and local codes. These guidelines have been modernised to reflect changes in technology, building codes, and users' needs.

As the baby boom generation ages, becoming 60 years old as of 2006, the need to continue to keep buildings accessible for all people has become critical. Interior designers and others in the design-build industry should not consider the design guidelines as impediments to good and creative design. The guidelines should always be viewed as a means to ensure that everyone can enjoy using those creatively designed buildings and interiors.

The new guidelines are expected to simplify many of the compliance requirements. This simplification will help designers do a better job of making commercial public buildings more accessible. It will also help determine whether spaces are not accessible when they should be. Spaces that were very restrictive in their design or lacked easy-to-apply standards will now be simpler to design.

Licensing and Registration of Professionals

The licensing of interior design professionals remains an important though sometimes contentious issue. Interior designers have sought to be licensed since the 1950s. The first state to pass legislation to license or register interior design professionals was Alabama in 1982. As of 2006, more than half of the states have some form of licensing, certification, or registration legislation that defines who may practice interior design or use the title interior designer. Other states continue to seek regulation of the work of the interior design profession.

The profession has become increasingly complicated, and responsibility for what is done to a commercial or residential interior to meet standards of safety is more complex than it was even 30 years ago. Interior designers are held responsible for providing safe environments for their clients and the users of commercial interiors. Technology in the construction of interiors continues to evolve and become more complex. Building and life safety codes demand critical decisions concerning space planning and product specification to ensure the safety and health of occupants of commercial interiors.

Sustainable design knowledge and criteria are necessary to reduce the harm to our environment and to avoid harming continuous users of commercial spaces. Security issues will continue to impact the interior design of all types of commercial facilities. These are critical issues for any interior designer who requires greater accountability. Licensing or registration ensures consumers that the interior designers they hire for their commercial projects have the education, experience, and competence to provide interior design services.

Jurisdictions that have legislation concerning the practice of interior design require intensive educational preparation related to the knowledge base and skill sets required during the phases of a design project. They also require passage of a competency examination whose minimum requirements to sit for the examination focus on education in interior design and work experience.

Licensing or registration legislation in a jurisdiction may also require the designer to keep up-to-date in the profession by mandating a specific number of hours and types of continuing education seminars, workshops, or classes. Continuing education offerings are commonly developed based on a specific number of clock hours, not semester-long classes, as in a formal academic setting. In many jurisdictions, the majority of the hours of continuing education must focus on topics concerning the health, life safety, and welfare of the consumer.

Competency Examination of Professionals

Competency examination of interior designers has been discussed by professional associations and educators since at least the 1950s. An examination was developed in the 1960s by the professional association that later became ASID. Today, the examination that is required in all jurisdictions that have any type of legislation is the National Council for Interior Design Qualification (NCIDQ) examination. Passing the NCIDQ exam is also a requirement of ASID, IIDA, IDC, IDEC, and Canadian provincial associations for members to be recognised at the highest professional level of their association. All professions require an examination to test minimum competency related to any type of licensure or registration.

In fact, an examination of competency is a criterion of any profession. Interior designers should place the goal of passing the NCIDQ exam at the top of their list, whether or not their jurisdiction requires it or whether or not they wish to be professional members of an association. Passage of the NCIDQ examination shows clients that the interior designer has the education, experience, knowledge, and skills sets required by the profession today. It is a personal achievement that interior designers should willingly pursue.

The NCIDQ examination tests the general knowledge and skills of the minimally competent interior designer who has achieved educational preparation and work experience over approximately six years. The six-part examination, given over two days, tests through multiple-choice questions and various design practicum tasks the full range of knowledge and skills that a minimally competent interior designer should have. Passing the NCIDQ examination provides the interior designer a certificate indicating successful completion of the examination. NCIDQ is not a member organisation like

ASID or IDC, and "NCIDQ" cannot be used as an appellation. The NCIDQ certificate is a practice credential indicating an individual's demonstrated competence in the knowledge and skills required of today's professional interior designer.

Ethical Behaviour in Interior Design

Ethical behaviour and ethical standards have been common themes in the news media in recent years. Corporate executives, government employees, and the media have come under scrutiny regarding how they do their jobs, what they say, or how they interact with their constituencies. Perhaps you might feel that ethics does not apply to the work of an interior designer. However, you would be mistaken.

Ethical standards and a code of ethics are part of one's application to a professional association. Ethical behaviour in interior design means conducting oneself in a manner that is considered right by and for those practicing the interior design profession. Ethical standards have been established by the professional associations and serve as a guide to those who choose to affiliate with an association. Ethical standards might also be in some way a part of licensing/registration qualifications.

Ethical behaviour is not hard, it is not overly time-consuming, and it is not inconvenient. Conducting oneself in an ethical manner is simply one more standard for judging oneself as a professional and allowing the consumer to see the value the interior designer places on his or her obligations to clients and the profession. We expect the professionals in law, accountancy, medicine, and real estate, for example, to behave ethically when we deal with them as clients and patients. They too should expect ethical behaviour from the interior designers they hire to design their offices, medical suites, hotel rooms, stores, and myriad other commercial spaces. Ethical behaviour is a responsibility of all interior designers as just one more way to improve the professional image and standing of interior design.

Professional Growth of an Interior Design

Obtaining an education in interior design, taking the professional competency examination, and completing other requirements toward licensure or registration are all important milestones in the professional growth of a commercial interior designer. Many designers also become members of a professional association such as ASID, IIDA, or IDC. Professional associations provide many benefits to members that enhance professional growth. Attendance at national meetings moves that networking opportunity to a national and even an international level. However, the old saying that you get back what you put in is important.

Certainly join a professional association for its newsletters, member meetings, benefits such as insurance programs, and many other reasons. But also join to become active by volunteering for a committee. Here the young interior designer in particular gains greater insights into group dynamics and leadership characteristics.

Active participation in an association is a great way to gain confidence in speaking and writing—important communication skills for any interior designer. Another way to gain professional growth is through continuing education. Education does not stop when one receives a diploma at the end of an interior design program. Professionals should seek additional information at seminars, workshops, and training programs that offer continuing education unit (CEU) credit. In fact, many jurisdictions with licensing or registration legislation require CEU credits to maintain the license or registration. Professional associations may also require, but in any case highly recommend continuing education for their members.

Continuing education seminars provide up-to-date information on a wide variety of topics in the profession. These seminars and workshops are short, most taking one day or less. Some are even available online or by correspondence so that the busy professional can obtain continuing education even with a busy work schedule. Successful professionals find numerous ways to continue to grow and add value to the work they produce. That added value will come back to the interior designer in a variety of positive ways.

4

Designing of Food Service Facilities

The foodservice industry continues to be more and more competitive, and the integration of marketing concepts into the creation of the atmosphere is desirable from the standpoint of increasing sales. One approach to this integration is to use attractive displays of food and beverages in the dining areas or lobby and lounge areas. Displays of wines, salads, desserts, or baked goods lend to the creation of a pleasing dining atmosphere as well as help increase the sales of these items.

The use of salad bars, dessert carts, carving carts, and refrigerated display cases are some of the methods used to accomplish this integration. Among other things, the atmosphere to be developed for a food facility should attract attention, be pleasing to the eyes, and provide an interesting change of pace. For example, an intimate, peaceful dining room provides welcome relief from noisy offices and industries. Likewise, a noisy cafeteria may actually be refreshing to students who are in quiet surroundings most of the day.

The warmth and glow of a fireplace provides a welcome change in cold weather. The development of the physical and psychological aspects of the atmosphere depends in great part upon the planners selected to design the facility. They must have a clear understanding with the owner of the particular needs and goals to be accomplished in developing the atmosphere.

In addition to knowledge of the functional operation of the facility, the planners should be keenly aware of the type of clientele to be attracted. Only then can they come up with a suitable design that will be attractive as well as functional. It is then up to management to develop the nonphysical aspects of the atmosphere to complete the total concept.

Atmosphere Planning

Comfort is one of the key considerations in atmosphere planning. If individuals do not feel comfortable in their surroundings, the atmosphere has not been properly designed. Comfort is created when individuals feel secure and at ease. Security may be psychologically imposed by the use of red and orange colours and by privacy, which can provided by booths and partitions.

One way of sing dividers to create private areas in the dining room. Dining rooms which have an expensive look may create feelings of insecurity because individuals feel status-conscious in such surroundings. Atmosphere planning is dependent on an understanding of the perceptual awareness of individuals as sensed through sight, touch, caring, smell, temperature, and movement. The primary considerations of these perceptions as related to a dining experience are summarised as follows.

Sight: The perception of visual space involving lighting levels, colours, eye contact with fixtures and decorator items, and the use of mirrors and screens to expand or contract the visual space.

Touch: Perception of seat comfort, body contact, and contact with floor, tables, tableware, and upholstery fabrics.

Hearing: Perception of noise levels of conversation, kitchen sounds, Aside sounds, and music.

Smell: Perception of cooking aromas, body odors, and material odors from fabrics such as linen and leather.

Temperature: Perception of air temperature, relative humidity, Ay heat, cooking heat, radiant heat, and heat of cooked foods.

Movement: Perception of muscle activity required for access to tables and chairs, movement of servers and other customers, movement outside as viewed through windows. It is important not to think of atmosphere as simply a combination of colours, lights, and spaces, but how the individual is affected by those factors. It is the perceptual concepts that should be kept in mind when developing atmosphere.

To clarify the concept of perceptual environment, consider the matter of space. A person's perception of space is measured more in terms of freedom of movement than in terms of physical dimensions of feet and inches. A dining room one hundred feet long means very little to diners. If persons can walk across a smaller room without encountering obstacles, it will be perceptually large.

On the other hand, if they must make their way around closely faced tables and chairs, it will be perceptually smaller. This is due the feeling of crowding when their movements are restricted. Temperature works in much the same way. It is measured in terms of contrast rather than by degrees on a thermometer. An individual, just coming in from the cold will require less heat to perceive a feeling of warmth than someone who has been exposed to a heated room for a long time.

The body heat of others is also an interrelated factor is how an individual perceives a crowded condition. Individuals who re in a cooler room may be seated closer together than those who re in a warmer room. A person's eyes are probably the most important yet deceptive tools of measurement in perceiving feelings. The structure of the eye exaggerates activity or movement that takes place on the periphery of vision.

Consequently, individuals can be in an uncrowded room, yet feel as if it is crowded if there is a great deal of action or movement round them. When obstructions are used to block out the activity or movement on the periphery of their vision, they will perceive the area as uncrowded. Thus, individuals measure the atmosphere with their senses and valuate it as desirable or undesirable.

The atmosphere must be tanned so that the individual's perceptions result in a feeling of com-art, ease, and acceptability. With these concepts as a guide, the food facility planner should evaluate the many physical components of atmosphere that can be manipulated and arrive at a combination that ill give the desired sensations. The following are the physical components that affect the perception of atmosphere:

1) Colours
2) Illumination
3) Noise
4) Ambient temperature, relative humidity, odors
5) Type of seating (tables, booths, counters)
6) Furnishings; floor and wall coverings, drapes
7) Table appointments; dishware, silverware, napkins
8) Shape and size of rooms
9) Layout of tables
10) Appearance and dress of employees
11) Menu design
12) Sanitary conditions

13) Exterior design

14) Landscaping

15) Age and dress of customers

Colour

This is one of the visual aspects of the atmosphere as perceived by individuals; it is also one of the best tools that planners have to create a variety of moods. Most people make a number of choices based on colour; they select their clothes, cars, houses, paints, and even foods by colour. Colour can be used to induce a feeling of happiness, to promote serenity, or to stimulate hunger. It can attract people to one type of dining room and drive them out of others. Certain colours are especially important to the development of dining areas.

Many experiments have shown that certain colours have a very strong emotional effect on most individuals. It is known that blue reduces excitability and therefore helps one to relax. Blue is also considered to be cooling and is "easy" on the eyes. Green is a colour that acts as a sedative. Yellow, on the other hand, is cheery, stimulating, and attention-drawing.

On dull, sunless days, people exhibit mental and physical sluggishness which is partially attributed to the absence of yellow, red, and other stimulating colours. Red is associated with excitement and violence. Gray suggests coldness and is very depressing unless it is combined with livelier colours. Colour sensations can sometimes produce physical reactions that are not just of the visual system but affect the entire body. For example, persons exposed to predominately red colours exhibit increased blood pressure, quickened muscular reactions, and greater emotions.

Red also tends to produce restlessness and makes time seem to pass very slowly. In comparison, persons exposed to predominately blue and green colours have been found to exhibit slower muscle response and quicker mental and conversational response. Blues and greens also make time seem to go faster. Some of the common emotional responses caused by exposure to various colours. These may be used to develop the type of response desired in various areas of the food facility. The colours have to be predominant in an area and individuals must be exposed to them for a period of time.

Features

The strong effect colours may have on individuals, care should be taken in selecting them to achieve the desired result. One if the aspects of good colour planning deals with contrast. A single predominant colour, no matter how pleasing, cannot function alone. A restful green that is predominant would strain the part of the eye susceptible to it and eventually lead to eye and body fatigue.

With a single predominant colour individuals would have to look harder to distinguish objects because of the lack of contrast. Extreme contrast between very light and dark colours is also undesirable since they too result in eyestrain. Achieving the right amount of contrast along with maintaining the desired emotional responses is necessary to the creation of a pleasing environment for dining.

Classification of Colours

Red, yellow, and blue are the primary colours. They are referred to is primaries because other colours are derived from them. In their pure form the primary colours are too strong to use on large areas and therefore are used as accents. The secondary colours are green, orange, and violet and are mixtures of two of the primary colours. Green is obtained by mixing blue and fellow, orange by mixing red and yellow, and violet by mixing red and blue.

Mixtures of primary colours and secondary colours result in the intermediate colours. Examples of intermediates are red-orange, yellow-green, and blue-violet. Colours are also classified as warm or cool. Red, orange, and yellow are the warm colours; they seem to advance and convey a feeling of warmth. The cool colours are blue, green, and violet; these are retracting colours and are cooling and relaxing. A combination of one warm colour and one cool colour results in the complementary colours used in colour planning.

The problem of selecting colours that go well together or harmonise is solved by using one of five rules. These rules are related to harmonies and are identified as monochromatic, analogous, complementary, split complementary, and triad. Monochromatic harmony uses a single colour and is the simplest of colour schemes. The single colour can be expressed in the following ways.

— As the pure colour itself

— As a tint of the pure colour (a tint is the pure colour mixed with white) is a shade of the pure colour (a shade is the pure colour mixed with black)

— As a tone of the pure colour (a tone is the pure colour mixed with both black and white).

— Analogous harmony is obtained by using any three or four consecutive colours on the colour wheel. Examples of analogous harmony are red-orange, orange, and yellow-orange; or red, red-orange, orange, and Glow-orange.

— Complementary harmony results by using any two colours that are directly opposite each other on the colour wheel. Red and green, red-orange and blue-green, or yellow and violet are examples of complementary harmony.

— Split complementary or near complementary harmony involves three colours. Any one of the two complementary colours and two colours adjacent to the omitted complementary colour are used. On the colour wheel, the split complementaries are in the form of a Y. Examples of split complementary colours are yellow, blue-violet, and red-violet; green, red-orange, and red-violet; and red, blue-green, and yellow-green.

— Triad harmony also involves three colours. These are selected by king every fourth colour on the colour wheel. Two examples of triads are red, yellow, and blue; and yellow-orange, red-violet, and blue-green.

— After a particular harmony is selected, then a decision regarding the tints, shades, or tones of the colours is made. One or two of the colours selected will be used for the walls and other major surfaces. The other colours will be used as accents on smaller objects like drapes, table cloths, and dinnerware.

The important points in colour selection are as follows:

— Pure colours are usually too strong and brilliant when applied to large areas or surfaces.

— Colours should be selected under the kind of lighting that they will be used under. Colours selected under fluorescent lighting will appear different under incandescent lighting.

— Colours selected from a small sample will appear brighter when applied to large areas.

— Complementary, split complementary, and triad harmonies always result in a combination of warm and cool colours. The desired atmosphere will dictate which colour is to predominate.

— Black, white, brown, and gold usually go well with any of the colour harmonies.

— Texture is closely related to colour application and usage is best considered at the same time the colour choices are made.

Light and Colour

As light modifies colours in many ways, the type of light source and systems of lighting should be considered when selecting colours. Pink lights, for example, have been shown to pale lipstick colours. Green lights have a tendency to show up wrinkles and should not be used in an atmosphere where a feeling of well-being is to be created. Another problem is the use of amber lights which tend to wash out colours.

A well-chosen colour scheme can be easily spoiled by poorly selected lights. Lights and colours for work areas are quite different from those desirable for dining areas and should be planned separately. The uses of colour in foodservice facilities are so numerous that space will not allow a complete presentation of all of them.

Lighting

As with colour, proper planning of lights can achieve dramatic effects and aid in the creation of the desired atmosphere. Both sexes enjoy a type of lighting that makes them look their best. This factor is of great importance in the planning and design of lights for dining areas, bars, rest rooms, and other public spaces.

The best system of lighting for restaurants appears to be a combination of indirect, direct, and spot lights. These lights can be arranged to accomplish the desired flexibility required for the various meal periods. Areas should be well lit for breakfast and lunch, while less lighting is desired for evening meals. The installation of rheostats will provide this flexibility. In considering the lighting system, the amount of daylight entering an area should be considered. Total glass area can be specified by the architect to adjust for this factor. The use of tinted glass may be considered for some situations.

The ultimate type of lighting for dining areas has traditionally been considered to be candlelight. The reddish flame of candlelight is flattering to people and to most foods. The flickering of the flame adds to the creation of a desirable atmosphere. Alternatives to candlelight are incandescent and fluorescent lights. The economy of operation of fluorescent lights favours their installation in large areas. Incandescent lights would be the best choice in dining areas because of their red colour enhancement. Properly selected fluorescent lights may also be used in dining areas if sufficient red tones are used in the colour scheme. The deluxe warm white fluorescent tubes are the closest in colour tint to incandescent bulbs and would be recommended.

As with colour, lighting can do much toward creating atmosphere by correcting spacial deficiencies and accenting desirable areas. To illustrate, a low ceiling can be made to appear higher if it is well-lit; high ceilings will appear lower if they are dimly lit. Care should be taken not to light the long walls brightly in a narrow room since it will appear to be even narrower. Dark walls will show up better with bright lights, and if the colour is to be accented, the illumination level has to be high.

Bright lights are placed above normal eye levels to minimise glare. The same concept applies to candles since they too can create glare. Candles may be placed in frosted globes if they are at eye level or slightly below. In dining areas, it is best to concentrate illumination on the seats and tables and perhaps on special design features. The ceilings and walls should not be so brightly lit that they detract attention from the room. Bright lights may be used to create a brisk atmosphere which, if service is fast, results in a high turnover of customers. Serving areas, should be well-lighted. Some operations may use full lighting for a high turnover at lunch and then dim the lights for evening meals in hopes of attaining higher check averages.

Colourful Lights

Careful selection of coloured lights will enhance the total atmosphere. The first consideration is to coordinate the coloured lights with other coloured objects and colour schemes used in the room. This is important, since certain colours will take on strange off-colours when subjected to coloured lights. Red colours will appear very dark under blue or green lights and olive-green colours look brown under yellow lights.

Coloured lights affect the appearance of the faces and clothes of people. Red lights have the advantage of flattering complexions and tend to enhance the colour of fabrics. Red lights also have a good effect on most foods. Green and blue lights are undesirable for illuminating areas where people will be present. These lights tend to distort the red hues and are unflattering because of this. Green and blue lights may be used for inanimate objects that serve as accent pieces. The use of pink, ivory, or amber lights is suggested for areas where skin tone is important, as they are warm and impart a friendly and inviting feeling. It is better to use tints of colours rather than strong hues.

Lighting should not only provide atmosphere but should reach a satisfactory level of illumination from a practical standpoint. If the lighting level is too high, individuals will have a feeling of exposure; or if too dim, they may feel fearful. For these reasons, there should be enough light so persons can see, yet not so much that they feel uneasy. One method of attaining such an arrangement is to lower the height of ceiling fixtures. This provides a sufficient amount of light and at the same time results in a comfortable soft effect.

Foodservice lighting levels typically will range between 5 and 50 foot-candles (53.8-538 lux), with 30-50 foot-candles (323-538 lux) usually used for breakfast and lunch. A level of 5-30 foot-candles (53.8-323 lux), depending on the atmosphere desired, is used for evening meals. The lighting level in all areas must be sufficient to make the other elements of the atmosphere visible. It is senseless to spend a great deal of time and money creating a striking colour scheme and then ruin it with poor lighting. Any area with less than 5 foot-candles (53.8 lux) of illumination may as well be colourless.

In reality, the excitement of good lighting comes largely from its shadows and variations in brightness. Flat, shadowless lighting is dull and monotonous. The general lighting system for an area needs the accents of bright areas which come from direct light sources. These may take the form of wall brackets, chandeliers, downlights, or spot lights. Recessed ceiling downlights of low intensity are very satisfactory for lighting dining areas.

Sound

Aside from dinner music, sounds are to play a passive role and never attract attention. The design goal is to create a balance between quiet and noise. Many people are uncomfortable in a room which is very quiet. A noisy room creates tension and irritability. For dining rooms, a satisfactory acoustical environment has a reverberant sound level that is high enough to be heard, but not so high that individuals at nearby tables can distinguish what is being said.

Correct planning for the acoustical environment contributes to the development of the desired atmosphere. The sensitivities of individuals to various sounds require control of undesirable noise and maintenance of desirable sounds at an acceptable level. Sound may be considered to be a pressure wave and is compared to the ripples spreading out from a pebble dropped in water. If the sound is not restricted, it will spread out in all directions. The speed of sound in air is about 1100 feet per second (335 meters per second).

Any sounds produced in open air will travel directly from the source to the listener. In a room, however, sound is reflected from the walls, floor, and ceiling and can build up a general sound level much greater than that which results from the same source in open space. Sounds that are repeatedly reflected become noise or unwanted sounds. Noise at a high enough level causes irritation and fatigue. It can interfere with communication and concentration and become very distracting and disturbing.

The intensity of sound is measured by the decibel. A sound intensity of one decibel is at the threshold of audibility for the normal human ear. A sound intensity of 20 decibels may be compared to a whisper. The normal speaking voice has an intensity of about 60 decibels. Any sound intensities over 100 decibels for any length of time are undesirable, and constant exposure can cause partial loss of hearing. When there is a source of sound in a room, the level of noise at any position is made up of two parts. The first part is the direct sound travelling straight from the source to the position under consideration. The second part is the reverberant sound, which is the sound reaching the position after multiple reflection from the room surfaces.

The intensity of direct sound falls off as the distance from the source increases. Direct sound is reduced by about 6 decibels each time the distance from the source is doubled. Reverberant sound levels will generally be at a uniform intensity throughout the room. Direct sounds are predominant at positions close to the source, while reverberant sounds will dominate positions remote from the source.

Controlling Noise Levels

The problem of controlling noise levels is basically a matter of suppressing the sounds from the source or reducing the amount of reverberant sounds. Sound-absorbing materials are used to minimise both types of sounds. In some instances, the source of the sounds can be isolated by coverings or baffles. Kitchen areas are very difficult to soundproof because of the materials used in the construction of the room and the large amount of metallic equipment present.

Hard, dense materials, like quarry tile or clay tile used for kitchen floors and tiled wall surfaces, reflect a large portion of the sound striking them. Stainless steel surfaces actually act as sound surfaces much like a drum. In these areas, it is desirable to increase the amount of sound-absorbing materials as much as possible to overcome the severe noise problem. Service doors leading to the kitchen can be vestibuled to reduce the noise level before reaching the dining room. This is a compromise between the additional square footage needed for the vestibule and the desirability of reduced noise levels. Thus a facility designed for professionals may include a vestibule while a facility to be designed for other segments of the market may not consider one.

The following things that can be done to minimise noise from the kitchen include the following:

1. Selecting mechanical equipment such as fans and compressors for quiet operation.

2. Using installation techniques that minimise duct noises, the sound of water flow, and water hammer.
3. Using silent closing devices on doors and drawers.
4. Providing rubber bumpers for mobile equipment.
5. Soundproofing walls between kitchen and dining areas.
6. Placing a service station between the entrance to the kitchen and the dining room.
7. Creating a quiet work environment to reduce employee noise.
8. Using the spread load dishwashing concept where an adequate inventory of china, silverware, and glassware are maintained to handle the entire meal period. Dishwashing begins after the meal period to clean the dinnerware for the next meal period. This concept has several ramifications in terms of soiled and clean dish storage requirements, dishwasher size, impact on employee scheduling, and the total size of the dishwashing area.

In addition to acoustical treatment of walls and ceilings, carpeting where permitted will also help. Local sanitarians should be consulted before specifying carpet for production areas. The sound-proofing of metal surfaces by undercoating will reduce the noise created. One method of handling noise problems in dining areas is to vary the spacing of tables. The distance between diners at one table should be appreciably less than the distance to diners at adjoining tables. If a greater density of seating is desired, the use of screens or partial partitions will reduce the sound levels. Bar areas tend to be noisy and can be partially partitioned.

Music

Music is a desirable sound is one way of enhancing the

audible environment. Music has a direct effect on the mood of individuals. Background music should be selected so it does not attract attention. It should be soft, inoffensive, and as characterless as possible. The correct use of background music can put customers in a good mood for dining.

Climate

This is one of the important factors affecting the comfort of people. Most individuals are very sensitive to thermodynamic phenomena and variations from an ideal climate are easily noticed and quickly lead to discomfort. Customers will quickly respond to environmental conditions that are too hot, too cold, too drafty, too stuffy, or too damp. The ideal climate for dining consists of temperatures between 70 and 75°F with a relative humidity of 50%.

Thermodynamic comfort is a function of activity and other factors such as age, sex, and the amount of clothing worn. Needless to say, the climate should be designed for the particular type of patron that the facility is to be planned for. Higher-priced operations will usually attract people who are accustomed to slightly higher temperatures.

Women prefer higher temperatures than men, and children require less heat than both men and women. People who are in active occupations prefer lower temperatures. The amount of clothing worn during the different seasons reflects the needs of different temperatures. People will be wearing lighter clothing in the summer; therefore, slightly warmer than normal temperatures would be appreciated. Clothing worn in the winter is heavier and temperatures should not be allowed to get too high. The effects of colours and lighting are evaluated before a particular temperature level is decided upon.

Temperature can be used to some extent to affect a desired turnover of customers. Many fast-food operations may want lower temperatures to keep the customers on the move and thereby increase the turnover rate. The opposite is true in more luxurious dining rooms where turnover is not stressed. Customers are inclined to be more relaxed in a higher temperature, and the warmth is conducive to a leisurely meal of several courses. The ideal design is to have a system where the temperature can be precisely adjusted for the particular situation. Climate control in most regions requires both heating and air conditioning. The systems should have sufficient capacity to maintain the desired temperature and relative humidity.

Control of Odors

Climate control also includes the control of odors. Odors are an important part of the atmosphere, because smell usually evokes much deeper memories in individuals than either vision or sound. People are often uncomfortable in odor-free surroundings, and pleasant odors can contribute to the desired atmosphere. The popularity of display cooking areas in the dining room is partially caused by the cooking aromas that are emitted.

Odors have to be controlled or they will blend and can become quite offensive. This is very noticeable in dining areas where the air circulation system may bring in varied kitchen odors. Mixing the odors of fish and steak, for example, is not at all appealing to the person eating the steak. Odors are very disturbing to individuals when dining because taste is largely a matter of smell. If the odors cannot be controlled and separated, or if they are undesirable, they should not be allowed to seep into the dining room.

One method of accomplishing this is to maintain the air pressure in the dining room at a higher level than the air pressure in the kitchen. Exhaust systems designed to rid the interiors of smoke, fumes, and odors should be positioned to avoid affecting the immediate exterior environment. This is especially important for exterior walks and entrances into the public areas.

Exterior Design

The term exterior, as used in food facilities design, is taken to include signs, landscaping, parking areas, building structure, doors, and windows. The objective of exterior design is to attract customers. To perform this function effectively, the exterior must convey the correct impression of the type of food facility into which the customer is being invited. Exterior design is to be coordinated with interior design to provide the total atmosphere.

Visibility Problem

One problem to be dealt with in exterior design is the matter of attracting initial attention. This is a problem of visibility as seen through the eyes of pedestrians and people in slow- or fast-moving cars. An attractive sign, large enough for the situation, is generally accepted as the best method of attracting attention. The placement of the sign must ensure that drivers are aware of the facility before it appears in view. In some locations, signs may have to be placed at considerable distances from the building. The most effective signs are those that are short and to the point.

Attraction is also gained by the exterior treatment of the building. This includes the size, shape, colours, and materials used in construction. The first impression of an interior of a facility is gained from the exterior. This impression- is derived not solely by the exterior design but from glimpses of the interior that are provided by windows. Windows are so located as to frame the parts of the interior that they expose. Colour usage on the exterior can follow the same general guidelines presented for interior use. An additional consideration is to let any natural landscaping provide much of the colour. In this case, the building elements can be finished as plainly as possible so as not to compete.

Floodlighting is frequently used with success when the architectural features of the exterior are appealing or dramatic. Care must be used in sizing and placing windows in floodlighted areas to prevent glare into the building. Some designers may prefer to rely on the elegance of simplicity and use little, if any, decorative detailing. On the other hand, facilities with perhaps a national theme may require carefully selected exterior details to complete the concept of total atmosphere.

Parking Areas

Parking lots and areas is important in creating the right impression with the customers. The ease of entering and leaving the parking lot as well as the individual parking space is critical to good design. Consideration should also be given to the placement of walkways from the parking lot to the building. The locations of exterior trash and garbage containers have to be selected carefully. It may be desirable to sacrifice a parking space or two to give special treatment to these undesirable areas.

The customers' first impression of a foodservice facility as they leave their cars should not be the sights and smells of trash and garbage. Management should stress the cleanliness of exterior areas at all times. The entrance door to the facility can form the climax of the exterior attractiveness. It should be selected in accord with the overall design of the building exterior. Doors may be all glass, half glass, wood, or metal, plain or with panels. Separate entrances to the bar are provided if the bar will be used by nondiners.

Entrance doors are located for easy access from streets or parking areas. Whether to provide an entrance area or not is largely a matter of choice. An entrance area can have several desirable functions: it can convey a sense of spaciousness and enhance the atmosphere. Entrance areas also provide a meeting place for people and can be used is waiting space during rush hours. Landscaping provides the setting for -he facility. Another use of landscaping is to hide undesirable service areas or views from dining areas that are not pleasant.

The landscape architect may use contours, plant textures, heights, rocks, pathway surfaces, or garden furniture to achieve the desired exterior appearance. In laying out the landscape, important views are selected and foregrounds and backgrounds are developed for them. The landscaping must harmonise with the exterior features of the building so that a good impression is created from all angles of view.

Layout Process

The layout process described in two separate stages that occur at the same time. One stage deals with the arrangement of individual pieces of equipment, work tables, and sinks into a unit which comprise a functional area or a functional department. The term department is sometimes associated with separate rooms, but this is not necessarily the case with food service operations. In essence, the designer is developing an area where related functions will be performed and may include as many or as few functions as deemed appropriate for the project.

To illustrate, one particular area may be developed for the functions of dessert preparation, salad preparation, and sandwich preparation, whereas another project may require three separate areas for these functions. The second stage of the layout process involves arranging the functional areas or departments into the total facility. For example, the receiving, storage, preparation, production, and warewashing areas and the nonproduction areas, such as rest rooms, lounges, and offices, are brought together to form the basic floor plan for the facility. There may be some question as to whether these two stages of layout are done at the same time. Even though the planner may be working on one stage or the other at any given moment, layout decisions must be considered in terms of both stages.

In essence, the layout of the total facility must be considered when laying out the component areas; and in turn, the layout of the component areas must be considered when laying out the total facility. The layout phase of planning is critical because it integrates most of the factors that affect the food service facility when it is operational.

Variable Flow

The planning of individual workplaces is followed by a logical grouping of several workplaces to develop work centers and departnents. The combining of workplaces including tables, sinks, and equipment is guided by different concepts of flow. The criteria involved may include employee flow, material or product flow, customer flow, or in some cases, combinations of these.

For example, the layout of a short-order cooking area to be staffed by one employee is best done by evaluating the employee's movements. This can be done by determining the frequency of movements anticipated between pairs of equipment and then placing the pairs of equipment that involve the greatest frequency of movement next to one another in the equipment arrangement.

This analysis leads to arrangements that will minimise employee movement and leads to increased productivity. In some instances it may be possible to place equipment in the same vertical plane to completely eliminate employee movements. The use of salamanders above a range or a microwave oven above a work table are examples of this concept. Consideration of combined or multipurpose equipment where appropriate is warranted.

The planning of a large dishwashing area to include a continuous dishwashing machine and where employees are primarily working in fixed areas such as the scrapping table, loading the dishwasher, or unloading the dishwasher may be guided by evaluating material flow. In some situations, the flow of two or more variables may be evaluated to determine the best layout. A salad preparation area may require evaluation of both the flow of foods and the movements of employees in order to arrive at the best layout.

In most cases, arrangements that minimise the flow of materials are also those that minimise the movements of employees. This is likely when the materials are moved primarily by workers, but may not be the case if mechanical conveyors are used. If there is any doubt, both flows should be evaluated. Regardless of the type of flow selected as the criterion for layout, the following principles can be applied:

— Flow should be along straight-line paths as much as possible.
— The amount of cross flow or cross traffic should be minimised.
— Backtracking should be minimised.
— Bypassing should be minimised.

These principles of flow, whether applied to the movement of materials or of people, can be used for all types of layout problems. The concept of keeping flow in a straight line is the most important because it results in movements over the shortest distance. To utilise this concept, the designer will visualise or chart the flow involved with several different arrangements and select the one that gives the best straightline pattern. Flow analyses for layout problems involving only a few pieces of equipment are easy to do. Layout problems involving numerous pieces of equipment or areas will require more extensive flow analysis.

Some planners find flow diagrams or string charts a helpful tool in evaluating complex flow patterns. With the great variety of materials and activities found in food service operations, the concept of minimising cross traffic is important because it results in layouts that are free of bottlenecks and congestion. This concept is especially pertinent to fast-food operations, which have peak periods of flow. Cross traffic is minimised by the proper location of aisles, passageways, and doors. Some cross traffic can be tolerated if it results in shorter flow patterns.

However, if the cross traffic creates a hazardous situation, it should be eliminated, even at the cost of increased distance of movement. Cross traffic between employees and guests is undesirable and should be eliminated. Backtracking occurs when a material or person moves from one piece of equipment or an area back to the point where the movement originated. The flow is back along the same path that was just traversed.

Of course, many of the tasks required in food service operations involve a sequence of movements that make it practically impossible to eliminate all backtracking. Many of the cooking and production tasks are of this nature. In those situations, minimising the amount of backtracking is all that can be done. This involves evaluating several different equipment or space arrangements to find the best one.

Bypassing is the result of a material or person passing one or more pieces of equipment to get to the next piece of equipment required in the sequence of movements. Several different arrangements of the equipment or areas may have to be evaluated to determine which one results in the least amount of bypassing. As with cross traffic, it is impossible to eliminate all bypassing except in the very simplest of layout problems. The ultimate goal of layout is to develop arrangements of equipment and spaces for the food facility that have primarily straight-line flow paths with a minimum of cross traffic, backtracking, and bypassing.

Layout Decisions

Although flow has been identified as the most important criterion of layout, other modifying considerations which may affect some layout decisions should be evaluated before the arrangement is finalised. These include the following items:

— *Efficient use of utilities*. All equipment requiring steam, for example, may be placed together to economise on installation and operating costs.

— *Efficient use of equipment*. Some individual pieces of equipment that will be used in two or more functional areas can be placed in central locations so they are easily accessible.

— Efficient use of skilled labour. This requires arrangements of equipment that will minimise the movements of skilled personnel. This may increase the movements of other employees or increase the movement of materials. The decision may be based on an economic analysis of different arrangements.

— *Safety*. Some layouts based on the concepts of flow alone may result in an arrangement of equipment that is hazardous. Placing a deep-fat fryer next to a sink creates a dangerous situation, and safety should override flow in this case. Other hazardous arrangements may result when high-temperature equipment is placed adjacent to a traffic aisle or near entrances and exits. If another location is not feasible, sufficient guarding and shielding of the equipment is an alternative solution.

— *Efficient use of space*. Building configurations and shapes may require rearrangement of some layouts to make full use of available space.

— *Environmental factors of noise and odor*. Some pieces of equipment or areas may be isolated from flow paths if they are objectionable and cannot be modified to render them environmentally acceptable. Garbage-can washers or incinerators illustrate this situation.

These modifying criteria may result in arrangements that are more expensive than those based on flow alone. They have to be used, however, to achieve many of the objectives of planning that were identified.

Layout of Storage Area

Layout of storage areas is based on convenience and accessibility. Arrangements that allow heavy and bulky materials to be moved title and as easily as possible are preferred. Central storage facilities with several satellite locations are good arrangements for many types of facilities. The storage space in the preparation, processing, and other functional areas should be planned so they do not interfere with efficient work methods.

The use of combination walk-in and each-in storage units may increase the convenience of these areas. It is best to plan walk-in storage areas in a manner which keeps the products at least 8 in. (203 mm) above the floor to facilitate cleaning. An alternative would be to use mobile bins and containers that can be easily moved when the area is cleaned. Storage areas for non-food supplies may be located in the various functional areas as required. Storage space for china, glass, and silverware may be provided in serving or dining areas. Linen and paper goods used for service are also stored in or near these areas.

Layout of Cooking Area

Laying out the main cooking area is the key to fast and efficient production of foods. The flow patterns affecting this area include inflow of foods from storage and preparation areas and utensils from the pot- and pan-washing area. Outflow of foods to the serving, salad preparation, and sandwich preparation areas is common. The cooking equipment should be arranged so that the most frequently used pieces ire close to the pick-up location. Other factors related to the design of the main cooking area include the following:

— All heat- and moisture-producing equipment, such as fryers, broilers, griddles, ranges, and steamers, should be placed under ventilating hoods or be equipped with individual venting systems.

— Steam cooking equipment requires special installation including depressed floors, or the use of curbs.

— Some types of equipment require air for ventilation or cooling of enclosed spaces; vents and grill openings should not be blocked by other pieces of equipment.

— Provision has to be made to permit venting of fuel-burning equipment directly to the outside.

— Location of the main building ventilation or air-conditioning inlets is important to effect adequate cooling of the air without cooling the cooking equipment or interfering with the equipment venting system.

— If remote banquet rooms are to be served, methods of transporting hot foods and appropriate space for loading have to be considered.

— The use of partially or fully preprocessed foods will increase the need for refrigerated space in the cooking areas.

Flexibility and efficient use of employees and equipment can be obtained in some operations where similar equipment is involved in baking and cooking. In this case the baking and cooking areas are placed in close proximity so that kettles, ovens, and mixers can serve both areas. This may even result in reduced exhaust requirements. Placing the baking and cooking areas adjacent to each other also guides the placement of the pot-washing area since these two areas generate the bulk of the soiled pots.

The layout of preparation areas is fairly easy because most of the functions performed in them follow a logical sequence, and thus the equipment is arranged in the same sequence. Vegetable preparation, for example, basically involves trimming, washing, and size reduction, in that order. A straight-line arrangement of a work table for trimming, a sink for washing and draining, and equipment for size reduction becomes the layout for the area. Since the inflow of vegetables is from storage areas, the trimming table is placed close to them; consequently, the size-reduction equipment is placed near the main cooking and salad preparation areas.

Provision for temporary storage of materials and removal of waste will complete the layout of the vegetable preparation area for a small facility. Salad preparation areas are planned in a similar manner. The foods should flow in a continuous path from the start of the preparation tasks, through the various workplaces and equipment, which are arranged in the order of the steps required, and on to the serving area. Operations that prepare a large number of the same or very similar salads may be designed by the concepts of mass assembly.

Design of Baking Areas

The volume and variety of baked items that will be produced in a particular food service operation determines the layout to be used. Operations that produce a minimum number of items such as pastries and desserts can combine the baking area with the cooking area. Employees' work shifts may be scheduled to avoid problems of equipment usage. Operations that will be involved in the production of a moderate amount of baked goods frequently locate the baking area adjacent to the cooking area so some equipment can be shared.

Food service operations that will produce the full line of baked items including breads, rolls, pastries, or even speciality items may need a separate baking area in order to minimise interference between the cooking and baking functions. The design of baking area layouts should follow the typical processing steps to assure a smooth work flow. For example, a proof box located near the ovens simplifies the loading of items into the ovens. Similarly, a landing table placed near the ovens simplifies unloading.

Baker's tables are centrally located with easy access to storage areas, mixers, and kettles, as well as the proof box and ovens. Sufficient space is provided for mixing, cutting, panning, rolling, and finishing the baked items. Storage space for baking supplies, utensils, and tools that are frequently used are best located at the work centers. Provision for storage of the finished baked items might take the form of mobile units for easy movement to the serving or pick-up areas.

Another possibility would be to use pass-through storage units between the baking and serving areas. Special requirements such as the freezing and storage of some baked items are considered so that space for freezers is provided either in or near the baking areas. Refrigerators are required for the storage of highly perishable items such as custard-filled or whipped cream desserts.

Layout of Serving Areas

The layout of serving areas is based on the method and speed of service desired. Serving equipment should be arranged in the order of use, and should be located so they are easily accessible to serving personnel.

Table Service

Hot food pick-up areas are located adjacent to the main cooking battery. Provisions for maintaining the temperature of hot foods at pick-up areas should be considered. Additional serving stations or pantries for salads, desserts, rolls, and beverages are located nearer the dining area to avoid congestion. Linen, flatware, water, and butter used for setups are best placed in inconspicuous areas of the dining room. These stations may also include facilities for depositing soiled linen and tableware.

Counter Service

Most of the cooking and serving facilities in typical counter-service operations occur at the back bar opposite the dining counter. A common layout is to have a straight-line back bar with straight-line or a series of U-shaped dining counters. Some operations offering a more extensive menu may require additional preparation and cooking facilities that can be located in a separate area.

An efficient layout in this case is to have the pick-up counter as a part of the back bar. This is also a good arrangement for operations having both counter and table-service sections. The pick-up area should be located for easy access to the table servers.

Cafeteria Service

Cafeteria counters are placed as close to the production areas as possible with due regard to the free flow of customers or users. The layout of cafeteria counters is based on the shape of the serving area and the anticipated traffic patterns. Counters may be arranged in a straight line, ell-shaped, U-shaped, hollow square, or combinations of these configurations, as dictated by the length of counter required. The design of the counter should allow displayed foods that are usually selected in combination to be placed together on the counter.

Merchandising concepts call for desserts and salads to be located at the beginning of the line; hot foods should be at the end of the line to minimise cooling. Special care is needed in providing for cashiering, since this is one of the bottleneck areas in commercial cafeterias. The entire design of the cafeteria service system is based on volume flow, and anything that will speed service should be incorporated into the layout. Silver, napkins, water, and condiments may be located in stations away from the main counter area. Islands placed between the serving and dining areas are frequently used for this purpose. Self-dispensing equipment for beverages will also help speed the flow of people.

Cook-to-order items cause delays and are best located in a separate area where patrons can pull out of the main stream of flow to wait for their orders. This can be easily accomplished with the open square arrangement of counters. The layout of dishwashing areas should follow the sequence of operations performed in washing. The arrangement has to provide for sorting, scraping or preflushing, and stacking, prior to loading the dishwashing machine. If glasses and silverware are to be washed separately, provisions for these operations have to be planned.

Preflushing of soiled dishes may be accomplished in one of two ways. One method is to use a continuous flow of water over the dishes as they are being scraped. A disposal unit is used to handle the food wastes. The other method uses an overhead spray and is suitable for dishes that are placed in dish racks. In either case, the soiled-dish table has to be designed so that water is quickly drained away. Raised edges on the table help prevent excess water spillage. Regardless of the type of dishwashing machine used, space for loading and unloading must be arranged. Rack-type machines are frequently loaded in a straight-line flow from the soiled-dish table. Rackless or peg-type machines require space for the loader to handle the individual pieces of dinnerware.

Clean-dish areas are arranged so adequate drying time is allowed before the removal and stacking of dinnerware takes place. The flow of dinnerware through the dishwashing area is planned to be continuous and over the shortest possible distance. The layout of other areas for the food facility should be accomplished in the same manner as given in the above examples. When all the preceding steps of the planning process are satisfactorily completed, the layout step becomes fairly easy.

Requirement of Food Processing Facility

Design and construction of a food processing facility requires a great deal of planning. Information must be collected from many sources and combined into documents that are simple to read and share with others. Planning sessions should involve persons that represent all aspects of facility activity. Examples are production, maintenance, supervision, sales, accounting, receiving, warehousing, distribution, human resources, management, engineering, research and development, key suppliers, government agencies, and consultants.

Consultants include engineers, lawyers, insurance providers, and other specialists that may not be regularly employed by the company. For large projects, it is recommended to hold scheduled planning sessions at a convenient location that is free from distractions. It is often desirable to obtain an unrelated, third party to lead and moderate planning sessions inorder to retain objectivity and purpose. An agenda should be drafted for each planning session.

There are many of the elements to consider when designing food-processing plants. Since each situation is unique, some elements will not apply and some important elements may need to be added. Relevant elements can form the basis for a planning session agenda. Elements listed are not in any particular order of importance and emphasise engineering design. Lists of design considerations are given below.

— Facility
— Process
— Product
— Other

5

Hotel Environmental Management

The increasing adoption of environmental management in hotel firms seems to have been sparked off by growing concerns over the impacts of tourism on the environment. The US hotel industry has not been left out of this scourge as a number of initiatives have been undertaken. Hotels are at the hub of the tourism industry and it is one sector of the tourism industry in which activities such as construction of buildings and landscaping, cooking and disposal

Of waste, use of water and energy tend to affect the environment adversely if not properly managed. Service sector businesses like hotels, resorts and restaurants have some inherent characteristics which exacerbate their impacts on the environment namely; time perishable capacity, heterogeneity, labour intensity and customer involvement in the production process. The size of hotel facility also influences the environmental impact. For instance the impact of a hundred room limited service hotel will be different from a six-hundred room full service hotel.

The forces exerting pressure on US hotels to be more environmental-conscious could be summarised as government regulation, changing consumer demand, advocacy/initiatives by NGOs and international organisations as well as ethics by professional associations. Globally, the tourism industry is under pressure to adopt more environmentally sound practices. This arose out of concerns that tourism could and often did have negative impacts on the host communities and their environments.

Increasing environmental awareness on the part of consumers has served as pressure on hotels to adopt sound environmental practices. Tourists are becoming more discerning, seeking activities, arrangements and experiences which depend crucially on a high quality physical and cultural environment.

Studies conducted by the International Hotels Environment Initiative (IHEI) and Accor revealed that 90% of hotel guests preferred to stay in a hotel that cared for the environment.

Corporate bodies are also using environmental considerations in their choice of venues for meetings, as from 1997 to 1998, the number of companies seeking a green hotel for their meetings increased by 10%. Also, in the case of the Saunders Hotels, they were able to attract more than $750,000 in new convention business in 1992 alone due to sound environmental practices.

Furthermore, regulation of the tourism industry by governments in the form of planning restrictions, mandatory Environmental Impact Assessment (EIA) and laws relating to business practice has exerted pressure on hotels to adopt sustainable environmental practices.

Rowe believes that government restrictions are not limited to EIAs. According to him, in some communities such as Lake Tahoe, the government sets strict visual guidelines that hospitality companies must observe. The developers of the Embassy Suites Resort in Lake Tahoe had to undertake a complex and lengthy planning process. The design of the hotel was 70% dictated by government agencies, including the style of the hotel, scenic thresholds and the selection of exterior colours. Non-compliance with such government restrictions has often not gone unpunished. In Europe, North America, Australia and New Zealand, such prosecutions can now result in heavy financial penalties, considerable clean-up costs or in worst instances, jail sentences. Commenting on fines imposed on firms, which flout environmental regulations, Zhao and Merna, claim that fines have escalated from $300,000 from 1982, to $11.7 million in 1989. Hotels must therefore comply with environmental regulations to avoid these fines.

Another force has been exerted by both national and international NGOs and professional organisations. International organisations like the United Nations Environmental Programme (UNEP), World Tourism Organisation (WTO), World Wildlife Fund (WWF) and the World Travel and Tourism Council (WTTC) are all actively involved in ensuring environmental improvement in hotels.

Also, NGOs and other pressure groups such as Tourism Concern, World-wide Fund for Nature (WWF), Equations and Friends of the Earth, among others, have also exerted pressure on hotels to become increasingly concerned about their environments. The case in which Greenpeace won a court suit against Sol Melia Hotels for ecodamage is a case in point. However, the pressure exerted by NGOs has not always been in the form of advocacy and suits but also conservation activities in collaboration with some hotels. Novotel and Hotel Ibis Homebush Bay of Australia are in a unique partnership with the WWF whereby a $1.00 from every room per night sold is donated by the hotels to the latter.

However, within the hotel industry, cost savings seem to be the prime motivation for the increasing adoption of environmental management practices in hotels.

There are examples of transportation companies, hotels and restaurants haven taken steps to recycle and reduce the consumption of energy, thereby reducing costs, increasing profits and taking some steps towards sustainability. Forte believes that energy-efficient lighting will reduce lighting costs by at least 60%. A survey carried out by the American Hotel and Motel Association (AH&MA) revealed that Hotel managers rated reduction of energy consumption as well as waste management through recycling to be their most important concerns.

Environmental Management in US Hotels

Environmental Management in US hotels started in the form of initiatives by various associations and activities which begun when the Prince of Wales launched the International Hotels Environment Initiative (IHEI) in 1993.

This involved 11 international hotel chains accepting a manual spelling out a comprehensive campaign to advance environmental performance in the hotel industry. However, Stipanuk is of the view that US hotels have responded to environmental issues as far back as 1920. In 1994, the Hotel and Catering Institute Management Association participated in Green Globe, an environmental management awareness programme initiated by the WTTC. Today, individual hotels Accor, Ramada Renaissance Hotel, Fairmont Hotels and Resorts among others are aggressively pursuing environmental initiatives.

Today, various types of environmental initiatives exist. However, there are no common standards for hotels, so these initiatives are being carried out by the hotels themselves, NGOs, International Organisations and government agencies. Such initiatives have been in the form of publications, certification, awards, ecolabels and codes of conduct.

Ecolabelling

Ecolabels have also been used to encourage the development of less-damaging and environmentally friendly hotels as well as to educate the customer. Ecolabelling started in Europe in 1985 with Blue flag however; the concept has been adopted by the tourism and hospitality industry to promote a clean and green image. Today, there are over 100 in the tourism and hospitality industry, operating in several countries, including the US. In the US, ecolabels for hotels include EcoMeet, Green Hotels Association, and Green Hotel in the Mountain State, Green Seal, and Energy Star. A hotel has to be a member of a particular association or go through a certification programme in order to use its logo. Most of the ecolabels therefore provide certification programmes. Green Globe 21 for instance uses an Environmental Management System (EMS) as its ecolabel criteria. It has developed benchmarks specific to hotels.

Certification Process

Certification which is a process by which a third party gives written assurance to the consumer that a product, process, service or management system conforms to specified requirements.

Though it originally started in manufacturing industries, it has crept into the tourism and hospitality industry. A number of global and national certification schemes are available for US hotels. The ISO 14000 was developed originally for the manufacturing industry but now covers hotels. It is aimed at standardising environmental management practices, audits, performance evaluation, labelling and life cycle assessments practices around the world.

Green Globe 21 is a global certification programme developed by the World Travel and Tourism Council (WTTC) in 1998 to address sustainable development issues in the tourism industry. Its standards include an environmental code, policy guidance, environmental management systems, and employee information and consumer tips.

Ecotel is also a global initiative involving international inns, hotels and resorts that define the concept of environmental responsibility in the hospitality industry. Another certification scheme is EcoHotel instituted by HVS International in 1991. It is based on five major criteria: environmental commitment, solid waste management, energy efficiency, and water conservation and employee education/community involvement. The Green Scal a Washington D.C based NGO is also a certification scheme for the hospitality industry. A number of US hotels are also seeking Leaders in Energy and Environmental Design (LEED 2.0) certification, which was developed in the late 1990s by the US Green Building Council. However, this certification is only limited to buildings, including hotel buildings.

Some states have also instituted certification schemes on the local level. These include Green Hotel designation in the Green Mountain State of Vermont and Green Seal's alliance with Pennsylvania State, Washington D.C and Virginia. In all these certification schemes, hotels need to apply, and then they will be assessed based on the standards set. Assessment is the process of examining, measuring, testing or otherwise determining conformance with requirements specified in an applicable standard. Hotels which do not meet the standards need to make adjustments before they can be certified, so they can carry a logo.

Building Awareness of Environmental Issues

August 29, 2003—During the month of September, hotels are showcasing existing or new social and environmental responsibility initiatives to guests and communities to help foster relationships that develop and address social and environmental issues. Guests staying at participating hotels can contribute to Hotel Environmental Action Month through various traveller philanthropy initiatives.

Over the past few years, more travellers have been looking for responsible and sustainable options while visiting destinations and seeking to 'put something back' into the community or make a positive difference to the lives of others. Many hotels contribute to local communities through charities, environmental management or education initiatives. Guests can also ask their hotels what activities or programmes are taking place and how they can contribute. Some initiatives that guests can participate in include:

— *Donating loose change to charity:* Hilton hotels place money collection envelopes in all guest rooms asking guests to donate any small change and hand it to the front desk. Money received is donated to Variety-the Children's Charity.

— *Contributing $1 USD (or local currency equivalent) at one of 120 participating Starwood Hotels.* The funds are used to immunise children against polio, diphtheria, tetanus, etc. Over 4 million children have been immunised to date.

— Participating in a new information session that has been created for guests about the hotels' iguana sanctuary At the Aruba Marriott Resort and Stellaris Casino, guests are able to feed iguanas once they have attended the information session about how the animals came to be protected, their history and facts such as life expectancy.

— Learning about the flora and fauna of the 'Cerro El Avila' (a mountain in Caracas) by taking a guided tour with the JW Marriott Hotel Caracas. The tours will be offered to showcase the area and ways to maintain it and keep it safe.

— Contributing to 'pancake action' at the Radisson SAS in Düsseldorf where pancakes will be sold to collect money for the Alle im Dienste Solidarische. V (A.I.D.S.) organisation that helps adults and children who have aids or HIV.

— Eating at Radisson SAS Grande Hotel in Sophia hotel where one Euro will be added to guests restaurant bill and proceeds will go to a local orphanage.

— Walking over the 'fringing housc reef' walkway in Radisson SAS Sharm El Sheik that was created in Cooperation with the National Parks of Egypt. Along the walk, explanation signs will give information about the flora, fauna and ecosystem of the tropical reef. This will help protect the reef from damaging corrals and disturbing unique marine wildlife as well as create awareness of the natural resources of the area.

— Taking a guided tour of garbage separation at the Hilton Otaru in Japan. Education flyers will be distributed to guestrooms to showcase the progressive action in this local community.

The International Hotel Environmental Initiative (IHEI) is coordinating Hotels Environment Action Month

(HEAM). The primary objective of HEAM is to build awareness of environmental and social issues that face each region and to raise environmental awareness among guests, staff and the public. These initiatives will not only communicate the need for responsible tourism but also demonstrate the practical and innovative action already being taken by hotels around the world. For more information about traveller's philanthropy, the October issue of greenhotelier, published by IHEI will feature case studies of how guests can get more involved.

Importance of Environmental Management

A "quiet revolution" is taking place in the Caribbean—one less visible than the construction of new hotels and the building of new cruise ships. Nevertheless, its advent is profoundly changing the nature and shape of the tourism and hospitality industry, in every hotel guestroom, housekeeping, laundry or maintenance facility, and in every tourism destination that elects voluntarily to join the environmental movement. This revolution is environmentally sustainable tourism.

The Caribbean hotel industry, particularly, is positioned to reinvent itself in a way that improves profitability, enhances guest relations, builds bridges into the local communities, and preserves the Caribbean's natural beauty. Over the past 2 years, this trend has been translated into results in Jamaica in the form of the Environmental Audits for Sustainable Tourism (EAST) project, sponsored by the Jamaica Hotel and Tourist Association and funded by the United States Agency for International Development (USAID).

Jamaica EAST Project Description

In 1997, the Jamaica Hotel and Tourist Association,

Government of Jamaica, Jamaica Manufacturers Association, and a number of tourism-related public and private-sector industry organisations committed to undertake the Environmental Audits for Sustainable Tourism (EAST) project. With funding from the U.S. Agency for International Development, Hagler Bailly implemented a programme of environmental audits within a corporate environmental management system aimed at the tourism and hospitality industry in Negril, with a smaller component focused on manufacturing industries in Kingston and St. Andrews. The project is a model for environmental action and voluntary audits for the tourism sector, combining promotion and outreach, training, audits, and investment. The objectives of the EAST programme are:

— to develop greater awareness and understanding of the benefits of environmental systems and audits among hotel and restaurant owners and allied tourism businesses;

— to upgrade the technical skills of Jamaicans who are expected to conduct the audits and advise on environmental management systems;

— to assist a select, representative number of tourism-related establishments in carrying out environmental audits, and

— to help finance in the tourism industry, on a cost-sharing basis, selected audit recommendations in order to demonstrate the financial benefits of the systematic application of environmentally friendly practices and, thereby, encourage others in the tourism industry to do likewise.

The activities of the EAST project include:

— institutionalising environmental management in the tourism industry;

— performance monitoring of EAST demonstration hotels;
— environmental assessments, audits, and certification; environmental awareness and training; regulatory assistance in environmental licensing;
— audits and technical assistance in the manufacturing industry;
— targeted environmental investment fund feasibility and financing; performance awards programmes, and international human resources exchange programmes.

An important next step for Jamaica is to sustain and expand this improved level of environmental management among government and private-sector organisations.

EAST Findings

When Hagler Bailly began in June of 1997, the awareness was quite high in Negril (the target area for the EAST project) due primarily to the influx of questionnaires and surveys sent by European tour operators such as Tui and British Airways Holidays. These inquiries were from European markets interested in buying the export products, e.g., travelling to destinations supporting environmental best policies and management practices.

Hagler Bailly started with a survey of hotels in Negril to ask hoteliers why they choose to become "environmentally friendly." The results showed a genuine concern about the impact their operations have on the physical environment and an appreciation for how this can be translated into cost savings. Interestingly, the government's enforcement of environmental laws and standards ranked lowest. This told us that hoteliers were interested in measurable results and that they would respond better to incentives than to government intervention. Initially, however, when we asked individual hoteliers what they thought "going green" implied, the most common answer was to replace plastic straws with paper straws. Since none of the respondents had achieved the "environmentally friendly" status, was what are the perceived barriers to becoming a green hotel. The results pointed to the up-front cost of learning how to make the transition, and then to the financing to implement it.

Environmental Management System (EMS)

One of the most critical elements of becoming an environmentally friendly hotel is the adoption of a new culture that extends throughout the hotel organisation, and between the hotel and its guest, local community, and even its vendors. We call this an environmental management system (EMS).

An EMS is defined as a comprehensive organisational approach designed to achieve environmental care in all aspects of operations. The International Standards Organisation (ISO) 14000 series is an international standard for EMS. The World Travel and Tourism Council's GREEN GLOBE international certification has developed an EMS standard specifically for the travel and tourism industry.

An effective EMS can help a hotel assure its guests of its commitment to environmental management as partners in programmes such as recycling, linen and towel reuse, etc. It can set specific and realis[illegible] performance objectives and targets, and all[illegible] to monitor to see if the objectives and [illegible] met. As mentioned earlier, it can en[illegible] in the marketplace an[illegible] Americans, as w[illegible] environmentally aware tourists from Europe and elsewhere interested in visiting environmentally friendly destinations and staying in accommodations with environmental policies and programmes in place. Most importantly, an EMS can improve efficiency and reduce operating costs. In fact, the savings alone should be sufficient for any hotel to commit to implementing an EMS.

Few hotels today have what we would consider an EMS. This is not to say that there are no hotels implementing environmental programmes such as water conservation and composting, but it is typically not done as part of a larger management system, nor is it integrated with other environmental programmes. There is a growing demand to have an EMS that meets international standards such as ISO 14001 and GREEN GLOBE. An EMS evaluation, because of its broad-reaching implications, will begin to encompass other concerns such as health, safety, and security, emergency preparedness, compliance with discharge and emissions standards, and employee training.

What constitutes an EMS? The principal components of an EMS, as defined by GREEN GLOBE, include the following: an environmental policy that clearly communicates the organisation's commitment to maintaining the social, cultural and physical environment; an action plan to guide the property's actions and expenditure of resources; the implementation or operations of the EMS that encompasses all of the
...tions relative to the environment, including
...aining, staff procedures, incentive
...munity outreach among other
...itoring to ensure that the
...wing for responsive

actions to capture things such as leaking toilets and chemical spills and review, typically by senior management, to determined how to improve the EMS and the level of compliance with the hotel's environmental policy.

EMS and Environmental Programmes

Many will say, we already have hotels in the Caribbean that are operating in an environmentally responsible manner. That is to say that the hotel is currently composting much of its organic solid wastes, or that guestrooms have low flow showerheads installed. We call these environmental programmes. An EMS is the integration of those programmes under a comprehensive organisational system. An EMS takes the following approach to addressing its environmental issues (or aspects as they are referred to in the standards).

— First, an assessment is done to determine what improvements can be made, how much they cost, and what types of changes in consumption or waste generation can be expected. The assessment also allows you to establish a baseline against which change can be measured.

— Next, the hotel sets objectives such as to reduce water consumption for the entire property by 10%. Each objective is supported by a set of specific targets, such as introduce towel and linen reuse programme by June 31st, or install low-flow showerheads in guest rooms and staff locker rooms by August 1st.

— The individuals, or departments, responsible for achieving the targets are identified in an action plan. It is important to remember that the greatest improvements are made through changes in staff procedures.

— Finally, the impact or results, in terms of changes from the baseline, must be measured and documented. This provides the necessary feedback to determine whether the EMS is working.

The EMS can be viewed as the integration of multiple environmental programmes. Environmental programmes are typically designed to address a specific environmental problem or issue such as recycling or composting solid waste; or are focused on a specific department such as a linen reuse programme in housekeeping and laundry. In some instances, particularly for smaller hotels, environmental programmes may involve multiple properties, such as sharing the cost of a bottle crusher for glass recycling

EAST Environmental Management Audit Findings

Hagler Bailly designed a specific audit protocol that combines the attributes of an energy audit, an environmental audit, and a management audit —the EAST Environmental Management Audit. We tested the audit protocol on the full range of hotel properties, from 15 rooms to over 200 rooms. The audits covered the following areas. energy use, water use, wastewater generation and disposal, solid waste generation and disposal, use of chemicals, and management and staff practices.

Summarised below are some of the general findings of the EAST audits.

Inefficient use of water—Leaking toilets accounted for 40% of the daily water use in one 35-room hotel. The cost of the leaks was US$600 per month. In another property, a defective drain valve on a washing machine increased laundry water use by more than 1 million gallons per year equivalent to US$6,000 of wasted water.

Inefficient use of energy—Loose louvers and doors and poor insulation force air conditioners to work continuously in order to keep guest rooms cool. This mode of operation increases energy consumption and shortens the air conditioner's service life. Excessive and unnecessary use of chemicals—Instead of manually cleaning the kitchen grease trap, a property used 420 gallons/year of sulfuric acid to do the job. This cost of this dangerous habit exceeded US$6,000 per year.

Excessive solid waste generation—A 25-room property spent US$1,700 per year to purchase large plastic trash bags. Many properties place all yard waste in plastic bags and pay to send this material to the dump. Organic wastes from kitchen and landscaping accounts for up to 50% of a property's solid waste and can be easily composted.

Staff not participating in environmental programmes—In 90% of cases, housekeepers automatically replace all used guest towels in properties that have towel reuse programmes.

Poor (or no) monitoring—Approximately 70% of audited properties had no effective utilities monitoring programme. Water and electricity bills are simply received and paid. A 20,000-gallon per day leak went undetected for more than a week because the property didn't check the water meter daily.

There was considerable variation in water use among 14 properties we audited ranging from 15 to 70 rooms. To provide a common base for comparison, we calculated each hotel's consumption in terms of Imperial gallons per guest night. The results are shown in Figure 1. The most efficient of the hotels used just one-third the water per guest night of the least efficient.

	Imperial gallons / Guest Night
Most Efficient Hotel	116
Average Efficient	216
Least Efficient	351

Figure 1. Water Use in Properties Audited by East

A similar comparison was also done among audited properties for electricity consumption. The results are shown in Figure 2. Again, the most efficient hotel used only one-quarter of the electricity per guest night of that of the least efficient hotel.

	KWH / Guest Night
Most Efficient Hotel	8.7
Average Efficient	21.4
Least Efficient	32.9

Figure 2. Electricity Use in Properties Audited by EAST

The water and energy use indices of a hotel are affected by occupancy rates as well as by its conservation efforts and investments in efficient technologies. As a general rule, water and energy indices rise during low occupancy months and drop during high occupancy months. Given the influence of occupancy and conservation efforts on efficiency, the monitoring data collected from the properties should be analysed in greater detail to ensure that efficiency gains result from improved environmental practices rather than better occupancy rates. This higher scrutiny is particularly important, for example, in the case of a hotel that reduced its water and electricity use indices by more than 25% while simultaneously increasing its occupancy by 16%.

The water and electricity use indices are consistently lower "after" the EAST audit, regardless of the actual occupancy levels, these graphs prove that the property's water and electricity savings are due to improved conservation practices rather than higher occupancy rates. The vertical distance separating the "before EAST" and "after EAST" trend lines represents the actual water and electricity savings achieved through the property's conservation efforts at any given occupancy level.

Improvement

So what did it take to improve performance in a typical Jamaican hotel?

Most of the recommendations made in the EAST Audit reports have the following characteristics. They have low implementation costs, rapid payback periods, and they are relatively simple and easy to implement.

The EAST auditors also found that the greatest environmental and financial benefits can be achieved by improving: frequent monitoring, particularly utility bills; management supervision, oversight to ensure that programmes are operating effectively; staff practices, training, and providing incentives for staff to implement programmes, and preventive and routine maintenance, particularly of energy- and water-using equipment. In the breakdown of EAST audit recommendations for a typical hotel, the following was evident. Over three-quarters of the recommendations cost less than US$10 / guest room, 19% of the recommendations cost between US$10—50 per guest room and only 3% cost more than US$50 per guestroom.

Payback period is defined as the length of time required before the savings from a measure equal the cost to implement the measure. In terms of payback period for

EAST audit recommendations: 62% of the recommendations had a payback of less than 2 months, another 36% had payback periods of between 2 months and 1 year, and only 2% had payback of greater than 1 year.

Another way to break down the EAST audit recommendations is by area of activity (or department) in the hotel. Auditors identified that the largest, by far, can be found in the maintenance and engineering department. We should note that more often than not, the problems lie in insufficient resources resulting in shortages of staff, parts, and supplies, and unwillingness to pay repair bills to fix a problem properly. Guest rooms (or housekeeping department) and restaurant and bar (or food and beverage department) accounted for 15 and 16 percent of the recommended actions, respectively. This is mainly due to the high degree of energy and water used in these areas.

During the visits to Jamaica, we became aware of one small hotel in Port Antonio—Hotel Mocking Bird Hill—that has made considerable strides in improving environmental performance. For purposes of the following example, we will refer to Mocking Bird Hill's consumption levels as that of a "green hotel." Using the average from the 14 EAST hotels audited for both water and electricity; we show the difference relative to the "green hotel."

Looking now at an illustration of the cost advantages of a green hotel, let's assume a 50-room hotel, with 60% occupancy, and 2 guest per room. Over the course of a year, the water savings are over3.6 million gallons, or savings of US$21,829 in water bills. The electricity savings are 186,000 kWh per year, or savings of US$23,886 in electricity bills. Total savings, for both water and electricity amounts to US$45,715 per year.

The savings can greatly improve a hotel's profitability. For example, if it takes US$10 of revenue to generate US$1 of profit, savings of US$45,715 in utility costs would have an impact equivalent to US$457,150 in additional revenue. Assuming average revenue of US$100 per guest night, the savings represent the equivalent to additional 4,571 guest nights worth of revenue.

Cash Flow Associated with "Going Green"

So how would the investment and savings look over an extended period of time? Most of the costs are incurred in the first 9 months. These include the cost of an external audit, energy and water savings equipment, and training of key staff. After the first year, the costs are only associated with preventative maintenance and preparing for the annual GREEN GLOBE certification. Over a 3-year period, the initial investment of US$40,000 will yield approximately US$112,000 in savings, or a net profit of about US$70,000.

Implications for the Jamaican Hotel Industry

Just to illustrate the point further, we asked the question: "What would becoming a green hotel mean for Jamaica as a whole?" Here we have used the Jamaican Tourist Product Development Company (TPDCo) hotel data for 1996, assumed 60% occupancy and 2 guests per room like the earlier example. Obviously, this over-simplifies the hotel industry, but the point is valid.

For all of Jamaica, the difference between an industry comprised of green hotels and one comprised of average hotels is over 930 million gallons of water per year. The green hotel industry will use 77% less water than the average, and 86% less than the inefficient hotel industry.

The reductions in water consumption also translate directly to the volume of wastewater coming from the hotel industry. We can do the same simulation for energy or specifically electricity consumption. For all of Jamaica, the difference between green hotels and the average hotel industry is over 47 million kilowatt-hours per year. The green hotel industry will use a third less electricity than the average, and two-thirds less electricity than the inefficient hotel industry.

6

Waste Reduction in Hotels

Waste reduction includes all actions taken to reduce amount and/or toxicity of waste. It includes waste prevention, recycling, cornposting and the purchase of products that have recycled content or produce less waste. Waste prevention is one of the easiest methods of reducing waste and can be controlled at the time of purchasing products and services. There is a direct correlation between what a hotel purchases and what throws away. In addition, all of the resources and economic costs of materials, manufacturing, labour, transportation, packaging, storage and disposal are wasted when a product is discarded.

Cornposting food waste and yard trimmings can save hotel money on hauling and landfilling fees. However, cornposting is limited by land space at the hotel and/ availability of commercial cornposting sites. Purchasing products made with recycled content creates outlets or markets for the materials collected in the hotel's recycling programme. As such, procurement sustains the recycling process and in turn, reduces the amount of waste going to the landfill.

Benefits of waste reduction:

— savings through reduced purchasing costs,

— reduced waste disposal costs,

— reduced energy consumption and pollution,

— conservation of natural resources.

Recycling Process

Recycling is the process by which materials, otherwise destined for disposal, are collected and used as raw materials for new products. Recycling prevents useful materials from being landfilled or combusted, thus saving energy and natural resources. There are three steps in recycling:

1) collecting the recyclable components of solid waste,
2) processing and manufacturing them into reusable products,
3) purchasing and using the products made with reprocessed materials.

Hotel recycling programmes focus on collecting recyclable materials from the hotel's waste stream for recycling and purchasing products made from recycled materials.

Benefits of recycling:

— reduces hotel waste disposal costs by diverting materials from the landfill,

— possibly provides revenues through the sale of recyclable materials,

— demonstrates a hotel's commitment to environmental protection to guests, businesses and employees.

Hotel and Motel Waste Reduction

Hotel and motel owners, managers and employees must make a commitment to the hotel's waste reduction and recycling initiatives if these programmes are to be successful. To be successful requires initial research in present purchasing and waste handling practices. This includes the cost of disposing of waste, research of products, packaging, vendors, recycling processors equipment and related areas. Further planning is needed in programme implementation and employee training. The following actions are suggested to assist in organising hotels waste reduction initiatives.

General Manager and Employees

— Inform appropriate people in the hotel's corporate structure of the programme's progress, emphasising the savings in waste disposal costs, revenue from material sales, the conservation of natural, non-renewable resources and pollution prevention. Seek their commitment and financial support.

— Appoint a waste reduction manager to provide leadership to each of these initiatives. Establish an accounting system that reflects monthly waste management costs. A monthly report is needed for tracking waste disposal and recycling information.

— Establish a budget for the recycling initiative. Funds may be needed for purchasing recycling containers, equipment and developing employee motivation programmes.

— Assist management and employees in establishing the hotel's waste reduction and recycling goals. Post the goals on bulletin boards so all employees are informed.

— Create employee interest. Involve them in the initial stages of the programme so they will take responsibility.

— Incorporate recycling procedures in employee position descriptions. Include recycling procedures in new employee orientation, employee training programmes and staff meetings. Inform the recycling programme manager of planned structural renovations and equipment replacements. These activities may require special arrangements with haulers and materials processors.

— Develop an environmentally green marketing plan for the hotel. Work with the hotel's marketing company to highlight the hotel's waste reduction efforts in all promotional materials.

— Inform employees of the programme's progress. Place copies of monthly recycling reports on employee bulletin boards and discuss in employee meetings.

Recycling Programme Manager

The recycling programme manager is usually appointed by the hotel's general manager. This position requires an individual with leadership and communications skills who is able to motivate employees. Knowledge of the hotel's present purchasing and waste disposal practices and contract procedures would be helpful. The following actions will assist in assuring success.

— Meet monthly with the hotel's general manager to inform him/her of the programme's progress.

— Present reports of programme progress at department managers meetings.

— Work with management to establish a budget for programme organisation, equipment purchases and employee motivation/rewards.

— Develop recycling procedures to complement the operational practices of the hotel.

— Work with the recycling materials processor to develop a training programme on materials preparation and train employees in recycling procedures specific for the hotel and various departments.

— Research recycling container types and equipment prices.

— With the assistance of department managers and employees, design materials collection and storage systems that complement employee work procedures.

— Issue bid invitations to waste haulers and intermediate processors for recycling materials removal/hauling and processing.

— Issue bid invitations for purchasing and leasing recycling containers and equipment.

— Review existing purchasing practices to determine how purchasing decisions impact the hotel's waste disposal costs.

— Develop a monitoring system that addresses employee compliance in the hotel's waste reduction initiative.

— Review guest comment cards monthly. It is important to know how guests perceive the programme.

— Inform employees of the programme's progress. Seek their ideas and opinions at meetings and in private conversations. Keep them in the loop.

— Evaluate the programme's progress often and make adjustments as needed.

Motivating Employees

No matter how well planned your waste reduction and recycling initiatives may be, they probably won't succeed without the support of the hotel department managers and staff. Successful hotel recycling programmes require employee involvement, training and recognition. Involve all employees in the recycling programme. They are already disposing of waste as they perform their daily jobs.

Recycling is simply disposing of job related waste in a different container from the one used for trash. Seek their ideas in organising the recycling programme and for methods of collecting and storing the materials. Employees are more likely to support a programme that they understand and have helped design.

— Develop motivational programmes that create opportunities for staff involvement and enthusiasm about the recycling programme.

Training programmes

— Develop employee training programmes that include recycling techniques specific for various departments.

— Include recycling information in new employee orientation programmes.

— Inform employees of environmental issues and laws. Employees want to know why the hotel is recycling.

Recognise employees

— Develop a system of on-the-spot, weekly and monthly incentives for employees who exhibit activity and leadership in recycling and waste reduction efforts.

— Recognise employees and departments that show exceptional involvement in the recycling programme.

Involving Guests

Hotel guests are becoming more environmentally conscious, They are becoming more inclined to support "green" initiatives in the travel and hospitality industry. Most guests are pleased to see the use of products made from recycled materials, energy efficient light bulbs, low-flow shower heads and recycling programmes in hotels and restaurants that they patronise. Hotel managers report that most guests are willing to participate in the hotel's recycling efforts.

To increase guest involvement in the programme, place recycling instructions in guest rooms and locate recycling collection containers in convenient locations in convention halls and public areas throughout the hotel. Always place a trash container along side of the recycling container in public areas to avoid trash being thrown in the recycling bin.

Waste Reduction Guidelines for Officers

Waste Reduction guidelines will assist hotel and motel management and employees in reducing the volume and toxicity of waste generated in offices. To successfully reduce waste disposal costs, conduct an audit to determine the types and volumes of waste generated in offices. Plan your waste reduction initiative to target specific products or materials that contribute the greatest volume and/or weight to the waste stream or which create disposal problems. Establish short and long term departmental goals for waste reduction.

The following check list provides a format for your department's audit and additional ideas for waste reduction.

Paper Waste

— Use a centrally-placed or electronic bulletin board for messages instead of making multiple copies of memos.

— Shred office paper and use it to package shipments.

— Eliminate fax cover sheets by using a rubber stamp or sticky notes designed for fax use. Reuse envelopes and folders for routing inhouse mail and correspondence.

— Include a statement requesting electronic addresses on all written correspondence. Electronic mail will save on postage, labour and paper.

— Decrease the number of hard copies of documents by establishing a central filing system to store documents.

— Use electronic mail for correspondence when possible.

— Prepare documents with small margins and double sided printing or copying.

— Make double sided copies when possible.

— Use the back side of paper that is printed on one side for drafts.

— Make scratch pads from paper used on one side by stacking paper and coating one end with rubber cement and cutting in half.

— Edit and proof read documents on computer screens before printing.

— Use staff routing slips when sharing information in-house to stop multiple copies.

— Purge mailing lists to reduce returned mail. This saves on paper use, postage and recycling costs.

— Avoid unnecessary print-outs by faxing directly from the computer.

— Reduce unsolicited mail by sending each solicitor a postcard requesting that they remove your hotel's address from their mailing list; reuse their original mailing label for your return address.

Reuse

— polystyrene peanuts, shredded newspapers and office paper for packing materials,
— obsolete forms and letterhead for drafts and note pads, file folders,
— mugs for coffee instead of disposable cups.

Reduce hasardous waste by purchasing:

— non-toxic inks,
— unbleached and chlorine-free papers,
— nontoxic, biodegradable correction fluid,
— equipment that does not require batteries,
— rechargeable batteries for small calculators communication radios and flashlights.

Support recycling by purchasing:

— paper products made from recycled paper, recycled office papers and cardstock for pocket folders, table tents, business cards, and guest cards,
— file boxes, clipboards, binders, and computer diskettes made from recycled materials, furniture, carpet and padding, trash cans, and recycling containers made from recycled plastic,
— bulletin boards and floor mats made from recycled tires,
— remanufactured toner cartridges for office machines,
— refillable pens and pencils rather than throwaways,
— services from contractors, printers, graphic artists, and other subcontractors who use recycled products and recycle at their businesses.

Other Reduction Strategies

— Combine office supply orders; ordering in bulk reduces packaging waste and saves time, energy and money.

— Chart the shelf life of items and purchase only the needed quantity.

— Request that vendors avoid excessive boxes, bags and wrappings when shipping to your property.

— Purchase plain paper fax machines. Most documents received on thermal paper are copied and the thermal paper fax is then discarded. Thermal fax paper is not recyclable.

— Organise a recycling programme to recycle all office paper including cardboard, magasines, brochures, telephone books and computer papers.

— Recycle typewriter, adding machine and computer ribbons and printer cartridges. When you purchase new office equipment, ask about their energy efficiency.

Waste Reduction Guidelines for Housekeeping Managers

Waste Reduction Guidelines will assist hotel and motel housekeeping managers in reducing the volume and toxicity of wastes generated in the housekeeping department. To successfully reduce disposal costs, conduct a departmental audit to determine the types and volumes of wastes generated for disposal.

Plan your waste reduction initiatives by targeting specific products or materials that contribute the greatest volume and/or weight to the waste stream or which create disposal problems. Establish short and long term department goals for waste reduction and implement appropriate waste reduction strategies.

The following check list will provide a format for your department's audit and provide additional ideas for waste reduction.

Reduce Waste

— Select vendors who take back reusable containers, pallets and other waste packaging.
— Request that manufacturers package products in returnable and/or reusable boxes and crates. Reuse plastic drums and buckets for recycling or trash collection containers in back of the house service areas.
— Use refillable bath soap, shampoo, hair rinse and hand lotion dispensers for guest rooms to eliminate soap pieces and plastic bottles
— Offer newspapers in centrally located places such as lobbies, restaurants, and news stands rather than distributing them to each guest room to reduce the volume of discarded newspapers and plastic bags.
— Eliminate plastic bags and stickers on newspapers.
— Eliminate the use of plastic liners in ice buckets.
— Refinish and reupholster damaged and dated furniture.
— Remanufacture worn mattresses. Mattress manufacturers will rebuild to the hotel's specifications.
— Replace tissues in bathrooms when they are almost empty or leave new rolls or boxes of tissues for the guest to replace. If company policy is to replace half rolls of toilet tissue, save them and donate to shelters or use in employee restrooms.
— Provide amenities such as shower caps, shoe wipes on request.

— Use the small concentrate empties for spray bottles for cleaning solutions by adding pumps.

— Redye stained bath towels and wash cloths for reuse as pool towels and cleaning cloths. Redye linens and carpet to match remodelled decor.

— Rotate draperies to expose different portions to sunlight and extend their useful life.

— Use reusable baskets or plastic containers for guest laundry, thus avoiding disposable paper or plastic wrap

— Use clothes hangers left by guests for employee uniforms or return to the dry cleaners and recycle plastic garment bags.

— Purchase cleaning and laundry products in concentrated form, dilute and pour into reusable containers for individual use.

— Purchase vacuum cleaners with reusable bags vs. disposables ones.

— Purchase sheets with a high thread count for longer wear.

— Provide reusable drinking glasses and coffee cups for guests instead of paper or plastic throwaways.

— Organise a recycling programme for metal, plastic, glass and paper materials.

— Use pump-style sprays instead of aerosol cans.

Reduce Toxicity

— Purchase cleaning products with less hazardous constituents.

— Train employees in proper use of cleaning supplies including the dangers of mixing bleach with other cleaning products.

— Label all cleaning supply bottles with appropriate labels.

— Use a hazardous chemical containment pan to prevent leaching of unused chemicals.

— Check chemical containers periodically for leaks and spills and replace as needed.

— Store unused portions in original containers in a cool, dry place away from equipment, and keep storage areas well ventilated.

— Dispose of chemicals per label instructions. Call your county environmental protection office if you are unsure of how to dispose of hazardous wastes properly.

— Collect dead alkaline, dry cell and rechargeable batteries used in department radios, flashlights and calculators at a central collection point and dispose of them at the battery recycling area in your county.

— Reduce the need for pesticide applications in guest rooms and employee work areas by removing food containers, garbage and recycling containers daily; clean employee break rooms daily to remove crumbs and spills; and report cracks around doors and windows to the engineering department for repairs to prevent crawling pests from entering.

— Check labels on room deodorizers for hazardous chemical content. Deodorizers are often used to mask smoke and mildew odors. Reduce the need for these products by implementing practices, such as changing air conditioning filters every three to four weeks; sealing cracks around windows, doors, and air conditioning units; and operating air conditioning equipment at temperatures recommended by the engineering department.

Support recycling by purchasing

— Toilet and facial tissues and paper towels made from recycled paper fibers.

— Housekeeping carts, waste containers, caddies, and mop buckets made from recycled plastics.

— Carpet, carpet padding, mats, vertical blinds, and furniture made from recycled materials.

Waste Reduction Guidelines for Food and Beverage

Waste Reduction Guidelines will assist hotel and motel food and beverage managers in reducing the volume and toxicity of wastes generated by the food service operations.

To successfully reduce waste disposal costs, conduct a departmental audit to determine the types and volumes of wastes generated for disposal. Plan your waste reduction initiatives by targeting specific products or materials that contribute the greatest volume and/or weight to your departments waste stream or which create disposal problems. Establish short and long term departmental goals for waste reduction and implement appropriate waste reduction strategies.

Reduce Waste

— Use reusable metal or nylon coffee filters. Use only reusable dishes and flatware in restaurants and employee cafeteria.

— Install a magnet on food waste containers to recover silverware accidently thrown away with food waste.

— Use paper towel dispensers in employee rest rooms that control the amount of paper being dispensed or use less than standard width paper to reduce paper waste as well as litter. Use filters in deep fryers to extend the life of cooking oil.

— Distribute condiments, paper napkins, and straws upon request instead of offering them self-serve for take-outs.
— Replace individually wrapped condiment packages with bulk dispensers in restaurants and employee cafeterias.
— Use washable hats and aprons for kitchen employees instead of disposable paper ones. Use only cloth napkins, tablecloths and china for restaurants, meetings, and conventions.
— Use stained wash cloths and towels for cleaning rather than paper towels.
— Redye tablecloths and napkins to match new color schemes when remodelling; reuse worn table linens as cleaning rags or remake into aprons, laundry bags, mattress covers.
— Use glass or plastic coasters to reduce cocktail napkin waste.
— Eliminate paper place mats and use cloth ones.
— Reuse five gallon PVC buckets.
— Request fruits, vegetables and meats to be packaged in reusable crates, or recyclable boxes.

Purchase:

— condiments in bulk and dispense the items in smaller, refillable containers.
— concentrate bar mixes; reconstitute and serve from reusable containers.
— dispenser beverages in concentrate or bulk and pour into reusable serving containers.
— milk in five (5) gallon dispenser bags delivered in reusable plastic crates, rather than by the gallon. If

milk is purchased by the gallon, select recyclable plastic jugs, not waxed cartons.

— frozen foods in bulk and store unserved portions in airtight reusable food containers.

— flours and grains in bulk and store properly in reusable food containers.

— draft beer in returnable/refillable kegs to reduce the quantity of bottles and cans requiring disposal.

— carbonated fountain beverages in refillable cylinders and dispense into reusable glasses.

— beverages with the least distribution packaging.

Reduce Toxicity

— Purchase cleaning products that contain the least amount of hazardous chemicals.

— Use pump-style spray containers for cleaning products.

— Dispose of unused portions of cleaning products according to the labels.

— Dispose of used appliances to scrap dealers who recycle CFC's.

— Purchase refrigerators, freezers, and coolers which are CFC-free.

— Use dry, concentrated dishwasher chemicals in dispensers to reduce chemical spills and waste.

— Reduce the need for pesticide applications by eliminating clutter where pests might hide; sealing cracks around doors where pests may enter; and removing garbage, recycling bins and open food containers at closing time.

— Wipe down all food preparation surfaces, tables and other areas which might contain crumbs to attract pests.

Support recycling by purchasing:

— recycled paper for menus, table tents, guest checks, inventory sheets, calculator and cash register tapes; use the recycling symbol on printed materials to inform guest of your hotel's commitment to the environment.
— paper napkins, place mats, and paper towels are used, purchase ones made from recycled paper.
— serving carts and food storage containers made from recycled plastic and recycle them when they need replacing.
— reusable food storage containers made from recycled materials.
— floor mats made from recycled rubber tires.
— carpet, vertical blinds, and furniture made from recycled materials. waste and recycling containers made from recycled plastics.

Energy Efficient Equipment

The hotel industry is equipped with energy intensive equipment and lighting. Air conditioning, heating, lighting, ventilation, refrigeration, motors, cooking, laundry, cleaning and office equipment are necessary for hotel operations. Choices made when purchasing equipment can have a major impact on the hotel's operating expenses and on the environment; therefore, it is important that efficiency be considered before purchasing energy intensive equipment.

A/C Efficiency

— Purchase A/C equipment sized for the area of use.

— Look for a high Energy Efficiency Rating (EER); a Seasonal Energy Efficiency Rating (SEER) of 10 or higher is recommended.

— Use high efficiency motors for A/C air handling unit fans (fan speeds).

— Install heat recovery units on large A/C systems to preheat water.

— Compare efficiency of gas and electric air conditioning systems before making a selection.

— Purchase washable, commercial grade A/C filters and change them every four weeks during hot humid months.

Lighting Efficiency

— In purchasing light bulbs, as a general rule, the bulb cost is the smallest cost. Energy costs over a bulb's useful life are many times the original purchase cost. Evaluate bulbs by comparing lumens per watt.

— Convert inefficient incandescent bulbs to efficient fluorescent bulbs in exit signs, guest room lamps and other areas where incandescent bulbs are used.

— The newer 95-watt incandescent bulb replaces the older type 100-watt incandescent bulb.

— Replace incandescent reflector bulbs with lower wattage ellipsoidal reflector bulbs.

— Install lighting controls (timers or occupancy sensors) to turn off lights in unoccupied areas such as storage rooms, employee rest rooms, walk-in coolers, etc.

Increase the energy efficiency of fluorescent lighting systems by purchasing:

— high efficiency fluorescent bulbs; for example, replace a T-8 with a T-12 bulb,

— energy efficient ballasts that provide a more efficient energy transfer,

— reflectors that direct more light out of the fixture into the room,

— high intensity discharge bulbs (Low Pressure and High Pressure Sodium and Metal Halide) for parking lot lighting, security lighting, and for select indoor use,

— photovoltaic lighting systems for lighting advertising signs, walkways, plants, trees, decorative water fountains and remote out-door areas.

Electric Motor Efficiency

— Choose high efficiency motors with variable speed controls.

— Consider the hours the system needs to operate before selecting motor sizes.

— Consult with a qualified energy engineer for a costsavings analysis; two small motors may operate more efficiently than one large motor.

Kitchen equipment considerations include purchasing:

— air-miser hoods that use outside air as make-up air instead of discharging conditioned inside air,

— a timer for the kitchen exhaust hood that turns off the system when the kitchen is closed,

— smaller convection ovens to replace oversized conventional ovens,

— an air-to-water heat pump water heater for kitchen use,

— refrigeration equipment with high energy efficiency ratings,

Water use considerations:

Water use in hotels varies depending on geographical location, occupancy, property type and season of the year. The average water use is 218 gallons per occupied room per day. Larger properties use more water due to the water intensive facilities often found in the larger hotels, i.e., pools, laundries and restaurants. Excessive use of water increases the cost of operation, increases electrical energy required for pumps, depletes the water supply and puts extra demands on waste water disposal plants.

Increase water use efficiency by purchasing:

— dishwashing machines that use final rinse water for the prewash of the next load of dishes,

— water-saving showerheads and sink faucet aerators: 2.5 gallons per minute (GPM) showerhead and 1.5 GPM aerators are recommended for water savings and guest satisfaction respectively. Showerheads with less water flow often increase the number of guest complaints,

— a food-thawing machine instead of running water over foods for faster thawing,

— laundry washers which use final rinse water for prewashing of the next load of laundry,

— Plan landscapes with plants requiring low maintenance. Xeriscaping ideas are available from the Cooperative Extension Service, The University of Georgia and/or The Georgia Water Wise Council.

Office equipment considerations include purchasing:

— computers, monitors and printers with power down features that consume 60% less energy when machines are idle.

— copy and fax machines which have power down/ stand-by features that operate when machines are idle.

Selecting Recycling Materials

All hotels and motels have sufficient quantities of recyclable materials to justify recycling. Nationally 50-65% of a hotel's waste is recyclable. The amount of recyclables generated in hotels/ motels depends on the following: the type hotel property, occupancy, number and size of meal functions, lounge/bar business, conventions, guest and employee activities and purchasing practices. The type and number of businesses operating in leased spaces in the facility also impact the volume of recyclable materials.

Leased Space

Hotels rent space to a variety of businesses but the most common ones are retail stores, business services and photography operations. Businesses leasing spaces in hotels are often overlooked in recycling programmes. Their waste is usually handled by the hotel; therefore, they increase the hotel's waste volume. Consider the amount and type of waste created by a business when negotiating a lease.

Cardboard and office paper are the most common and most desirable types of waste created by these businesses. If a tenant produces hazardous waste, the hotel may want to require them to handle their own waste disposal. Hazardous waste usually requires special disposal containers and transportation. Inquire about how they plan to handle it and request proof of proper disposal. If hazardous waste is thrown into the hotel's waste collection or recycling containers, the hotel may be held responsible for disposal problems.

Waste Audit Identification

A waste audit identifies the types and approximate quantities of materials for recycling and potential savings due to waste disposal cost reduction. An audit helps identify the size containers needed for collecting and storing the recyclable materials at specific sites in the hotel and at the Central Recycling Center.

Although an estimate of the amount of recyclables can be done by direct sorting and weighing of waste, previous hotel recycling programmes have proven that an acceptable estimate of recyclables can be made from reviewing purchasing and waste removal records and by evaluating the amount and types of waste generated in each department.

The amount of waste and recyclables produced in a hotel is affected by variables that differ every day. A hotel waste audit, depending on type, produces only information related to the waste and recyclables generated on the day of the audit. The variables mentioned earlier affect the volume of waste on a specific day. These records can be reviewed internally.

Marketing the Materials

Before a hotel recycling programme can be implemented, a decision must be made about where the recyclable materials are to be taken for processing. This decision can make the difference between simply disposing of recyclables and receiving money for them. Processors may require different amounts of material preparation required for recycling. This important decision usually involves public or private processing facilities. An intermediate processor collects, consolidates, and prepares quantities of recyclable materials for shipment to manufacturers.

Some processing facilities are owned and operated by mills or manufacturers and others are operated by small companies and individuals. Processors offer different levels of services. Some processors operate buy-back centers where materials are weighed and payment is made for specific materials. Full service processors accept all recyclable materials and may offer other services such as container leasing or loan and materials transportation.

A Materials Recovery Facility (MRF) accepts commingled recyclable materials for processing. Most MRFs accept glass, plastic, paper, aluminum and steel materials. Each operation is different so contact MRF managers for information about acceptable materials and the preparation required. Paper must be kept clean and dry and this is not possible if paper is thrown into collection containers filled with bottles and cans. MRFs may be owned and operated by private industry or by city or county governments.

In some states, MRFs are owned by counties and operated by private industry. MRFs may or may not pay for recyclable materials and occasionally there may be sorting or processing fees. Government owned MRFs do not usually pay for recyclable materials. The majority of the privately owned MRFs do not charge for sorting and pay for some of the materials.

Each operation is different so a thorough research is advisable before selecting a MRF. Before choosing a processor for your hotel's recyclable materials, investigate the laws, rules and regulations governing hauling and tipping fees in your area. In some areas recycling may be included in waste hauling franchise agreements with cities and counties.

Recycling is exempt from waste franchise contracts in most areas. Intermediate processors are listed in the yellow pages of telephone directories. New companies or smaller companies may not be listed, Contact the Georgia Department of Community Affairs in Atlanta or your local Keep America Beautiful affiliate for a list of processors in your area of the state.

Central Recycling Center

The Central Recycling Center (CRC) is an area outside the hotel where recyclable materials are stored until they are transported to a processor. In larger hotels CRCs may be located in the dock or receiving area.

CRC Location

Consideration should be given to the location of the CRC. For convenience, locate it outside the hotel near an employee service exit. Easy access to the container(s) is needed for vehicles picking up and transporting the materials. The CRC is usually located outside the hotel because of the amount of space required for containers. Odors, insects and rodents are also reasons for locating CRCs outside. The hotel's design, space limitations and vehicle access may make it impossible to locate CRCs conveniently.

Local zoning ordinances may regulate the CRCs location. Visibility of the CRC is a concern for some hotel management. They are concerned with the visibility of recycling equipment and stored materials creating an undesirable appearance for the guests. However, guests are expressing interest in preserving the environment and recycling is one way for the hotel to create a positive environmental image. Well kept CRCs that are visible to guests create a positive image for the hotel. In areas with zoning restrictions CRCs can be concealed with fences, walls or landscaping.

CRC Equipment

Equipment is needed in the CRC to prepare materials and store them until they are hauled to the recycling materials processor. Equipment usually found in the CRC are storage containers such as a large recycling roll-off, dumpster and/or portable 92-gallon containers. The type materials storage container(s) needed depends on the available space, volume of materials to be recycled and the requirements of the processor.

Hotels with food and beverage operations need a baler for reducing the volume of cardboard created from food and drink packaging. A large trash container for disposing of non-recyclables should be placed in the CRC. If a trash container is not available, nonrecyclable materials may be thrown into recycling containers or on the ground.

Materials Storage Containers

Roll-off Containers

Large recycling roll-off containers are the most popular recycling containers for hotel Central Recycling Centers (CRCs). A roll-off container may be compartmentalised for sorted recyclables or simply one large compartment for commingled materials. They are designed with a closed top and conveniently located doors. The top keeps the materials from blowing out of the container when it is moved and provides security for the materials. A locking system is usually optional, but highly recommended to keep out unwanted garbage and recycling material thefts.

Roll-off containers are available in different sizes. To reduce the number of times the container is hauled and/or emptied at the processor, select a roll-off recycling container as large as space permits. If the hotel is paying for each container pull, the savings from recycling is reduced when containers are pulled too often or half full. Recycling roll-off containers are available through manufacturers, waste hauling companies and some material processors and may be purchased or leased.

Before making a final decision on storage containers for the hotel's CRC, compare cost benefits of container leasing, purchasing and availability from processors. A worksheet is included in these materials to help in the research of storage containers for your CRC.

Dumpsters

Dumpster waste containers are commonly used at smaller hotel/motel properties for storing waste. They are also being used for storing specific recyclable materials such as newspaper, cardboard and office paper. They work satisfactorily for storage of office paper and newspaper. However, dumpsters do not have adequate space to store cardboard or all of the recyclable materials from large hotels. Dumpsters require more frequent emptying, thus increasing the cost of recycling if the hotel is charged for the number of times per week/month the dumpster is emptied.

A recycling dumpster is emptied into a larger container on the back of a truck. The dumpster is not removed from the hotel. Drivers may pick up materials from several locations and dump them into the same container before hauling to the processor or mill. This creates a question as to how the weights are determined. Weights of recyclable materials in dumpsters are usually estimated. Materials are not weighed before dumping into the large container on the truck. If the hotel expects payment for recyclable materials, ask how the weights are determined.

If dumpster type containers are used for collection of recyclables and waste materials at the same location, paint the recycling dumpster a different color and label it. This will help prevent trash/waste materials from being thrown into the recycling container. Dumpster recycling containers may be provided at no cost by some companies or they may be leased or purchased from a waste hauler or intermediate processor.

Portable rolling containers

Large 92-gallon portable rolling containers are the third type of container used in hotel Central Recycling Centers (CRCs) for collecting and storing materials. These containers are convenient for small hotels/motels that recycle only a few items such as aluminum cans and office paper. They are also used at larger properties for collecting and storing newspaper and office papers. Individual containers have limitations on transportation and storage capacity. This smaller container is usually transported by a recycling company or by a hotel vehicle.

Recycling Materials Flow Plans

Designing

Once sites for recycling containers have been identified and storage containers selected, establish a materials flow plan-routes to move the recyclables from the temporary storage sites to the Central Recycling Center. Developing a materials flow plan is a very important step in setting up the recycling programme.

The flow plan establishes the type materials to be recycled at each location, where materials are to be stored, where collection containers are to be used, which employees perform the work tasks and the direction the materials are to be moved through the property. Complete materials flow plan worksheets for every department and mark the directions the materials are to be moved on a property floor plan.

1. The first step in developing the recycling materials flow plan is to review the hotel's floor plan. Locate the storage spaces, hallways, equipment placement and employee traffic patterns in all departments.
2. Identify collection points at work stations and storage areas. From this information a decision can be made on the placement of storage containers and the size containers for each location.
3. Establish people traffic patterns and routes for moving the recyclables through the hotel. The traffic movement routes should be the ones with the least amount of interference with hotel guests and employee activities. Materials flow plans should start at the point where the recyclables are generated and continue until the materials are placed in the recycling storage container(s) in the CRC.

Placing Collection Containers

Involve employees in deciding where the recycling collection containers will be located in their work areas, For greater employee participation in the recycling programme, locate collection containers in or near work areas where recyclables are generated. This method is called collecting at the source or point of waste generation. For example, place a recycling collection container near the can opener in the kitchen. When cans are opened and emptied they are easily placed in the appropriate recycling materials collection container.

Hotel design, equipment placement and traffic patterns may prevent the containers from being placed in convenient locations in some departments. In this case, place the containers as close to the work area as possible. To reduce the labour costs of recycling, handle the materials as few times as possible. However, in offices and on guest room floors it is necessary to add an intermediate storage center where materials are temporarily stored during the day until they can be moved to the Central Recycling Center (CRC).

Waste Reduction Programme

Step 1 - Secure support. A successful waste reduction programme requires both a philosophical and financial commitment from facility managers. Without this commitment, employees may be reluctant to fully embrace the programme. Designate a "green team" comprised of representatives from each facility operation to provide support and input for the waste reduction activities.

Step 2 - Conduct a waste characterisation study (waste assessment or audit). This study will help determine waste stream composition by identifying waste volumes, existing waste management practices, and the associated costs. It will help identify which portions of the waste stream could be recycled, reduced, or eliminated altogether.

A waste audit also will help to identify disposal costs. Using a full cost analysis approach, taking into account complete lifecycle costs such as procurement, use, and final disposal, can further clarify the true costs of different materials and practices.

Step 3 - Develop a waste reduction plan. Based on the waste assessment findings, set waste reduction priorities and goals for the facility. Goals should identify the extent to which each waste stream is to be reduced, reused, or recycled.

Step 4 - Implement the programme. Once waste reduction goals have been set, educate employees on the waste reduction activities that will become a part of their jobs or responsibilities. Continually monitor, evaluate, and fine-tune waste reduction efforts by identifying more effective and efficient methods of reducing waste, increasing reuse and recycling, and identifying additional opportunities to remove or eliminate materials from the waste stream.

Turning Solids into Soil

The Cherokee Indian Reservation, located in western North Carolina, attracts 5 to 8 million tourists annually. After opening its casino in November 1997, the Eastern Band of Cherokee Indians (EBCI) initiated a pilot project, assisted by $69,500 in EPA grant funding, to evaluate windrow and particle screening processes for composting food waste from their new casino and its three restaurants.

EBCI already had an established composting programme for wastewater treatment sludge (biosolids) and vegetative waste, and used their experience to develop a progressive system to compost food waste. EBCI collects approximately 1,200 pounds of food waste a day from the casino and its restaurants for composting. The Tribe distributes the final product to landscapers, nurseries, and individual homes both on and off reservation.

Mohegan Sun Casino

The Mohegan Tribe of Indians have experienced tremendous success with their waste management efforts. The Tribe's Integrated Pollution Prevention (P2) Programme resulted in recycling more than 44 percent of the solid waste stream of the Mohegan Sun Casino and Tribal Office in 1997. Before the casino was built, the Mohegan P2 Team transformed waste disposal costs into revenue through the sale of recyclable materials such as corrugated cardboard, paper, plastic, cans, and glass. Even more waste was prevented by reusing clothing, toys, books, and other household materials.

The casino itself was constructed through adaptive reuse of existing, older buildings. Since the casino's opening, the Tribe has pursued additional environmental initiatives. Automotive emissions from reservation visitors, for example, are voluntarily offset by the Tribe's purchase of emission offset credits from other facilities.

Food waste was a major problem for the Tribe, constituting 37.5 percent of the waste stream before waste reduction efforts. The Mohegans now send more than 2,190 tons of food waste produced each year in the casino's restaurant operations to an offreservation piggery for use as feed, avoiding $184,000 in hauling and landfill disposal fees. Pig waste and bedding from the piggery are composted and reimported onto the reservation for landscaping use, thus "closing the loop" on food wastes.

The piggery does not need to grow grain to feed the pigs and the Tribe does not need to purchase peat moss for mulch. The Tribe also sells waste fat, bones, and grease to a renderer for use in the production of animal feed and other products. For example, the sale of approximately 52 tons of cooking grease earns $3,000 annually and avoids $84 a ton in disposal fees, saving another $4,368 a year.

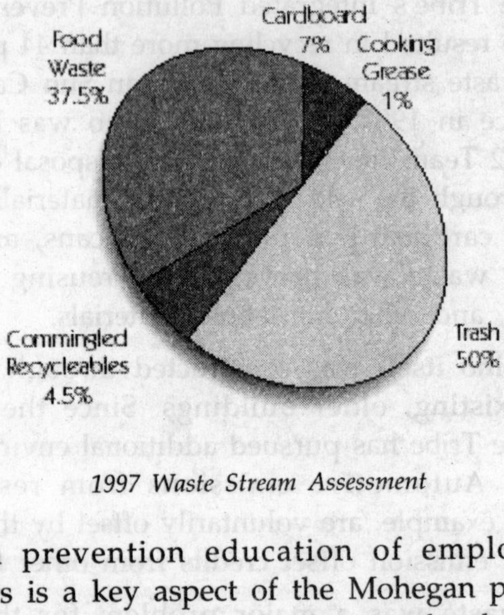

1997 Waste Stream Assessment

Pollution prevention education of employees and contractors is a key aspect of the Mohegan programme. More than 6,000 individuals involved in waste management have been through a P2 training programme. The Mohegans also practice environmentally preferable purchasing, buying recycled-content products whenever possible.

Foxwoods

Eight years ago, Foxwoods was nothing more than a bingo hall housed in a two-story building in the Connecticut woods. Today, Foxwoods Resort and Casino is bigger than most small towns, employing 11,500 people and hosting more than 55,000 visitors during peak season. According to Mike Van Splinter, Foxwoods' director of environmental services, the Mashantucket Pequot Tribe was able to incorporate environmental designs from the start-rather than having to retrofit an established resort complex-because the Tribe was building in an undeveloped, rural environment.

The Tribe made environmental protection a priority well before Foxwoods reached its current size and popularity. According to Van Splinter, Foxwoods recycles everything that is practical, including glass, steel, aluminum, plastic, and paper. To find the most profitable outlets for common materials such as corrugated cardboard, Foxwoods issues Requests for Proposals (RFPs) to secure vendors. To ensure maximum return on recyclables, Foxwoods purchased a baler to pack the corrugated cardboard and a combination can rinser/ crusher to process steel cans.

The facility uses more than 260 tons of steel cans in one year, but it recycles about 99 percent of them. The baler and rinser/crusher minimise the volume of Foxwoods' recyclables, increasing both dollar return and the number of vendors willing to accept the materials. To further facilitate its recycling efforts, the Tribe is creating two "mini-MRFs," or materials recovery facilities, which, in addition to processing Foxwoods' materials, also will accept materials from surrounding areas.

The Tribe also has employed a number of waste prevention measures. It has, for example, arranged for used wooden pallets to be picked up by their vendor and house wine to be delivered in bulk recyclable barrels rather than individual bottles. In addition, the Tribe composts its yard trimmings on site and is looking into new technology that can convert its food residuals into energy.

To reduce the weight of its waste, the Tribe has invested in dewatering equipment, commonly used by the pulp and paper industry, to extract water from its waste stream. Van Splinter cites two important aspects of Foxwoods' waste management practices: separation of recyclables at the point of generation and a strong commitment from the Tribe and the Foxwoods staff.

7

Hotel Housekeeping and Sanitation

In recent years, hotels, motels, camps, and recreational and RV parks affiliated with national chains have been growing rapidly. To the traveler, familiar chain establishments represent dependability and quality at predictable rates. National corporations own many chains, although several others are independently owned but affiliated with a chain through a franchise agreement. Increases in competition and in the sophistication of travelers have induced the chains to provide lodging to serve a variety of customer budgets and accommodation preferences.

In general, these lodging places may be grouped into properties that offer luxury, all-suite, moderately priced, and economy accommodations. The numbers of limited-service or economy chain properties—economy lodging without lobbies, restaurants, lounges, and meeting rooms—have been growing. These properties are not as costly to build and operate. They appeal to budget-conscious family vacationers and travelers who are willing to sacrifice amenities for lower room prices.

While economy chains have become more prevalent, the movement in the hotel and lodging industry is towards more extended-stay properties. In addition to fully equipped kitchenettes and laundry services, the extended-stay market offers guest amenities such as in-room access to the Internet and grocery shopping. This segment of the hotels and other accommodations industry has eliminated traditional hotel lobbies and 24-hour personnel, and housekeeping is usually done only about once a week. This helps to keep costs to a minimum. All-suite facilities, especially popular with business travelers, offer a living room and a bedroom.

Lodging Facilities

Lodging facilities that were used for economic purposes were built along transportation routes where travelling parties found it convenient to make rest stops en route to their destinations. In Marco Polo's time, rest areas were strategically placed at a distance of a day's ride by caravan. Polo was able to travel from Venice to the Mongol Empire of Kublai Khan in Central Asia by making scheduled stops along the way, where food and safe shelter were available. Chaucer's Canterbury Tales, written around 1390 in England, contains lively descriptions of inn-keeping practices of the time.

In Don Quixote, many of Cervantes' ideals are put into practice at an inn in La Mancha, Spain. What we know today as inns had their origin in England some centuries ago, the term meaning "a public house that provides lodging for travellers and others." These taverns with rooms for rent were usually located along highways to provide a convenient overnight stay for those travelling by coach.

The introduction of railways in the nineteenth century created the need for a large number of these hostelries along the numerous lines that crisscrossed the country. Today, the term inn implies a small hotel, although properties called "inns" often contain a large number of rooms; for example the Holiday Inn Crowne Plaza in New Orleans has 439 guestrooms. The term hotel derives from the French hostel. The modern French word hotel suggests "a more or less commodious establishment with up-to-date appointments," though this was not necessarily true one hundred years ago.

Today, the term hotel defines a lodging establishment offering accommodation, food and beverage, and amenities to guests. The New Orleans' Windsor Court Hotel, which consumers have rated as one of the best hotels in the United States, advertises meeting facilities, outdoor pool, health club, ballrooms, concierge services, five-diamond dining room, chamber music, and 24-hour suite service. Nightly rates at the Windsor Court range from $320 for regular guestrooms to $990 for two-bedroom suites. The first spas were operated in Europe and consisted of resorts located by mineral springs, which were believed to have curative powers. Today, spas offer a wide array of health-related services ranging from curative massage and mud baths to weightloss programmes.

Lodging properties can be independently owned, owned by a multi-unit chain, franchised, or managed by a management company. Properties that are independently owned are not affiliated with any multiple -property entity and are usually managed by their owners. This type of property still represents the largest segment of the lodging industry. A typical in dependently owned establishment is small in size and is located in a relatively small community. There are advantages and disadvantages to independent operation: on the positive side, independent lodging establishments can provide guests with unique, personalised service while saving royalty and management fees that otherwise would have to be paid to franchisors and/or management companies.

On the negative side, such properties may not have name recognition to travellers, they lack collective advertising power, and they are unable to benefit from a national/international reservation system. Often, independently owned and managed properties join reservation referral systems and marketing associations, such as Best Western International, Leading Hotels and Resorts, or Utell International. Chain properties operate under the direct control of the chain's headquarters. Establishments belonging to the same chain display the same logo and offer identical services by category. For instance, a Hilton four-star hotel must provide similar service and amenities whether it is located in Florida or in Oregon. This assures guests of consistency in price, room layout, menus, sports facilities, and so on.

Lodging properties can also be categorised by service. Economy or budget properties focus on meeting the basic needs of the travelling public-that is, clean, comfortable rooms that are not expensive. The market segments typically attracted to economy properties are guests travelling with children, bus tours, and budget-minded retirees. Many of these properties do not offer food and beverage services except for breakfast, although they all feature TV and some have a swimming pool, whirlpool, and tennis courts. Mid-market properties offer all the amenities expected in a "home -away-from -home setting."

Restaurants, coffee shops, bars, luggage service, meeting rooms, health club, and room service are generally offered in such properties. The quality of bed linen, towels, room furniture, lobby decor, and customer service must be good or very good. Travellers who frequent properties of this type are business people, individual tourists, conventioneers, and guests wishing to receive a guaranteed level of excellent service. Often, mid-market properties feature suites that consist of a bedroom, adjacent living room, and a kitchenette with refrigerator. Suites are very appealing to families with children or to two couples travelling together.

Luxury properties offer world-class service, which includes any type of convenience that would be expected by any traveller in any country in the world. Committed to the ultimate in hospitality, luxury properties may feature extravagant amenities like Godiva or other imported chocolates, speciality toiletry items, slippers, silk robes, and special services like executive floors, concierge, foreign language translators, nanny, and private secretary. The American Automobile Association (AAA) is the most common rater of lodging establishments in the United States. As a service to its members, this organisation provides travel guides that are updated annually describing the properties and evaluating their services.

The ratings are determined by field inspectors who base their decisions on thorough evaluations of the properties' design, decor, fittings, comfort, and of their levels of service, cleanliness and upkeep. In general, AAA awards three diamonds to economy establishments while mid-market properties are assigned four diamonds. Invariably, luxury hotels and resorts receive a rating of five diamonds.

The housekeeping categories used by the housekeeping department usually include: housekeeping salaries and wages, payroll taxes and benefits, and other expenses. Salaries and wages include those of the entire housekeeping department; payroll taxes and benefits include the operator's share of additional costs related to payroll; the category of other expenses encompasses any other cost incurred by the housekeeping department that is not payroll-related. The buying function in lodging chains is often centralised. Items like soap, linen, mattresses, pillows, furniture, and fixtures are procured by the company's purchasing department and shipped to the different units on request.

Purchasing in large independent properties is done by the purchasing agent, who is a specialised buyer in charge of procuring products for all departments in the property. Smaller properties often allow the department heads to purchase goods for their respective areas of responsibility. In any case, it should be the job of the executive housekeeper to always pretest and approve all items used in the housekeeping department and decide the quantities and the specifications of the products to be bought. It should not be the job of the purchasing agent, or any other person for that matter, to purchase material and supplies without the consent of the executive housekeeper. It is also important to solicit the input of janitors, section housekeepers, housepersons, and laundry personnel on the appropriate characteristics of the items that in the end are to be used by them.

All merchandise purchased should have precise specifications, which are descriptions of the products' quality and factors that should reflect precisely the performance needs for each particular institution. Specifications should be stated clearly, giving the information needed to assure proper identification. For instance, a luxury resort does probably require the best bed linen money can buy, while a small, inexpensive motel may just need bed linen of fair quality. Before buying a product, prices should be obtained from at least three different vendors. Product price and vendor dependability and service should be reviewed once or twice every three months. Purchasing decisions should be made based not only on price but on quality, suitability, and storage availability as well.

The executive housekeeper must control the function of purchasing by defining clearly what is to be procured, who will be in charge of the buying, what specifications are to be considered, and what quantities will be needed. The person in charge of purchasing must consistently provide the needed quantities of products in housekeeping inventories. Although in some cases purchasing is done by the corporate office or by the property's purchasing agent, the executive housekeeper is ultimately responsible for the cost and results of what is purchased.

For some products, linen for instance, pars need to be established; for others, for example soaps and paper products, maximum and minimum quantities are set up. Pars can be defined as the number of required on-hand items to perform housekeeping operations. In the case of linens, for instance, the optimum number of pars is 4. This means that ideally the property should have on hand one set of sheets and pillowcases set up in the guestroom beds at any given time, another set being laundered, an additional set ready to go in floor closets and room attendant carts, and one final set on reserve. For guest and cleaning supplies, the maximum quantity is the greatest number of units that should be in stock at any given time, while the minimum quantity refers to the fewest number of units.

For example, the maximum and minimum number of cases of soap could be 35 and 25 respectively. That means that if at any given time the soap inventory is above 35, the product is overstocked. On the other hand, if the number of cases falls below 25, additional supplies must be ordered. This system eliminates the risk of overstocking or of running out of products. The receiving function of goods ordered must also be controlled. Unless adequate inspection and receiving procedures are used, the best purchasing system may fail because it is at this point that determination must be made of whether or not the products meet the specifications and quantities of the order previously placed.

Failing to inspect the merchandise adequately may result in higher costs, lower quality, theft, and fraud. On receiving a shipment, the goods should be compared with those listed on the receiving sheet or purchase order to verify the correctness of the delivery. If the goods meet the prearranged requirements, they are accepted by signing the invoice or delivery memo. If the products do not meet inspection requirements, they should be refused and a notation indicating the reasons for refusing the delivery made. The function of storing merchandise must also be controlled adequately. Access to storerooms must be limited to authorised personnel only. The storeroom should be locked off -hours and a record should be kept of the person entering it and of the merchandise taken. Valuable items like towels and some guest supplies should be stored in an area that remains locked at all times.

The storage area should be designed to hold the specific products stored in it; bottom shelving levels should be at least 10 inches off the floor to ensure adequate ventilation and to allow for cleaning underneath. A rotation system should be established by which oldest stock is placed in front and issued first. In large properties, housekeeping items may be stored in the main storeroom. In this case, the housekeeping department will need to fill a requisition form to request products.

Floor closet storage should also be locked at all times and access limited to the section housekeepers, housepersons, or supervisors in charge of the area. To account for the cost of housekeeping operating assets used, physical inventories are conducted regularly, in most cases monthly. Linens, uniforms, and cleaning and guest supplies inventories are taken by counting all items on hand and listing them on a physical inventory form. Laundry chemicals may be included in the cleaning supplies category or counted separately for better control. The purpose of taking physical inventories is to find out what amount of items for each category is on hand and to work out its current market value.

Physical inventories are difficult to conduct as all items that need to be accounted for must be counted one by one. In the case of linens, for instance, linens are found in guestrooms, laundry room, linen room, floor closets, room attendant carts, etc. To keep tight control on valuable items, for example imported chocolates for special guests, a perpetual inventory system may be implemented. Executive housekeepers must administer and maintain their proprieties' fixed assets classified as Furniture, Fixtures and Equipment (FF&E), Software, and Department Equipment. Although new establishments are usually handed over to the management team equipped with allitems needed for operation, the executive housekeeper is directly involved in the replacement, refurbishing, and upkeep of most fixed asset items in the property. For this reason, executive housekeepers must have appropriate knowledge of the assets that are under their control.

Regardless of their type of service, lodging properties must maintain interior design consistency standards throughout the building. Whether a property has been classified as economy, mid-market, or luxury, its guestroom and public area design, colour patterns, fabric and upholstery quality, and overall appearance must befit the category they represent. Doing piecemeal refurbishing or renovating must always be avoided. Colours, for instance, must be complementary. In general, blue is a complement of orange, green of red, and yellow of violet. Using several light tints and shades of the same colour makes rooms seem larger, while full-intensity hues tend to make the room seem compact. Adjoining walls should be painted the same colour to provide a sense of continuity.

Executive housekeepers are generally responsible for the refurbishing and upkeep of the furniture in guestroom, public, and employee areas. Furniture should be solidly built, easy to maintain, functional, and attractive. It is not advisable to purchase pieces of furniture directly from a catalogue; instead, the executive housekeeper should carefully examine samples to ensure that the products have been built to withstand repeated rough use. All furniture tops should be plastic-laminated or finished with water-repellent polyurethane to avoid scratches, rings, and stains caused by abusive treatment and spilled liquids.

Desk chairs should have padded backs to provide comfort to guests and prevent wood from hitting desktops. Furniture dotted with glides or casters will prevent carpet damage when pushed or pulled around the room. Luggage racks are better if built-in and fitted with wall-protecting panels, as there is a greater likelihood that the luggage will bump against and deteriorate walls when detached racks are used. Desks should be large enough to accommodate a desktop computer and a fax machine.

TV/VCR units should be an actual piece of furniture, rather than simply a conventional metal stand, and should be fitted with 180-degree swivels so that guests can see the screen from anywhere in the room. Case furniture such as chests of drawers, credensas, armoires, desks, and bureaus also should be purchased with durability in mind. Drawers should be equipped with nylon ball bearings and slide glides so that they don't jam when opening and closing. In general, guestrooms should provide a warm residential look; for instance, love seats and armchairs can replace the standard chairs so often found in hotel rooms. Upholstery fibers may be natural, synthetic, or plastic.

Natural fabrics, such as cotton, linen, silk, and wool, are rich looking and long wearing but expensive and delicate to maintain because they stain easily. Synthetic fibers are less expensive and easy to clean but they are less elegant and more likely to generate static electricity. Often, upholstered materials are a blend of natural and synthetic fabrics. The greatest advantage of upholstery plastic materials such as vinyl is that they can be easily cleaned by just wiping with a soapy cloth; however, they generally have a duller appearance than natural or blended materials.

Upholstery fabrics should be strong enough to withstand repeated shampooing. Treating fabrics With soil-retardant sprays can decrease the need for dry-cleaning the material. It is also important that upholstery fabrics be treated with flame-retardant finishes. Before putting upholstered furniture fabrics into use, they should be pretested to ascertain the best way to clean the pieces without causing shrinkage or discoloration. Some fabrics can be cleaned with solvent, others can be cleaned with water and detergent, and some only allow for vacuuming. In general, synthetic fabrics such as nylon and plastics such as vinyl are the most stain-resistant and easy-to-clean upholstery materials. Beds are the central attraction in guestrooms and often a big selling point for travellers when choosing a lodging property. When asked to pay an average of $70.00 per night per room, guests expect to receive a clean, well-maintained sleeping area and a comfortable bed.

In commercial operations, beds consist of a frame to support the springs and mattresses and unattached headboards. Bed frames usually consist of metal bars with legs attached to each corner or of a metal or wood platform. The main advantage of platform frames is that room attendants don't have to vacuum underneath the box frame, thus saving time when cleaning the room.

Headboards are mounted on the wall and should match the general design of the room's furniture. It is important to know the composition of the bed structure of each property in order to figure out the maximum member of people that the property can house.

Knowing the different types of beds and how many guests can stay in the rooms will help executive housekeepers plan for bed and bathroom linen and supplies. Another type of sleeping equipment is the mobile bed. Families on vacation and travelling high school or college groups often require additional sleeping accommodations in guestrooms. The rollaway, or bed on wheels, consists of a folding frame with an attached bed spring body. The mattress in rollaways must be made of latex foam or have very light, flexible innersprings so that they too can fold with the frame. Because rollaways are unable to provide a comfortable surface to hold the weight of an adult person, they should be recommended only for children or young people to avoid legitimate complaints about the property's not providing adequate acco-mmodation.

Cribs are also essential to have in order to accommodate infants or young children. While cribs should be collapsible to save storage space, their extension mechanisms should be kept in good working order to prevent the crib from collapsing when being used. Dual-purpose sleeping equipment is common in guestrooms. These pieces of furniture provide both seating space and extra sleeping capacity, eliminating the need to roll in a mobile bed on short notice. Sofas, couches, chair-beds, and in-wall beds are the most common dual-purpose pieces of furniture found in lodging properties. Sofas, couches and chair-beds convert into beds by removing the cushions and pulling out the folding frame and mattress or by dropping the back to the level of the seat. In-wall beds, also called Murphy beds, are concealed in the wall behind a panel, giving the room the appearance of a studio or parlour rather than a bedroom.

Surveys of favourite guest amenities conducted regularly by hospitality magazines consistently show that guests put comfortable mattresses at the top of the list, second only to cleanliness. Most mattresses used in lodging operations are of the innerspring type; they have metal coils that support the weight of the sleepers while conforming to their body contours. The strength and number of coils determine the mattress firmness, which may range from medium to super firm. Heavy-gauge steel wire coils are best, allowing for weights to flex down a specific area without disturbing the space surrounding the pressure points. This allows for two persons of different weights to lie side by side and each get different levels of buoyancy.

The firmness of the mattress is determined by the gauge of steel used, the number of turns of each coil, and the way the coils are attached to the mattress frame. Preferably, the springs should be encased in fabric pockets to provide independent coil action, rather than being attached to each other with wire or hooks. Good mattresses have sufficient padding to cushion the springs beneath and provide a smooth surface. The padding should be nonallergenic and comply with the government flame-spread regulation, which states that a lighted cigarette should not be able to ignite the insulation.

Water-filled mattresses (waterbeds) became quite popular with the public when they were first used in the 1960s, but they soon proved to be inconvenient with lodging operators because they often leaked and because the water had to be heated, which became costly. Although today's waterbeds are efficiently built with individually filled cells that do not need to be heated because of an insulating foam layer, there doesn't seem to be a great demand for them from lodging guests. Lodging properties, however, should have a few waterbeds to fulfil the request of interested travellers. Guestrooms and lodging property lobbies are also furnished with accessories such as mirrors, decorations, pictures, and lights, to complement the furniture.

For instance, strategically placed mirrors can give small rooms an illusion of depth; serene motifs in paintings will provide a feeling of tranquillity; triple magnification make-up mirrors and wall-mounted hair dryers in bathrooms are a welcome amenity; a well-stocked mahogany bookcase in the lobby will provide a homey feeling to guests who enjoy reading. Beautiful carpeting can enhance the appearance of lodging properties and make a lasting impression on guests. On the other hand, discoloured, worn, or dirty carpets are usually sources of guest complaints. The first step in selecting the right carpet is to match its colour, texture, and pattern with the design of the area where it is to be installed.

Then, other factors need to be considered, such as determining the anticipated level of wear and tear caused by the intensity of traffic, the location of the carpet, and the budget allocated for it. When heavy traffic is expected, carpets should feature strong resistance to abrasion, as well as texture retention and anti-soiling and staining characteristics. The location of the carpet should determine specifications such as enhanced colourfastness, antimicrobial protection, resistance to snags, and resilience under rolling loads.

Besides durability and stain resistance, carpets in lodging properties should be capable of withstanding repeated cleaning treatment. Before purchasing carpet, be sure you fully understand the warranty coverage offered by the manufacturer or installer. Warranties for commercial carpets should include protection for wear and tear, colourfastness (fading from sunlight and atmospheric contaminants), tuft bind deterioration, static charges, backing strength, ravelling of seams and edges, and any other manufacturing defects.

Executive housekeepers should have sufficient knowledge of carpet construction to ensure that the right carpet is selected for each area in the property. There are three main elements in the composition of carpets: the pile, or face; the backing, or material to which the pile is secured; and the padding, or cushion on which the carpet rests. Most commercial carpets are tufted, that is, the yam is threaded through the backing material to form loops. The backing material usually is woven jute or polypropylene with a layer of adhesive latex extended over the material to anchor the tufts. Knitted carpets are made by interlacing together the pile yam and the backing.

The process of embedding the pile fibers electrostatically into a layer of adhesive material applied to the backing is called flocking. Weaving is the old-fashioned way of making carpets using conventional looms. The yarns are interlaced together to form the pile and the backing. As with linen, the yarns woven lengthwise are called the warp and the yarns going across are the wefts. The process of making carpets by compacting the fibers and the backing by mechanically punching them together is called needle punching. Improper lighting in rooms may discourage guests from staying in a particular establishment.

Guests, particularly business travellers, expect to find adequate lighting to be able to work over flat surfaces such as tables and desks, or to read in bed or sitting on a couch or armchair. Lights of adjustable intensity should be placed strategically so that guests can arrange their preferences to suit their needs; for example, subdued lighting for relaxation or bright lighting for working or entertaining friends. Having three-way lamps or lights activated by rheostats give guests the option to set the mood of the room to their liking. Floor lamps are not recommended in guestrooms because they can be easily knocked over and they create tripping hazards. Desk lamps should have the on-off switches at the base to reduce the risk of guests burning their fingers on the light bulb or upsetting the shade's balance when reaching around to locate the switch.

One advantage of fluorescent lights is that they use less energy and last longer than regular bulbs. In all cases, sufficient wattage must be provided in lamps that guests will use for reading or working purposes. Long gone are the days when hoteliers could sell rooms equipped with a minimum of basic features. Today's business traveller is putting a new spin on the concept of guestroom equipment. Lodging chains that cater to corporate clientele offer in-room or satellite office support services including computers and fax and copy machines. Guestrooms are often equipped with multi-line telephones complete with voice mail and PC compatibility; some hotels even provide cellular phones and 24-hour access to translators and information in other languages.

Refrigerators and microwave ovens are quite common in suite hotels, and coffee-makers, together with selections of coffee and tea blends, are now available in the rooms of most properties. Wide-screen television sets and high-quality clock radios are a must in four- and five-diamond properties, as are in-room safes. In-room strongboxes are seen as a last-ditch defence for the guests' personal belongings, including items as large as lap-top computers. The locking systems of in-room safes range from ordinary keys to programmable push-buttons, magnetic-lock devices, and the guest's credit card. Some microprocessor safes automatically lock for 30 minutes after four false attempts to open them. Besides being a great convenience for guests who don't want to line up for safety deposit boxes, in-room safes are effective against thieves and even employees who may use stolen keys to burglarize rooms.

Valuables can be stored by guests themselves and remain secure during trips to the pool, jogging around the block, or going out to dinner. Some safes have built-in memory, which enables the front office personnel to read the date and time of the most recent safe openings and closings. This can provide convincing evidence in case of a loss claim against the property. Some up-scale lodging properties, particularly resorts and first class hotels, offer minibars in their guestrooms and suites.

Stocked with beverages and snacks, minibars can be profitable because guests are often tempted to have a last drink before going to bed or first thing in the morning. Fully automated minibars can electronically sense when an item is removed, sending the corresponding charge to the guest's room account. Non-automated units must rely on the honesty of the guest to notify the front desk just before checking out if goods have been consumed. Depreciable fixed assets that are not furniture or equipment, such as bedspreads, mattress covers, blankets, pillows, and window coverings may be categorised under the classification of software.

As with mattresses, bedspreads should be purchased with the qualities of durability, comfort, maintenance, and fire safety in mind. Bedspreads are an important component in the decor of guestrooms and should complement the motif, colour, and design of the room. Fabrics made of 100 percent polyester offer excellent resistance to fading, staining, shrinking, and wrinkling.

Polycottons, a blend of polyester cotton, are less expensive than fabrics made of 100 percent polyester, but their life span is shorter, they have fewer fire-retardant qualities, and they fade more easily. While the normal recycling life span of a good bedspread should be at least 5 years, polycotton bedspreads only last from 2 to 3 years. Other factors to consider when specifying bedspreads are their fill and seaming. Fill is one of the key elements that determines the appearance of bedspreads. The number of ounces of fill per square yard should be 7 or more. Non-compressed fills are better than mechanically packed fills because of their ability to spring back to its original 'loft is greater.

Wide, seamless bedspreads are preferred to those constructed with seams because they don't come apart as easily. Bedspreads can be large enough to reach to the floor or just to cover the mattress. In this case a pleated cloth skirting called a dust ruffle may be placed between the mattress and the box spring to extend around the sides and foot of the bed. Washable bedspreads should be purchased with the guarantee that they will not shrink, fade, or wrinkle. Par levels for bedspreads should be one plus 10 percent to allow for washing and replacement.

The purpose of blankets is to act as insulators. A heavy blanket does not necessarily keep the warmth of the body from escaping through it. On the other hand, a material (even if it is light) that is tightly woven will retain body heat. However, all blankets should be porous enough to allow any moisture buildup under them to escape to the surrounding air. Wool is a delicate natural fiber that is very warm but that requires extreme care when laundered.

Cotton, on the other hand, washes easily but it is a poor insulator and shrinks up to 15 percent if not purchased preshrunk. Synthetic fibers such as acrylics and polyester, if properly constructed, are suitable to commercial operations. Acrylic fibers are warmer than polyester but not as strong. Because guests may fall asleep while smoking in bed, blankets should be fire retardant. The size of the blanket should be large enough to cover the length and width of the mattress and have some additional inches for tucking.

All mattresses should be fitted with moisture-proof covers at all times to prevent staining. Vinyl plastic covers are impermeable and can be washed like any other fabric. Their use is recommended for cribs or small cots for young children and hospital beds. Felt pads made of moisture-proof, flame-retardant, 100 per cent polyester resist shrinkage and are quite durable.

Most commercial pillows axe filled with synthetic fiber, mainly polyester. Synthetic pillows are quite common in commercial properties because they are inexpensive, easy to launder, and nonallergenic. When purchasing pillows, it is important to make sure that the fill is of good quality so that it springs back into shape easily; lumpy, heavier fills are an indication of inferior grade. The synthetic covering of the pillow must be fire retardant and stain proof and able to withstand frequent washings. Pillows with natural fills such as down and feathers are very expensive, particularly goose down.

Lodging properties should stock a few natural-fill pillows to meet the occasional request for them. Because of the price, down and feather pillows should be provided to guests on a loan basis, that is, a record should be kept in the housekeeping department of the room number where the pillows were delivered and then should be recovered after the guest's checkout. The first consideration for selecting wall coverings is that they match the general decor of the room; the second, and just as important, consideration is their durability and ease of maintenance. The two most common forms of wall coverings are paint and vinyl. The paint used to finish walls should be easy to wash with soapy water and of very good quality so that the surface doesn't require repainting after a short period of time.

Vinyl wall coverings are available in several thicknesses to suit the area to be covered; for instance, walls covered with thin layers are vulnerable to bumps from baggage and carts and should be used only to cover no-traffic areas. Heavier vinyl can withstand heavy impacts and can be used over surfaces susceptible to abrasion. Although far more expensive than paint, vinyl wall coverings generally pay for themselves because they require very little maintenance. Vinyl coverings are made by laminating the material to cotton or polycotton backings and are glued to walls using an adhesive paste. To prevent mildew from loosening the vinyl from the adhesive, the glue should contain a mildewcide. Fabric wall coverings can provide rooms and hallways with a luxurious, elegant look but they should be avoided in commercial operations because of the difficulty of cleaning or replacing them when soiled. Wallpaper should be used only if it is stain and water-resistant and allows for damp cleaning with soap and sponge.

Windows in offices, lobbies, and employee areas are usually fitted with vinyl blinds. Because of their susceptibility to fading, fabrics used for curtains must be resistant to direct sunlight. As curtains attract dust and odours, they require frequent washings and dry cleaning; for this reason, it is advisable to purchase good-quality, vinyl-coated fabrics that can retain their shape and colour for long periods of time. Curtains should be flame retardant to comply with local fire departments specifications. Drapery can be simple or quite ornate. Valances, and shirred or pinch-pleated fabrics, can add elegance and warmth to rooms, although they will require more cleaning time to keep them dust free.

In all cases, the curtain rods and cords must be sturdy to avoid damage; having batons instead of cords

scrubber, 37-inch squeegee assembly, and can service 44,000 square feet per hour.

When large lodging properties use drinking glasses made of glass (rather than plastic), glass washers are necessary. The practice of washing housekeeping glasses in the kitchen's dishwashers is not an effective one as it is usually seen as an "encroachment" by the food and beverage department personnel. When operating a glass washer, the right type of detergent and the correct water temperature as determined by the local health department must be provided. Rather than transporting trash, soiled linen, and supplies in plastic bags, lodging properties should use light trucks or hoppers.

The three major purposes of chemicals used in the housekeeping department are to remove dirt, to destroy harmful microorganisms, and to preserve and beautify furniture, fixtures, and surfaces. Chemical cleaners are manufactured to remove soils from surfaces through chemical action. The stronger the chemical is, the better effect it will have on getting the job done. The strength of cleaning chemicals is measured on the pH scale. pH is the symbol for the logarithm of the reciprocal of hydrogen ion concentration in gram atoms per liter. Cleaning chemicals that have been enhanced with alkalis or acids to strengthen their cleaning powers can be dangerous to humans and often cannot be used on certain surfaces.

A neutral cleaner can be used for all types of jobs but its cleaning power is limited. The executive housekeeper should have adequate knowledge of the department's needs to select cleaning chemicals appropriate for each type of cleaning job to be performed regularly in the housekeeping department. Generally speaking, high-alkaline cleaners are effective degreasers while acidic cleaners are good for fighting lime and rust, which are always found in urinals and toilets. Another name for cleaners is detergents.

Detergents act chemically to emulsify dirt, holding it in suspension so it can be removed away from the surface. Synthetic detergents are easy to rinse off and often have excellent cleaning, deodorizing, and germicidal characteristics. Most cleaning detergents are made from mineral oils. All-purpose cleaners have neutral pH-balanced formulas for general-purpose cleaning jobs. They usually are synthetic detergents, often vegetable oil based, of which pine oil is very popular because of its pleasant scent and strong deodorizing power. All-purpose cleaners may have corrosion inhibitors to protect metal surfaces.

Single-purpose cleaners are heavy-duty cleaners used for specific cleaning jobs. Abrasive cleaners are cleaning powders or pastes combined with silica for tough cleaning jobs. These cleaners will scratch soft surfaces like fiberglass or porcelain. Gentler cleansers made with nonscratching calcite instead of silica greatly reduce their abrasive action.

Degreasers are highly effective cleaners, often biodegradable, that remove grease, tar, ink, food deposits, smoke film, fats and other grimy soils. Degreasers can be highly effective on concrete floors. It is important to remember that some products advertised as degreasers may be toxic and therefore not suitable for use on kitchen surfaces.

Although most all-purpose cleaners can be used as deodorizers, stronger chemicals are needed to counteract stale odours. Deodorizers can be purchased as mists, wall and urinal blocks, cup and wick, and aerosols. Glass cleaners are ammonia- and alcohol-based products that clean and provide a protective coating to glass surfaces. Glass treated with good-quality glass cleaners resist fogging caused by moisture and temperature changes and in some manner repel dust, dirt, fingerprints, and smudges. Most glass cleaners can also be used as multipurpose cleaners on chrome, stainless steel, enamel, formica, ceramic tile, and other washable surfaces.

Effective Sanitising

Effectiveness sanitising is dependant upon a number of factors including: initial contamination load, humidity, pH, temperature, and time. The use of steam as a sanitising process has limited application. It is generally expensive compared to alternatives, and it is difficult to regulate and monitor contact temperature and time. Further, the byproducts of steam condensation can complicate cleaning operations. Hot-water sanitising—through immersion (small parts, knives, etc.), spray (dishwashers), or circulating systems—is commonly used. The time required is determined by the temperature of the water.

The primary advantages of hot-water sanitisation are: relatively inexpensive, easy to apply and readily available, generally effective over a broad range of microorganisms, relatively non-corrosive, and penetratesinto cracks and crevices. Hot-water sanitisation is a slow process which requires come-up and cool-down time; can have high energy costs; and has certain safety concerns for employees. The process also has the disadvantages of forming or contributing to film formations, and shortening the life of certain equipment or parts thereof (gaskets, etc.).

The registration of chemical sanitisers and antimicrobial agents for use on food and food product contact surfaces, and on nonproduct contact surfaces, is through the U.S. Environmental Protection Agency (EPA). Thus, any antimicrobial agent and its maximum usage level for direct use on food or on food product contact surfaces must be approved by the FDA.

Prior to the sanitisation process, all surfaces must be clean and thoroughly rinsed to remove any detergent residue. An unclean surface cannot be sanitised. Since the effectiveness of sanitisation requires direct contact with the microorganisms, the surface should be free of cracks, pits, or crevices which can harbor microorganisms. Surfaces which contain biofilms cannot be effectively sanitised.

Generally, the activity of a sanitiser increases with increased concentration. However, a leveling off occurs at high concentrations. A common misconception regarding chemicals is that "if a little is good, more is better". Using sanitiser concentrations above recommendations does not sanitiser better and, in fact, can be corrosive to equipment and in the long run lead to less cleanability.

Sanitisers are dramatically affected by the pH of the solution. Many chlorine sanitisers, for example, are almost ineffective at pH values above 7.5. Organic and/or inorganic inactivators may react chemically with sanitisers giving rise to non-germicidal products. Some of these inactivators are present in detergent residue. Thus, it is important that surfaces be rinsed prior to sanitisation. The microbiological load can affect sanitiser activity. Also, the type of microorganism present is important. Spores are more resistant than vegetative cells. Certain sanitisers are more active against gram positive than gram negative microorganisms, and vice versa.

Chlorine, in its various forms, is the most commonly used sanitiser in food processing and handling applications. Commonly used chlorine compounds include: liquid chlorine, hypochlorites, inorganic chloramines, and organic chloramines. Chlorine-based sanitisers form hypochlorous acid (HOCl, the most active form) in solution. Available chlorine (the amount of HOCl present) is a function of pH. At pH 5, nearly all is in the form of HOCl. At pH 7.0, approximately 75% is HOCl. The maximumallowable level for no-rinse applications is 200ppm available chlorine, but recommended usage levels vary.

For hypochlorites, an exposure time of 1 min at a minimum concentration of 50ppm and a temperature of 24°C (75°F) is recommended. For each 10°C (18°F) drop in temperature, a doubling of exposure time is recommended. For chloramines, 200ppm for 1 min is recommended. Chlorine compounds are broad spectrum germicides which act on microbial membranes, inhibit cellular enzymes involved in glucose metabolism, have a lethal effect on DNA, and oxidise cellular protein.

Chlorine has activity at low temperature, is relatively cheap, and leaves minimal residue or film on surfaces. The activity of chlorine is dramatically affected by such factors as pH, temperature, and organic load. However, chlorine is less affected by water hardness when compared to other sanitisers. The major disadvantage to chlorine compound is corrosiveness to many metal surfaces. Health and safety concerns can occur due to skin irritation and mucous membrane damage in confined areas.

At low pH (below 4.0), deadly Cl_2 (mustard gas) can form. In recent years, concerns have also been raised about the use of chlorine as a drinking water disinfectant and as an antimicrobial with direct food contact (meat, poultry and shellfish). This concern is based upon the involvement of chlorine in the formation of potentially carcinogenic trihalomethanes (THMs) under appropriate conditions. While chlorine's benefits as a sanitiser far outweigh these risks, it is under scrutiny.

Chlorine dioxide (ClO_2) is currently being considered as a replacement for chlorine, since it appears to be more environmentally friendly. Stabilised ClO_2 has FDA approval for most applications in sanitising equipment or for use as a foam for environmental and non-food contact surfaces. Approval has also been granted for use in flume waters in fruits and vegetable operations and in poultry process waters. ClO_2 has 2.5 times the oxidising power of chlorine and, thus, less chemical is required.

Typical use concentrations range from 1to 10ppm. ClO_2's primary disadvantages are worker safety and toxicity. Its highly concentrated gases can be explosive and exposure risks to workers is higher thanthat for chlorine. Its rapid decomposition in the presence of light, or at temperatures greater than 50°C (122°F) makes on-site generation a recommended practice. Use of iodine as an antimicrobial agents dates back to the 1800s.

This sanitiser exists in many forms and usually exists with a surfactant as a carrier. These mixtures are termed iodophors. The most active agent is the dissociated free iodine. This form is most prevalent at low pH. The amount of dissociation from the surfactant is dependent upon the type of surfactant. Iodine solubility is very limited in water.

Generally recommended usage for iodophors is 12.5 to 25ppm for 1 min. It is generally thought that the bactericidal activity of iodine is through direct halogenation of proteins. More recent theories have centered upon cell wall damage and destruction of microbial enzyme activity. Iodophors, like chlorine compounds, have a very broad spectrum: being active against bacteria, viruses, yeasts, molds, fungi, and protozoans.

Iodine is highly temperature-dependent and vaporizes at 120°F. Thus, it is limited to lower temperature applications. The degree to which iodophors are affected by environmental factors is highly dependant upon properties of the surfactant used in the formulation. Iodophors are generally less affected by organic matter and water hardness than chlorine. However, loss of activity is pronounced at high pH. Iodine has a long history of use in wound treatment.

Since Quaternary Ammonium Compounds (QACs) are positively charged cations, their mode of action is related to their attraction to negatively charged materials such as bacterial proteins. It is generally accepted that the mode of action is at the membrane function. The carbon length of R-group side chain is, generally, directly related with sanitiser activity in QACs. However, because of the lower solubility in QACs composed of large carbon chains, these sanitisers may have lower activity than short chain structures. QACs are active and stable over a broad temperature range. Because they are surfactants, they possess some detergency. Thus, they are less affected by light soil than are other sanitisers.

However, heavy soil dramatically decreases activity. QACs generally have higher activity at alkaline pH. While lack of tolerance to hard water is often listed as a major disadvantage of QACs when compared to chlorine, some QACs are fairly tolerant of hard water. Activity can be improved by the use of EDTA as a chelator. QACs are effective against bacteria, yeasts, mold, and viruses. An advantage of QACs in some applications is that they leave a residual antimicrobial film. However, this would be a disadvantage in operations such as cultured dairy products, cheese, beer, etc. where microbial starter cultures are used.

QACs are generally more active against gram positive than gram negative bacteria. They are not highly effective against bacteriophages. Their incompatibility with certain detergents makes thorough rinsing following cleaning operations imperative.Further, many QAC formulations can cause foaming problems in CIP applications. Under recommended usage and precautions, QACs pose little toxicity or safety risks. Thus, they are in common use as environmental fogs and as room deodorisers.

However, care should be exercised in handling concentrated solutions or use as environmental fogging agents. Like QACs, acid-anionic sanitisers are surface-active sanitisers. These formulations include an inorganic acid plus a surfactant, and are often used for the dual function of acid rinse and sanitisation. Whereas QACs are positively charged, these sanitisers are negatively charged. Their activity is moderately affected by water hardness. Their low use pH, detergency, stability, low odor potential, and non-corrosiveness makes them highly desirable in some applications.

Fatty acid or carboxylic acid sanitisers were developed in the 1980s. Typical formulations include fatty acids plus other acids (phosphoric acids, organic acids). These agents also have the dual function of acid rinse and sanitisation. The major advantage over acid anionics is lower foaming potential. These sanitisers have a broad range of activity, are highly stable in dilute form, are stable to organic matter, and are stable to high temperature applications. These sanitisers have low activity above pH 3.5 - 4.0, are not very effective against yeasts and molds, and some formulations lose activity at temperatures below 10°C (50°F).

Peroxides or peroxy compounds contain at least one pair of covalently bonded oxygen atoms (-O-O-)and are divided into two groups: the inorganic group, containing hydrogen peroxide (HP) and related compounds; and the organic group, containing peroxyacetic acid (PAA) and related compounds. The primary mode of action for HP is through creating an oxidising environment and generation of singlet or superoxide oxygen (SO).

HP is fairly broad spectrum with slightly higher activity against gram-negative than gram-positive organisms. High concentrations of HP (5% and above) can be an eye and skin irritant. Thus, high concentrations should be handled with care. Peroxyacetic Acid (PAA) has been known for its germicidal properties for a long time. However, it has only found food-industry application in recent years and is being promoted as a potential chlorine replacement.

PAA is relatively stable at use strengths of 100 to 200ppm. Other desirable properties include: absence of foam and phosphates, low corrosiveness, tolerance to hard water, and favorable biodegradability. PAA solutions have been shown to be useful in removing biofilms. While precise mode of action mechanisms have not been determined, it is generally theorised that the PAA reaction with microorganisms is similar to that of HP. PAA, however, is highly active against both gram-positive and gram-negative microorganisms. The germicidal activity of PAA is dramatically affected by pH. Any pH increase above 7-8 drastically reduces the activity. PAA has a pungent odor and the concentrated product (40%) is a highly toxic, potent irritant, and powerful oxidiser. Thus, care must be used in its use.

Role of Cleaning Workers

Maids and housekeeping cleaners perform any combination of light cleaning duties to maintain private households or commercial establishments, such as hotels, restaurants, and hospitals, clean and orderly. In hotels, aside from cleaning and maintaining the premises, maids and housekeeping cleaners may deliver ironing boards, cribs, and rollaway beds to guests' rooms. In hospitals, they also may wash bedframes, brush mattresses, make beds, and disinfect and sterilise equipment and supplies with germicides and sterilising equipment.

Janitors, maids, and cleaners use various equipment, tools, and cleaning materials. For one job they may need a mop and bucket, for another an electric polishing machine and a special cleaning solution. Improved building materials, chemical cleaners, and power equipment have made many tasks easier and less time consuming, but cleaning workers must learn the proper use of equipment and cleaners to avoid harming floors, fixtures, and themselves. Cleaning supervisors coordinate, schedule, and supervise the activities of janitors and cleaners.

They assign tasks and inspect building areas to see that work has been done properly, issue supplies and equipment, and inventory stocks to ensure that an adequate amount of supplies is present. They also screen and hire job applicants, train new and experienced employees, and recommend promotions, transfers, or dismissals.

Supervisors may prepare reports concerning the occupancy of rooms, hours worked, and department expenses. Some also perform cleaning duties. Cleaners and servants in private households dust and polish furniture; sweep, mop, and wax floors; vacuum; and clean ovens, refrigerators, and bathrooms. They also may wash dishes, polish silver, and change and make beds. Some wash, fold, and iron clothes; a few wash windows.

Supervisors conduct inspections to ensure that the building is cleaned properly and the team is functioning efficiently. Building cleaning workers usually work inside heated, well-lighted buildings. However, they sometimes work outdoors, sweeping walkways, mowing lawns, or shoveling snow. Working with machines can be noisy, and some tasks, such as cleaning bathrooms and trash rooms, can be dirty and unpleasant. Janitors may suffer cuts, bruises, and burns from machines, handtools, and chemicals. They spend most of their time on their feet, sometimes lifting or pushing heavy furniture or equipment.

Janitors and cleaners work in nearly every type of establishment and held about 2.3 million jobs. They accounted for about 57 percent of all building cleaning workers. About 28 percent worked for firms supplying building maintenance services on a contract basis, 21 percent were employed in educational institutions, and 2 percent worked in hotels. Other employers included hospitals, restaurants, religious institutions, manufacturing firms, government agencies, and operators of apartment buildings, office buildings, and other types of real estate.

Maids and housekeepers held about 1.5 million jobs. Hotels, motels, and other traveler accommodations employed the most maids and housekeepers-27 percent-while private households employed the second most: 25 percent. Eight percent were employed in hospitals; and, a similar percentage worked in nursing and other residential care facilities.

Most building cleaners learn their skills on the job. Usually, beginners work with an experienced cleaner, doing routine cleaning. As they gain more experience, they are assigned more complicated tasks. In some cities, programs run by unions, government agencies, or employers teach janitorial skills. Students learn how to clean buildings thoroughly and efficiently, how to select and safely use various cleansing agents, and how to operate and maintain machines, such as wet and dry vacuums, buffers, and polishers.

Sanitation and Health

In addition to facility, food, and water cleanliness, personal cleanliness is essential to maintain a healthful work environment. Inflammation of the skin (dermatitis) is an ever-present problem in an industrial or laboratory setting. Adequate washing and prevention of contact with agents harmful to the skin are the most effective measures of skin care.

— Wear clean clothing. Change clothing that has been contaminated with materials which may be harmful. Use disposable clothing as necessary.

— Use the proper personal protective equipment such as chemical gloves, face shields, aprons, etc.

— For minor exposures to relatively inert materials that cause excessive soiling, hand-protective creams may be applied before the job is started.

— Thoroughly wash after any job that causes excessive soiling of the skin and particularly after contact with agents harmful to the skin. Use hand-cleansing creams —not acetone, mineral spirits, and other such solvents —to remove greases, dyes, carbon, paints, resins, or other adhering materials. Hand cleansing creams do an excellent job and are available from stock.

— Solvent use can cause irritation of the skin. After excessive washing and contact with cleaning solutions and agents, handconditioning creams should be used to replace oil in the skin.

— Emergency showers and eyewashes are for emergency use to dilute and wash away contaminants in those critical seconds right after an accident in which you may be sprayed or splashed with a chemical. Employees should know the location of and how to use the emergency equipment nearest their work areas. Emergency showers and eyewashes are checked periodically by Plant Maintenance and Engineering. Emergency eyewashes should be flushed at a minimum of once per month.

8

Eco-friendly Hospitality Business

Tourism is "the temporary movement of people to destinations outside their normal places of work and residence, the activities undertaken during their stay in those destinations, and the facilities created to cater to their needs". It is often difficult to distinguish between tourism and recreation, as they are interrelated. Tourism involves travelling a distance from home, while recreation is defined as the activities undertaken during leisure time. Outdoor recreation is even more closely related to tourism.

The extent of the overlap depends in part on the length of time of the activity and its location. For example, a boater who uses his or her boat for one day and who stays near his or her home may be considered a recreational boater; while a boater who travels on his or her boat overnight to a destination may be considered a tourist.

The degree of environmental impact varies, depending on the type of tourist and the intensity of site use. There are day tourists, who visit a destination for a day and then leave; summer residents who are in effect tourists for a season; and tourists on bus tours and other trips that may visit a location for a few minutes or a number of days. Day tourists have an impact on the environment through their transportation to their destination as well as their activities once there. This is true for summer residents, but these tourists also have a cumulative impact, as they are in one place for a longer period of time. For example, nutrients leaching from the septic systems of tourists' waterfront homes can accelerate eutrophication and contribute to depletion of dissolved oxygen supply of the adjacent water body.

On the other hand, summer residents often are an important force in preserving the natural beauty of an area. Tourists who visit an area for longer than a day and choose to stay in hotels contribute to the impacts that the lodging industry has on the environment. In addition to the length of stay, tourist impacts depend on the type of activity undertaken. Passive activities such as birdwatching have different impacts than more active pursuits, such as snowmobiling or boating.

There are environmental impacts from the travel to a destination, the tourist activities in and of themselves at that destination, such as hiking or boating, and from the creation, operation, and maintenance of facilities that cater to the tourist, such as hotels.

Transportation Industrynm

Air Transportation Industry

In 1995, twenty percent of U.S. commercial air travel was attributed to leisure, including rest and relaxation, sightseeing, and outdoor recreation. Table 1 illustrates the total and tourism-related contribution of air pollutants from the air transportation industry. Aircraft emit the most carbon monoxide of any of the five listed air pollutants, but it is a small amount relative to other modes of transportation. In total, aircraft are responsible for approximately one percent of the total ground-level emissions from mobile sources; therefore tourism-related air travel is responsible for only.2% of total ground-level emissions. Furthermore, tourism-related air travel contributes less than 1% of total U.S. emissions of each of the listed criteria pollutants.

Although aircraft contribute only a small amount to total air pollution, emissions from this source is increasing. Between 1970 and 1995, hydrocarbon and NOx emissions from aircraft sources have grown 53%. Projections to 2010 indicate that aircraft emissions will continue to increase. Aircraft emissions in nonattainment areas with large airport facilities in particular are projected to represent a growing percentage of regional sources of air pollutants.

The projections indicate an increase in the aircraft component of total regional emissions between 1990 and 2010 in ten metropolitan regions (nine of which are currently not in attainment of the National Ambient Air Quality Standards (NAAQS) for ozone; the tenth city has attained the ozone standard, but is considered an ozone "maintenance" area). The 2010 percentages are still relatively low, ranging from 0.2% volatile organic compounds (VOC) in Philadelphia to 5.1% VOC in Charlotte; and 1.8% NOx in Philadelphia to 7.6% in Charlotte. The percentages are higher in Charlotte in part because other sources contribute less.

The EPA has had regulations for smoke and hydrocarbon emissions from aircraft engines in place since 1984. In 1997, the agency promulgated new emission standards for nitrogen oxides and carbon monoxide. This rule was adopted to codify the existing voluntary emission standards of the United Nations International Civil Aviation Organisation (ICAO). The DOT's Federal Aviation Administration (FAA) is responsible for enforcing these aircraft emissions standards.

Table 1: Air Pollutant Emissions of Tourism-related air transportation in 1997

Pollutant	*Total Aircraft Emissions (in million short tons, or mst)*	*Tourism-Related Aircraft Emissions*	*Total U.S. Emissions (in mst)*	*Tourism-Related Aircraft Emissions % of U.S. Total*
Nitrogen Oxide	.178	.0356	23.582	.15%
Carbon Monoxide	1.012	.202	87.451	.23%
Volatile Organic Compounds	.187	.0374	19.214	.19%
Sulphur Dioxide	.012	.0024	20.369	.01%
Particulate Matter (PM-10)	.041	.0082	33.581	.02%

Source of Noise Pollution

In addition to air pollution, aircraft contribute to noise pollution. The FAA is responsible for addressing the noise abatement issue. The 1990 Airport Noise and Capacity Act authorised the FAA to reduce aircraft noise by requiring replacement of louder planes with quieter aircraft. In fact, airlines have spent billions of dollars to address this problem. Stage 2 aircraft are now being replaced by Stage 3 aircraft, which are 50% quieter; and the goal was to have only Stage 3 planes flying by 2000. There are also noise impacts from air tour operators, such as those that take 800,000 passengers a year on scenic overflights of the Grand Canyon.

In an effort to reduce unnatural noise, the FAA proposed new rules in August 1999 that would cap the number of overflights in the Grand Canyon. However, again, as tourism-related travel represents only 20% of commercial air travel, and airplanes are only one source of noise pollution, tourism's contribution to total noise pollution is minor.

Ground Transportation

Much of the tourism-related air pollution comes from automobiles. Thirty-five percent of people travelling for leisure in 1995 used personal automobiles as their means of travel. Four-hundred million leisure trips are taken in automobiles per year in the United States; 80% of those trips are 250 miles or less. In 1997, light duty vehicles emitted an average of 1.53 grams of exhaust hydrocarbons per mile, 19.86 grams of carbon monoxide per mile, and 1.51 grams of nitrogen oxide per mile. Automobiles emit by far the most carbon monoxide, nitrogen oxide, and volatile organic compounds in comparison to other transportation.

Personal automobiles emit 32% percent of the total national carbon monoxide emissions, and 12% of total national nitrogen oxide emissions. However, it is difficult to separate the amount of tourismrelated automobile travel from all automobile travel.

One area where it is possible to distinguish between tourism-related automobile travel and other travel is within national parks. Exhaust from tourists' cars affects air quality and vegetation in some national parks. Adverse impacts on vegetation have been attributed to automobile exhausts in Yosemite.

Almost three-quarters of national park superintendents surveyed cited exhaust from tourists' cars as a significant factor affecting air quality within the parks. Indeed, one national park report noted that "the impact of automobiles (air and noise pollution, acreage for roads, gasoline stations) may be more significant than the impact of the visitors themselves.".

Tour buses have an impact on air quality as well. Often referred to as the motorcoach industry, the tour bus industry includes 3,000 companies and 25,000 vehicles. Companies are classified as intercity or charter-tour. The latter constitutes more than 50% of the market. Charter-tour bus trips have increased, while intercity trips have declined. Specific emissions data on tour buses are not available, but most tour buses belong in the category of heavy-duty diesel vehicles. In 1997, these vehicles emitted 1.468 million short tons (mst) of carbon monoxide, and 1.886 mst of nitrogen oxide.

Another form of ground transportation that has grown in the past twenty years is the recreational vehicle (RV) and off-road recreational vehicle (ORV) sector. Table 3 illustrates the amount of air pollutant emissions from these vehicles. These non-road recreational vehicles do not include sport utility vehicles, or SUVs. These data suggest that this segment of tourism-related transportation does not contribute significantly to air quality problems, as land recreational vehicles contribute less than 1% of U.S. total emissions of each listed pollutant.

Ground transportation can also have an impact on natural habitat. This impact occurs primarily through road construction. However, some vehicles such as ORVs can have a direct impact. As noted earlier, the distinction between tourism and recreation is a difficult one to make. While ORVs can be considered to be primarily recreational, some ORV users travel significant distances to participate in a recreational activity. When ORV use occurs during a trip away from home, it can be considered a tourist activity as well as a recreational one.

Off-road vehicles have damaged dune systems and salt marshes in Barnstable, and Provincetown, Massachusetts.

Table 2. 1997 ir pollutant emissions of light-duty gas and heavy duty diesel vehicles

Pollutant	*Light-Duty Gas Vehicles (automobiles) in million short tons (mst)*	*Heavy Duty Diesel Vehicles (in million short tons)*
Nitrogen Oxide	2.863	1.886
Carbon Monoxide	26.847	1.468
Volatile Organic Compounds	2.719	.221
Sulphur Dioxide	.128	.084
Particulate Matter (PM-10)	.056	.154

A study done by the National Park Service Cooperative Research Unit at the University of Massachusetts found that even low-level use can cause severe environmental degradation. Only 50 passes of an ORV at the foot of dunes halted growth of beach grass that stabilises the dune. This causes erosion of the dunes, which in turn increases the risk of damage from flooding, as dunes provide natural flood protection.

In addition, the use of ORVs by tourists has proven destructive to wildlife in some areas. Cape Cod National Seashore has had to initiate seasonal and spatial permits for ORV users to protect Piping Plovers during their nesting period. An ORV race across the deserts of California and Nevada has been permanently cancelled as a result of the damage the vehicles were doing to the desert tortoise populations.

Table 3. Air Pollutant Emisison of Recreational Land Vehicles in 1997

Pollutant	*Recreational Land Vehicle Emissions*	*% of Total U.S. Emissions*
Nitrogen Oxide	.009	.04 %
Carbon Monoxide	.392	.45%
Volatile Organic Compounds	.137	.71%
Sulphur Dioxide	N/A	N/A
Particulate Matter (PM-10)	.004	.01%

Recreational Marine Vehicles

Recreational marine vehicles, can, therefore, affect air quality during transit to a destination and while their owners boat in and around that destination. Recreational marine vehicles do not emit as much carbon monoxide as automobiles, but they do emit significantly more of it than recreational land vehicles (such as off-road vehicles) and aircraft. The EPA found that nonroad hydrocarbon emissions represent 10% of urban summertime HC emissions.

Recreational marine engines were responsible for 30% of the nonroad engine emissions. addition, two-stroke engines, such as those found on personal watercraft, are rather inefficient and typically release 25-30% of oil and gas into the surrounding water. However, emissions from marine recreational vehicles represent only a small percentage of total national emissions; therefore their effects are less pronounced than with automobiles.

The Clean Air Act Amendments of 1990 gave the EPA authority for the first time to regulate emissions from nonroad engines and vehicles. The EPA set emissions standards for new spark-ignition gasoline marine engines in 1996, including outboard engines, personal watercraft engines, and jet boat engines. These are designed to reduce hydrocarbon emissions from these types of engines 75% by 2025. These emissions standards do not apply to inboard motors, as they emit fewer pollutants, but they do apply to outboard engines sold starting in 1998, and to personal watercraft (such as jetskis) engines sold starting in 1999.

Development and Land Use

The environmental impacts of the construction and development of facilities needed to support the industry are both immediate and gradual. Development associated with tourism includes accommodations, roads, retail stores and restaurants, tourist attractions, tourists' seasonal waterfront homes, water supplies, and waste disposal facilities. Cumulative effects over time are particularly problematic because the developer in question is often out of the picture before impacts become obvious. An example of a gradual impact is the leaching of nutrients from septic systems of tourists' waterfront homes into the waterbody, accelerating eutrophication and depleting dissolved oxygen supplies.

Tourist infrastructure can also adversely impact water quality because more wastewater is created in one place and reduced someplace else, putting more pressure on sewage treatment plants or septic systems in the tourist destination. When a sewage treatment plant receives more effluent than it can treat, the excess can flow directly into water bodies untreated, creating a potential health hazard. The sewage problem with tourist facilities is further exacerbated by the seasonal nature of many tourist areas. An area which off-season may have the capacity to properly treat sewage may be overburdened during the tourist season.

Sewage effluent can damage coral reefs because it stimulates the growth of algae, which cover the filter-feeding corals, hampering their ability to get food. Furthermore, the algae impede the transmission of sunlight to the plant cells (zooxanthellae) living within the corals' tissue, hindering their ability to grow and provide the coral with needed nutrition. This damage has occurred on the Hawaiian island of Oahu, where the discharge of partially treated sewage effluent stimulated the growth of a particular algae, destroying parts of the reef. However, it is difficult to separate the effects of rapid urbanisation of Oahu on the sewage treatment plants with the effects of an increase in tourists to the area.

An area where the degradation of coral reefs due to sewage discharge can be attributed to tourism is in Jamaica. Damage to the corals there resulting from sewage discharge from tourist resorts along a 160-kilometer stretch of coastline was observed as early as 1973.

Tourist facilities increase the amount of impervious surfaces, causing more runoff to reach water bodies. This runoff contains nutrients, suspended particles, and oil and gas. Excess nutrients added to a water body can accelerate the process of eutrophication, causing an overgrowth of algae, which in turn uses up excess dissolved oxygen as the algae decays, causing fish kills. The overgrowth of algae is also a nuisance to swimmers. Furthermore, if masses of algae wash up on shore, they can create a foul-smelling area and a breeding ground for biting flies. A relevant example is the accelerated eutrophication of Lake Tahoe since the 1950s.

Increased development to accommodate tourism and recreation contributed to the degradation of water quality for two primary reasons: (1) the increase of impervious surface, which in turn led to increased runoff of nutrients into the lake, and (2) the destruction of wetlands needed to filter those pollutants. Construction of facilities supporting the tourism industry can damage wetlands, mangroves, coral reefs, and estuaries. Wetlands have been destroyed to make way for roads, airports, marinas, sewage treatment plants, and recreational facilities.

In Cancun, Mexico, the natural environment of mangrove wetlands was almost completely destroyed by the development of tourist hotels and their associated infrastructure. Similarly, in Jamaica over 700 acres of wetlands have been destroyed since the 1960s for tourism development. In the Rocky Mountain National Park, the construction of a high-level road increasing human accessibility led to the destruction of 95% of the vegetation cover in some areas close to the road.

Although tourism has been the impetus for much destructive development, it has also been the motivation for preserving sensitive ecosystems. Some of this motivation stems from economic benefits, as natural parks serve as attractions for tourists. An example on an international level is the Parc des Volcans in Rwanda, which provides ecological benefits through protection of the local watershed, and economic benefits, as it is the country's third largest source of foreign exchange. Everglades National Park in Florida is a domestic example of a sensitive wetland and estuarine environment where tourism has spurred preservation efforts.

Tourism with an emphasis on cultural and historic sites has been called "heritage" or "cultural" tourism, and is one of the fastest growing trends in the industry. Heritage tourism focuses on sharing the historical and cultural resources of an area with travellers, while still maintaining the integrity of each site. This type of tourism has been the impetus for the rehabilitation of existing historic sites, buildings, and monuments, such as the facelift that historic houses, lighthouses, and piers received on Cape Cod in the name of tourism.

Similarly, the 18th century capital of the former British colony of Virginia, Williamsburg, has been transformed from ruins to a thriving historic site and tourist destination. Renovations to the Custer House at Fort Abraham Lincoln State Park in North Dakota were completed in part to attract additional tourists. A final example where heritage tourism has been the catalyst for improvement is the rural, somewhat neglected farm town of Fort Benton, Montana. It was transformed into an international tourist attraction because of several historic sites that were restored, including a Lewis and Clark memorial, the Museum of the Northern Great Plains, and the Museum of the Upper Missouri.

A related benefit of tourism can be the revitalisation of derelict urban areas. Two examples are the Gas Lamp District of San Diego and the South of Market Area (SOMA) in San Francisco. The Gas Lamp District was transformed from an area resembling skid row to a thriving tourist area, thanks in part to municipal funding. City officials took advantage of the area's prime location between downtown and the city's convention center by building restaurants, clubs, and other tourist attractions that were subsequently also used by local residents.

Similarly, in San Francisco's South of Market Area, an area dominated by abandoned warehouses grew into a thriving tourist destination due in part to the construction of a convention center there in 1983. The tourist development led to residential development, and now SOMA is considered a good place to live. Other urban centers such as Washington, D.C. and New York City have also benefited from an expansion of tourism. The revenue generated from tourists and their activities allows these areas to maintain sites and buildings that would not otherwise be as well kept.

Another benefit of tourism development is its role in fostering an appreciation and understanding of nature. Tourism development can facilitate an increasing awareness and appreciation of the natural world. For example, the development of mountain railroads and athletic resorts in Switzerland made it possible for people to visit and appreciate the previously unknown area. Similarly, tours into the Canadian tundra have increased their visibility to people other than hunters and scientists.

Development undertaken to cater to tourists in coastal areas can have adverse impacts. Jetties and breakwaters built to create artificial harbours can increase erosion of those areas on the downstream side of the littoral drift (i.e., the movement of sand along the nearshore underwater propelled by the prevailing current). In addition to their physical impacts, these structures can detract from the aesthetics of an area. The construction of marinas can alter water levels and nutrient concentrations, as well as destroy habitat.

However, tourism-related development can benefit a coastal zone as well as harm it. Public access, for example, often increases with tourism development, as some states have legislation requiring developers to maintain some public access with development. Furthermore, tourism injects the resources along a coast and adjacent waters with political and economic value, helping to ensure their protection. The political value stems from the significant constituency of summer residents and day tourists who want to maintain their recreation area. Slightly more obvious are the economic benefits from fostering tourism along the coast, as revenue is generated from entrance, parking, and other fees, as well as from sales and employment.

Tourism-related development has an impact on wildlife, also. Development in the lower elevations of mountain resorts (where it usually is located) restricts the migratory winter range of certain wildlife. Impacts on wildlife associated with tourist development can be indirect as well as direct. For example, automobile headlights, streetlights, and resort illumination on beachside roads can disorient marine turtles. This disorientation causes them to head inland instead of towards the sea. The growth of tourist communities can affect wildlife habitat.

Impacts on National Park Gateway Communities

Communities adjacent to national parks that cater to tourists are called "gateway communities." Development of these areas is often undertaken without consideration of the natural landscape. Indiscriminate and scattered development tends to detract from the local character of such areas and homogenizes the experience for the visitor. For example, Tusayan, the gateway town to the south rim of the Grand Canyon, is "dominated by a gaggle of fast-food restaurants, motels, and trinket shops along the highway, [and] has been likened to a strip mall on the entryway to the Vatican". An example of new development that is not integrated into the natural landscape is a resort community currently being built around an IMAX theater in West Yellowstone. It is important to note that development adjacent to national parks is a trade-off for less development within the parks. If it is a question of one or the other, then it is preferable to develop outside of the parks. However, there is no reason why areas adjacent to the parks cannot be developed in accordance with the natural environment and local character.

Many resorts have ribbon or sprawl developments that are unattractive and are not well assimilated into the surrounding area. High-rise hotels along the coastal zones of Atlantic City and Miami are examples of visual pollution. Hawaii was one of the first tourist destinations in the United States to experience this problem, prompting articles about it as early as 1969. Becker noted that "statehood and the jet airliner have transformed the Hawaiian capital from a picturesque crossroads to something approaching an outpost of Southern California." The character and architectural beauty of Jerusalem was similarly marred by the construction of several high-rise hotels in an attempt to stimulate tourism.

A more subtle impact of tourist facility development is the gradual yet persistent transformation from a natural to a built environment. As the number of tourists in an area increases, the demand for facilities increases, and thus their supply. Eventually, the built environment almost wholly subsumes the natural environment, with contrived, artificial attractions becoming the focus of tourists. Relph described this process as "the destruction of the local and regional landscape that very often initiated the tourism, and its replacement by conventional tourist architecture and synthetic landscapes and pseudo-places." For example, visitors to the Dells,

Wisconsin initially went there to see the natural sandstone cliff formations. However, the increasing number of tourists every year led to an expansion of the built environment, and the attractions now receiving the most attention from tourists have names such as "Western World" and "Robot World," along with water parks and a greyhound racing track. The natural sandstone cliffs are a peripheral attraction, if they are seen at all.

There are positive economic impacts associated with tourism in gateway communities and host communities. More visitors can mean increased employment opportunities and an improved standard of living. Other economic benefits of tourism reported in the literature include improvement of public utilities and transport infrastructure, and an increase in tax revenues.

Impacts of the Lodging Industry

Energy Use

The lodging industry consumed slightly below 0.5 quadrillion British thermal units (Btu) of energy in 1995. This amount was approximately 9.4 % of the total energy consumption of all commercial buildings. In that same year, the lodging industry consumed 125 thousand Btu per square foot, which was more than the average of 90.5 thousand Btu per square foot for all commercial buildings. The lodging industry has the fifth highest rate of energy consumption according to principal building activity (out of 13 categories). The lodging industry consumes less energy than both the health care and food service industries. While some hotels have been successful in reducing energy usage since the early 1970s, it remains a concern of the lodging industry. There is increasing pressure to reduce energy use further because of the greenhouse gas emissions associated with energy use.

Water Use

Water is used at lodging facilities for drinking, cleaning, recreation (if there are pools), fire safety systems, and bathing and sanitary purposes. Water usage depends on the size and type of the hotel. Larger hotels often offer amenities that use large quantities of water, such as swimming pools and extensive landscaping. Furthermore, large hotels are more likely to have a central chilled water plant, which consumes a large quantity of water. Stipanuk and Roffman estimated that hotel water usage ranges from 101 gallons per available room per day in a hotel with less than 75 rooms, to 208 gallons per room per day in a hotel with 500 or more rooms. This amount averages out to 154 gallons per available room per day, or 56,210 gallons of water per room per year. Since tourists constitute about 30% of the total number of guests in U.S hotels, tourism is responsible for about 16,863 gallons of water per room per year.

The entire lodging industry has been estimated to use 154 billion gallons per year, with tourism therefore accounting for about 46.2 billion gallons per year. Total freshwater withdrawal for offstream uses in the United States in 1995 was 340 billion gallons per day, of which tourism-related hotel water use was less than.04% of the total.

Solid Waste Generation

The amount of solid waste generated is dependent upon the size and type of the hotel, as well as the existence of waste management facilities. A pilot study by the Florida Department of Environmental Regulations, the Central Florida Hotel and Motel Association, and the University of Florida found that the average rate of solid waste generation at hotels ranged from 132.7 pounds per room per month for a Comfort Inn to 220.3 pounds per room per month at an upscale Hilton in the Walt Disney World Village. Therefore, waste generated from tourism would range from 40 pounds per room per month to 66 pounds per room per month (at 30% of total).

Impacts of the Cruise Industry

The cruise industry is the fastest growing segment of the tourism industry, moving from 500,000 passengers a year in 1970 to over five million in 1995. Industry statistics suggest an increase in those numbers to seven million passengers in 2000. The United States has an interest in the potential environmental impacts of the cruise industry in part because six of the world's eight leading cruise markets are in or adjacent to U.S. waters.

Solid Waste

As with recreational boats, the amount of solid waste generated by the cruise industry is difficult to document. A cruise ship carrying 2,700 passengers can generate at least a ton of garbage per day. An average passenger generates 2 pounds of dry garbage, 1 and a half pounds of food waste, and disposes of two bottles and two cans. One estimate had the industry generating only 1.1% of the total annual garbage generation by U.S. maritime sectors, with recreational boaters generating the most. However, the National Research Council developed its own estimates and found that cruise ships produce the second most garbage by weight, followed by recreational boaters.

The NRC believed that Cantin, et al. underestimated the amount of garbage produced by the cruise industry because they underestimated the number of passengers, and because the fleet has increased substantially since 1990. These discrepancies reveal the importance of assumptions in using data, and how different assumptions can lead to very different results. In addition, as with recreational boating, these figures represent the amount of garbage generated; it is even more difficult with cruise vessels to determine how much gets tossed overboard. It is nearly impossible to monitor the vessels, and it is difficult to distinguish shipboard waste from landgenerated waste once onshore.

Evidence of illegal dumping of solid waste must therefore come from passengers on board or other vessels. For example, passengers on board a Princess Cruise Lines vessel, the Regal Princess, witnessed the illegal dumping of 20 trash-filled bags overboard during the late evening in October 1991 5 miles off of the Florida Keys. Under the Marine Plastic Pollution Research and Control Act of 1987, any willful discharges of plastic within 200 miles of the United States shoreline are punishable by up to $500,000 in fines for the company involved. Princess Cruise Lines receieved the maximum fine.

Cruise vessels have addressed the waste issue through the use of onboard waste incinerators that meet the requirements of the International Maritime Organisation (IMO). The cruise industry is attempting to move towards zero discharge of these materials. Total waste on cruise vessels has been reduced by almost 50% over the past 10 years.

Air Pollution

The cruise industry has the potential to affect air quality through engine emissions. Most marine fuels are residual fuels with higher concentrations of contaminants such as sulphur. Recent studies have suggested that ocean-going vessels have the potential to affect air quality in coastal regions, port areas, and heavily traveled trade routes where annual sulphur emissions from ships equal or exceed land-based emissions. However, passenger vessels (cruise ships) contribute only 5% of nitrogen emissions from ships and 6% of sulphur emissions from ships.

The cruise industry contributes the least of all categories of ocean-going vessels to total nitrogen and sulphur emissions. The IMO approved global emission limits in September 1997, with NO_x regulations applying to new ships or major ship conversions after January 1, 2000. Sulphur fuel levels are currently limited to 4.5% of the total fuel mixture.

Oil and Chemical Effluent

Cruise ships also produce toxic chemicals and hazardous waste from dry-cleaning procedures, used batteries, and paint waste from brush cleaning. Waste oil is produced from normal leakage from the main engines and generators, the cleaning of fuel filters, losses during maintenance, and leaks from hydraulic systems. In 1997 passenger vessels (cruise ships) had 136 oil spills in U.S. waters, totalling 1,778 gallons. This amount represents only 1.6% of the total oil spills in the United States that year. While this is a small percentage, it is important to note that these figures represent only incidents reported to the U.S. Coast Guard. It is more difficult to discern how many illegal discharges occur.

There has been a recent example of illegal discharges. The world's second largest cruise line, Royal Caribbean, recently plead guilty to 21 felony counts for dumping oil and hazardous chemicals from its cruise ships and then lying about it to the Coast Guard. The cruise ships used bypass pipes to illegally discharge these materials, usually in the middle of the night, and crewmembers constantly falsified logbooks. One of the chemicals the company admitted to illegally dumping was perc, a toxic dry-cleaning fluid. While this may not be the norm in the cruise industry, it is important to consider the unreported incidents that have an impact on the environment. Based on the available data for reported incidents, however, it does not appear that the cruise industry's impact on the environment through oil spills is as significant as other sources.

Introduction of Non-native Species

The introduction of non-native species through discharge of ballast water is another potential environmental impact of the cruise industry. The Council on Environmental Quality found that over 130 non-native species have been introduced to the Great Lakes since 1800, with almost a third thought to have been carried by ships. It is impossible, however, to distinguish how many of those ships were cruise ships. Introduced species cause problems because they can disrupt the food web of the ecosystem and clog the intake pipes of power plants and water treatment facilities. The International Maritime Organisation has recognised these problems, and promulgated guidelines to minimize transfer of organisms.

Cruise Industry

The cruise industry is highly regulated. The International Convention for the Prevention of Pollution from Ships, or MARPOL 73/78 as it is called, is the primary regulatory framework for the industry. MARPOL comprises five annexes that describe the discharge regime of certain substances. The three annexes most relevant to the cruise industry are Annex one (I), Annex four (IV), and Annex five (V). Annex one prohibits the discharge at sea of oil in designated "special areas," and limits other discharges to a specified percentage of the cargo. Bilge water can only be discharged outside 12 miles from the U.S. coastline, established in the Law of the Sea Treaty.

In addition, oil discharged from cruise ships must be no more than 15 parts of oil per million parts of oily water mixture. Oily waste that does not meet this standard must be kept on board and/or taken to a reception facility. Annex IV prohibits the discharge of untreated sewage within 3 miles of the nearest land, and allows only treated and disinfected sewage to be released between 3 and 12 miles from land. Annex V prohibits disposal or dumping of any garbage (solid wastes, excluding sewage) within 3 miles of the United States. From 3 to 12 miles it is illegal to dump plastic, dunnage, paper, rags, glass, crockery, metal, or food not ground to 1 inch in diameter. From 12 to 25 miles it is illegal to dump plastic and dunnage, and it is illegal to dump plastic anywhere.

The United States ratified Annex V in 1987, and passed implementing legislation called the Marine Plastic Pollution Research and Control Act. The Coast Guard is responsible for enforcing these standards, and has promulgated regulations to that effect. They inspect vessels four times a year to check for properly operating marine sanitation devices and oily water separators.

Positive impacts of the cruise industry

It is important to comment on some of the positive impacts of the cruise industry. The industry contributes to the economy of destination areas. For example, Holland America line, which carried 178,822 passengers in 1995, estimated that their passengers spent $90 million in Alaska (primarily Anchorage, Juneau, and Fairbanks), their crew spent around $1.4 million on shore, and the combined in-state payroll of the Holland America partners was about $18 million.

In addition, the exposure of tourists to beautiful, pristine areas such as those in Alaska can improve understanding of the need for conservation. To that end, both Holland America and Norwegian Cruise Lines (NCL) have programmes to foster environmental awareness. Holland America has shore excursions that focus on ecology, nature, indigenous culture, and environmental responsibility, and NCL offers the same through their "Dive Into Adventure" programmes. Holland America donates time, money, medical materials, and other resources to the Alaska Raptor Rehabilitation Center; in addition they also donated 17 acres of recently purchased land to the center.

The cruise industry can aid in raising awareness of threatened or endangered species. For example, Discovery Cruise Line has adopted the "Manny T" as its mascot to increase recognition of the plight of the manatee. The line also donates money raised through shipboard sales of selected items and other shipboard events to the Save the Manatee Foundation, and is participating in a television public service campaign concerning the manatee.

Tourist Activities

Hiking, Snorkeling and Diving

Many tourist activities occur in fragile ecosystems, such as coral reefs. While snorkeling and diving in and of themselves do not cause much damage, inadvertent related activities, such as stepping on coral do cause damage. With such activities, it is the cumulative nature of the damage that is most problematic. One or two tourists may not cause much harm, but hundreds of them over time can do considerable damage to an ecosystem. Coral reefs are also affected by tourism as a result of the market for souvenirs. Tourists break off pieces of coral themselves, or the reef is dynamited by locals to sell the pieces. The cumulative effect is relevant here as well, as one tourist may not understand her impact when aggregated with other tourists. Damage to coral reefs from tourists in the above-mentioned manners has occurred in Tanzania, Kenya, and Madagascar, among other places.

Tourists hiking along mountain ranges can harm the ecosystem by littering and by trampling vegetation. The greatest impact of tourists on vegetation usually occurs during initial contact with an area, with the most sensitive species affected first. The cumulative impact of tourists on vegetation gradually shifts species composition, because only the most resilient plants can survive in an area under constant pressure from tourist activities. Excessive hiking on trails has caused damage to the sequoia redwoods in California. Increased visitation at Arches National Park has contributed to the deterioration of the soil there, which can take up to 250 years to recover after being trampled. Alpine tundra in the Rocky Mountain National Park also has been damaged by human trampling.

Hiking on the soil can also damage wildlife habitat. Constant pressure can damage or destroy the burrows of reptiles, mammals, and underground-nesting birds. Tourists' use of trees for firewood and tent poles has diminished tree populations, altering the age structure of the plant community. In addition, fires started by tourists for camping have caused major damage in the forests of California. Littering not only contributes to visual pollution, but can also change the nutrient composition of soils and prevent light from reaching plants. Furthermore, tourists have unwittingly carried exotic species to ecosystems, thereby upsetting their balance. Littering by tourists has caused wildlife, such as bears, to frequent the garbage area of campsites to scrounge for food. As animals become accustomed to human food, their behavior becomes more aggressive and can be potentially dangerous to humans. When Glacier National Park implemented management plans to restore normal feeding patterns for bears, there was a decrease in injuries to tourists.

Recreational Boating

The most significant problem associated with recreational boating and water quality is the discharge of sewage into waterbodies with limited flushing or nearby shellfish beds. Sewage contains pathogens which can adversely affect human health and contaminate shellfish. Diseases that can be potentially transmitted through human contact with fecal discharge and/or ingestion of contaminated shellfish include typhoid fever, dysentery, infectious hepatitis, and nonspecific gastroenteritis.

Significantly higher fecal coliform counts have been found in waters with a high recreational boating population during peak usage. One study reported that at three different sites on Puget Sound 70%, 91%, and 62% of shellfish sampled had levels of contamination higher than that allowed at the commercial wholesale level. Two of the three sites failed to meet the Washington State Department of Ecology Class AA Extraordinary Water Quality Standard.

The lack of other sources of contamination at these sites suggested to the authors that the contamination resulted from boat sewage discharge. Under Section 312 of the Clean Water Act, the EPA requires vessels to have Marine Sanitation Devices (MSDs), that physically and chemically treat boat sewage before it is released into the water. The three types of MSDs each provide a different level of treatment, depending on the vessel's length. A vessel must be equipped with one of the three types of MSDs, if it has an installed toilet as of January 30, 1980.

In addition to sewage discharges, recreational boats can impact the environment through oil spills. In 1997, recreational vessels were responsible for 535 oil spills in U.S. waters with a total volume of 4,217 gallons, and an average spill of 8 gallons. This represents 6.2% of total spill incidents in U.S. waters. While this is a small percentage, it is important to note that the data represent spills reported to the U.S. Coast Guard. It is likely that some spills are not reported. However, given the available information, oil spills from recreational boats do not seem to be a significant threat to the environment.

Another way that recreational boating can adversely affect water quality is through the discharge of solid waste (garbage). The National Research Council has listed some of the adverse impacts of marine debris in the environment:

- aesthetic degradation of surface waters and coastal areas;
- physical injuries to humans;
- ecological damage resulting from the interference of plastics with gas exchange between surface waters and deeper waters;
- alterations in the composition of ecosystems because opportunistic organisms use debris as their environment;
- entanglements of birds, fish, turtles, and cetaceans; and
- ingestion of plastic by marine mammals.

It is difficult to determine the amount of solid waste generated by recreational vessels. One study estimated that recreational boats generated 51.4% of the total annual garbage generated by U.S. maritime sectors. However, the National Research Council estimated that recreational boats contributed only 19% of the total.

Although the amount of waste generated on a daily basis is minimal due to the relatively short duration of trips, the cumulative effect has the potential to be significant. There are approximately 7.3 million recreational boats in the United States, more than in any other maritime sector. Recreational boaters operating within 3 miles of shore are required to store their garbage on board and dispose of it onshore.

Recreational boating can cause damage to marine habitat and animals such as coral by running aground or dragging anchor over the habitat. This damage has happened within some national parks with marine or freshwater components. For example, in 1997, 161 vessels ran aground in Biscayne National Park in Florida. These events damaged 8,000 square meters of submerged seagrass beds, which are important because they serve as a nursery for many commercial and sport marine species. In addition, seagrass beds help stabilise sediments, reduce wave energy, and filter pollutants. The manatee in Florida has been threatened by the propellers of powerboats.

The wash generated by motor boats can induce erosion of plant roots, and propellers can cut macrophyte growth. Although there are no data currently available on the effects of wakes from boats, these impacts are confined to localised and sensitive areas. The movement of tourists' vehicles can also adversely affect wildlife by separating the young from their parents. It is possible that whale-watching boats have this impact because studies have shown that, if young whale calves lose contact with their mothers, they sometimes attach themselves to the side of a ship. The noise made by these boat engines and propellers are also thought to interfere with the whales' communications systems.

Recreational boating can have positive impacts on the environment as well. Recreational boaters provide funding indirectly for conservation and recreation efforts through a tax on motorboat and small-engine fuel. This tax is mandated in the Intermodal Surface Transportation Efficiency Act, which earmarks the funds for the Federal Aid in Sport Fish Restoration Programme of the U.S. Fish and Wildlife Service. Revenue from this fund is used by states to stock fish, acquire and improve sport fish habitat, fund fisheries research and education, and to provide recreational access to water through boat ramps and piers.

Tourist Activities Within National Parks

Visitor and traffic congestion exists in many tourist destinations, and national parks have been greatly impacted by this problem. Over 2.5 million people visit Zion Canyon each year, with half of those driving in the park. A summer day can see 2,000 vehicles in the canyon corridor, creating congestion, air pollution from vehicle exhaust, and vegetation damage along overflow parking areas. To help alleviate this problem, the park plans to launch a shuttle system in 2000. Although this system is expected to reduce some of the trafficrelated impacts and provide a higher quality experience, it could also have the effect of increasing the number of visitors to the park.

The entrance to Yosemite National Park in California has had to be closed several times due to gridlock during the summer months when visitation is at its peak. With over 5 million visitors a year, Grand Canyon National Park suffers from congestion as well. The huge volume of traffic is more than just an inconvenience. There are physical impacts, such as air pollution from exhaust, and there are social impacts that also degrade the overall experience, such as honking horns and blaring radios.

The superintendent of Grand Canyon National Park has commented that "we've taken this special place that is different from everything in your life and we've homogenised it so it's just like your life. It's full of cars, you're constantly looking for parking spaces, you're standing around in lines."

An increasing number of tourists have been using snowmobiles as a form of recreation while visiting some national parks. Snowmobiles have the potential to adversely affect air quality over time because they use two-stroke engines that produce relatively high emissions of carbon monoxide and unburned hydrocarbons, and they are not equipped with pollution control equipment. Recent studies by state and federal agencies and the University of Denver found that snowmobiles account for 94% of the annual hydrocarbon emissions at Yellowstone National Park, 78% of carbon monoxide emissions, 37% of particulate matter, and 3% of nitrogen oxide emissions at Yellowstone. Currently, no federal law regulates these emissions.

Tourist activities can alter the integrity of cultural resources. This damage includes vandalism and looting of sites of cultural significance. Historic structures and archeological sites were harmed by tourist activities at Gettysburg National Military Park. Damages to cultural resources can be more serious than those to natural resources, as the natural resources can recuperate over time.

While the environmental impacts on the parks from tourists and their activities are important and significant in some areas, it is important to note that many parks do not experience these problems. As always, there is scientific uncertainty about the effects of visitors on park ecosystems.

Upstream and Downstream Influence

Tourism service providers such as hotels and travel agents to leverage their influence on other parts of the supply chain to encourage more environmentally responsible tourism. The "supply chain" in the tourism industry consists of those industries that supply accommodations, transportation, and make arrangements for travellers. "Upstream" influence refers to a sector's ability to influence an actor "above" them in the tourism services supply chain. A hotel's influence over a supplier's products is an example of upstream influence. "Downstream" influence refers to the influence an industry has over other sectors (including tourists) or industries "below" them in the tourism services supply chain. An example of this type of influence is a travel agent's influence over a tourist's choice of vacation type and destination.

Selected Components of the Industry

The tourism industry is not one industry, but rather a conglomeration of many industries and sectors. A full characterisation of this complex and fragmented industry is beyond the scope of this paper. However, the structure of selected components of the industry is presented to demonstrate the potential for upstream and downstream influence. This discussion focuses on the lodging and cruise industries, travel agents, tour operators, and some nonprofit groups that offer trips. Figure 1 illustrates the relationship among the different sectors and indicates where upstream and downstream leverage is possible.

The tourism industry has changed substantially in the past ten to fifteen years, with more change likely. The airline industry is expected to consolidate further, along with continued decreases in fares. Development of new technology such as the Internet has already had some effect on the distribution of travel, and it is very likely that more change will occur.

Lodging Industry

The lodging industry is in and of itself large, with over 51,000 establishments and over 3.1 million rooms in the United States.

The industry employs over 1.6 million workers, and accounts for 1.3% of the gross national product. It comprises hotels, motor hotels, motels, bed and breakfasts, and condos. There has been a trend in the lodging industry over the past thirty years of consolidation, as the number of chain and franchise affiliations has increased and the number of independently owned and operated properties has decreased. However, industry predictions suggest a decrease in the franchising trend, with a subsequent increase in control over properties by the chains. The fastest-growing segment of the industry is the bed and breakfast sector. This segment has the ability of generating tourism revenue in smaller communities where larger chains do not have a presence.

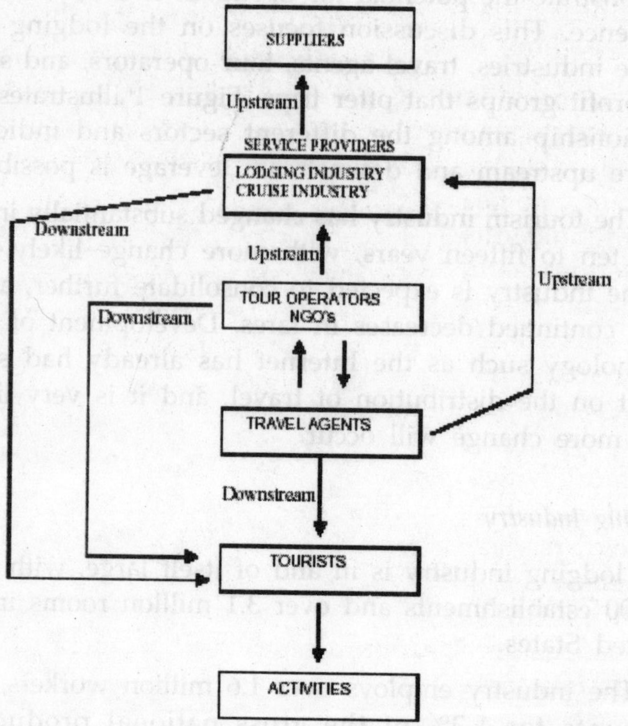

Figure 1: Relationships among selected sectors of the Tourism

Cruise Industry

As mentioned previously, the cruise industry is the fastest growing segment of the tourism industry, moving from 500,000 passengers a year in 1970 to over 5 million in 1995. This growth is also reflected in the increase of the number of berths, with 5,000 new berths added during the first half of 1996. The industry is planning on adding 41 new vessels by 2002, increasing passenger capacity by 57%. An average of 113 cruise ships visited or operated from U.S. ports between 1990-1995. The industry has a significant economic impact, creating $11.6

billion in expenditures in goods and services in 1997, including passengers and suppliers. The most visited U.S. ports of call for cruise ships are all in Florida: Miami, Everglades, Canaveral, and Tampa. Other U.S. ports of significance are located in Alaska, California, Louisiana, New York, Texas, and Massachusetts.

Travel agents

There are currently around 39,000 travel agencies in the United States. Traditionally, the industry has comprised many smaller agencies, with an average agency employing seven people. There is an increasing trend, however, of consolidation and concentration within the industry, as an increasing number of large networks of agencies act under a common brand name. Two-thirds of travel agencies belong to co-ops or consortiums. While there are more small agencies (with sales less than $2 million), two-thirds of the sales are done by agencies with $2 million or more in bookings. The development of technologies such as the Internet has spurred this consolidation, as small agencies need to combine with others to make a profit.

Large travel agencies get the majority of their revenue from commissions paid by airlines, with airlines spending $6.4 billion each year on travel agent commissions. Slightly less than 66% of the total dollar volume of travel agents comes from the sale of air travel. However, this allocation is changing as airlines move to cap commissions to travel agents. For example, instead of the previous flat rate of 10% for domestic trips, Delta airlines has limited commissions for these tickets to $50 regardless of the ticket price. Airlines are doing this for economic reasons, as commissions are now the fourth largest operating expense for U.S. carriers after labor, fuel, and maintenance.

Travel agents book 95% of cruises, 90% of airline tickets, and only 25% of hotel rooms. There is an emerging trend in the travel agent industry where the larger agencies focus on corporate clients, and the smaller agencies focus primarily on tourists and small businesses. These smaller agencies are inclined to concentrate on revenues from tours and cruises, rather than airline revenues.

Tour operators

Tour operators have an interesting niche in the tourism industry because they act as an intermediary between travel agents and suppliers of travel services. Tour operators plan and organise all aspects of a vacation by putting down large deposits for block reservations (e.g., at hotels and other lodgings), and then usually sells them to the public through travel agencies or airlines. This industry has grown from around 300 operators in 1975 to over 1,500 in 1990, with the 50 largest having 50% of the business. It comprises three segments: the independent tour operator, the airline working with a tour operator business, and the travel agent that packages tours for clients. Operators generate more than $10.5 billion annually in North America.

Other Organisations Functions

Organisations such as the American Automobile Association (AAA) and nongovernmental organisations (NGOs) perform many of the same functions as traditional travel agents and tour operators. Although AAA is primarily known for its automobile services, it generated travel sales of $2.15 billion in 1995, with leisure travel accounting for 81% of that. It has significant potential for downstream influence on its customers, as it can reach a large audience. AAA has 960 agency locations and around 35 million members in the United States. Industry representatives believe AAA has not yet realised its full potential as a travel agency.

AAA executives hope to increase their hotel, airline, and cruise line sales through a Windows-based booking system that will allow easy access to its members travel data. They currently have 23 preferred cruise and tour suppliers, and three airline preferred suppliers. In fact, AAA signed a 5-year preferred supplier deal with Carnival Cruise Lines in 1996. The organisation could use its growing influence in the travel industry to work with and promote environmentally friendly suppliers.

NGOs that have ecotourism links and/or conduct nature, adventure, and eco-tours include the World Wildlife Fund, the Nature Conservancy, the Audubon Society, Conservation International, Africa Wildlife Foundation, and the Sierra Club. These organisations use the trips as a way to raise money, and to increase awareness and understanding of natural systems. The Audubon Society offers trips to places such as the Galapagos Islands, Greenland and Hudson Bay, and the Pacific Northwest. World Wildlife Fund (WWF) takes travellers to Alaska, Antarctica, and Africa, among other destinations.

Upstream and Downstream Influence

The tourism industry has potential for upstream and downstream influence on the environmental impacts of tourism. The three primary types of influence are supplier relations, channeling of activity, and education.

Supplier relations

The lodging industry can leverage its influence "upstream" on suppliers by demanding products that have less of an environmental impact. For example, a hotel chain can wield its influence on a supplier by requiring paper towels made out of recycled materials for their bathrooms. The extent to which a hotel can leverage its suppliers depends upon several factors, including type of hotel (e.g., large chain or small independent) and type of supplies. Some larger hotel chains have national corporate purchasing agreements with different vendors. Often these chains will purchase supplies based only on these corporate purchasing agreements for the sake of convenience or because it is less expensive to do so. It might be most effective, then, to exert upstream leverage at this national level because franchises follow whatever contract is negotiated by their larger chains.

An example of an organisation exerting upstream leverage is the Green Seal programme; an independent, nonprofit organisation dedicated to protecting the environment by promoting the manufacture and sale of environmentally responsible products. The organisation has a pilot project underway to negotiate contracts where suppliers provide environmentally friendly cleaning products to large hotel chains and their franchises. The Green Seal programme has also published an environmental purchasing guide for hotels, providing specific product and brand recommendations.

Another programme underway to encourage environmental responsibility through supplier relations (among other things) in the lodging industry is the International Hotels Environment Initiative (IHEI). Created in 1992, this is a nonprofit organisation developed by the international hotel industry that serves over 8,000 hotels. It is governed by an International Council of 12 multinational hotel company executives, whose goal is to promote the benefits of environmental management as an integral component of hotel business. The group influences supplier relations with hotels through its supplier programme, created in 1998. This programme facilitates hotels' leverage on suppliers in three ways:

— by creating a "Registry of Industry Suppliers" who have an environmental policy and can also demonstrate that their products meet the best environmental standards (accessible to hotels through a CD-Rom, the Green Hotelier magazine (quarterly publication focusing on hotel environmental issues), and directly through IHEI to the corporate Vice Presidents responsible for purchasing in each member hotel group);

— by establishing and publishing environmental specifications for products or product groups; and

— through the creation and disbursement of a comprehensive buyers guide with a list of all registered suppliers, guidelines for purchasing of products that minimize their environmental impact, and profiles of products.

IHEI suggests several ways hotels can influence their suppliers. These include insisting on buying products made from recycled material or that are recyclable, writing to competing suppliers to explain why the hotel chose to do business with a more environmentally aware supplier, and demanding that suppliers minimize their packaging. In order to determine how environmentally friendly a supplier is, a survey can be distributed to them.

A third organisation dedicated to fostering environmental stewardship within the lodging industry is the Green Hotels Association (GHA). This mail order business and trade association was founded in 1993 to help hotels develop and maintain environmentally friendly practices. Like the IHEI, the GHA facilitates hotels' leverage on suppliers through publication of a catalog of environmental products for the lodging industry, with items such as a toilet-tank fill diverter, which saves around three-quarters of a gallon of water per flush. The GHA currently reaches less than 1% of all U.S. hotels. The cruise industry has a similar ability to influence upstream suppliers. There are several large firms that supply products to cruise lines. A large cruise line such as Carnival Cruise Lines generally has a good deal of influence on its suppliers because competition for business is strong.

Upstream leveraging efforts are focused primarily on the environmental quality of the shipboard products they purchase. They can encourage suppliers to use more environmentally friendly packaging. Recently, cruise lines belonging to the International Council of Cruise Lines have begun replacing plastic products such as cups, shampoo, and straws with biodegradable, reusable, or recyclable material. Carnival Cruise Lines has reduced the amount of plastic brought on board their ships through working with their suppliers. To further reduce the amount of plastic on board, Carnival has eliminated plastic from the shotgun shells used for skeet shooting and has completely eliminated driving golf balls off the ships.

Royal Caribbean Cruises is another example of a cruise line using leverage with suppliers to encourage use of products that minimize environmental impact. Through a Quality Supplier Development Programme (QSDP), the cruise line has convinced suppliers to reduce packaging and substitute more environmentally benign materials. In the last five years they have reduced packaging by 35% through several different routes including ordering ketchup and chili sauce in 5-gallon pouches instead of tin cans, ordering some beer in kegs rather than cans, putting fountain syrup in 5-gallon boxed bags, which saves 250,000 syrup cans annually, and purchasing soda in cans without plastic rings.

Travel agents are intermediaries between providers of the tourist product (including airlines, cruise lines, and hotels) and the tourist, and, as such, are able to influence the decisions of suppliers. Their influence is currently stronger with cruise lines and airlines, as they book the majority of those trips. However, the relationship between travel agents and hotels has strengthened, with travel agents' bookings constituting a growing segment of the hotel industry. This growth has occurred for several reasons. The hotel business has become more competitive, therefore hotels need to explore more marketing avenues. Secondly, the shift in business for hotels from large group sales to transient business has benefited travel agents because they are better able to target the transient client.

Finally, automated systems (computer reservation systems, or CRS, currently more commonly called Global Distribution Systems (GDS)) are making the distribution of travel services (such as the purchase and disbursement of tickets) easier and more efficient. These computer reservation systems were first developed by airlines for their internal operations in the 1970s.

As the efficiency of these systems became increasingly obvious, airlines opened them up to travel agencies. GDS allow travel agents to access and compare centralised information such as flights, hotel descriptions, and seat and room availability on one screen. By 1994, four systems were providing computer reservation services to travel agencies. Ninety-five percent of existing travel agents are now automated with a computer reservation system, and over 80% of airline reservations are routed through one of the above four primary GDS. Use of the GDS has expanded to include booking entire vacation packages electronically. Travel agents, therefore, may be able to exert influence on hotels by steering clients towards hotels that are known to have sound environmental management programmes and policies.

The proliferation of travel suppliers provided the impetus for the development of "preferred supplier" relationships, where travel agents tend to book with a supplier known to be reliable. This relationship is often based on economic incentives. Commissions paid to travel agencies vary among suppliers. Thus travel agents sometimes steer their clients to suppliers that pay the highest commission. This could make it more difficult for travel agents to recommend suppliers that have demonstrated more environmental awareness, unless those suppliers can compete financially with other suppliers. However, travel agents' capacity to exert upstream leverage may be increasing as a result of the increase in the number of large networks of agencies. These larger networks can leverage their influence on travel suppliers because of their size. One of the recommendations at a 1990 conference of the American Society of Travel Agents was to book clients into hotels and on cruise ships that properly dispose of waste material.

In addition, ASTA presents an ASTA/Smithsonian Environment Award to organisations that demonstrate "outstanding skill, originality, and effectiveness in preserving and/or protecting the environment". Past recipients of the award include Inter-Continental Hotels and Maho Bay Camps in the U.S. Virgin Islands. ASTA also provides a link on its Website to ecotour operators and destinations.

Channeling of activity

Sectors of the tourism industry have the opportunity to "channel" activities of both tourists and employees toward more environmentally responsible activities. This type of influence has been termed "downstream" leverage. The lodging industry exerts downstream influence on tourists by encouraging environmentally sound practices. Ramada International Hotels and Resorts distributed 20,000 copies of "50 Simple Things You Can Do to Save the Earth" to guests as a method to encourage environmentally responsible behavior.

In addition, the hotel chain established a children's menu that encourages protection of endangered species. The Green Hotels Association provides member hotels with a towel rack hanger and a sheet-changing card to give guests the option of using their linens more than once. The association estimates that this practice alone can save 5% on the cost of hotel utilities.

It has been suggested that an effective way to implement changes favorable to the environment is by starting with hotel employees in areas such as laundry, housekeeping, and engineering. These employees have first direct contact with some aspects of the hotel business that have an impact on the environment. The Saunders' Hotel Group solicits employee input and recognises their input through its SHINE programme, or Saunders Hotels Initiative to Nurture the Environment. This programme began in 1989 as a recycling programme and has since grown into a much more comprehensive environmental programme, with investments in energy-efficient lighting and windows as well as an improved recycling programme.

The cruise industry has a significant opportunity for downstream influence on the environmental behavior of its passengers, as the industry's vessels carried over 5.5

million North American passengers in 1997. Cruise vessels determine where their passengers travel, and they can exert downstream influence to minimize environmental impact by limiting the number of tourists that go ashore at sensitive destinations, and by avoiding environmentally sensitive areas. Orient Cruise Line limits the number of tourists for certain shore excursions, such as visiting an albatross colony. Cruise lines also influence personnel and passenger environmental behavior by:

— making announcements over the public address system and putting daily notices in ship newsletters that caution against throwing trash overboard;

— placing signs in crew and passenger areas encouraging environmental protection;

— offering training programmes in pollution prevention;

— placing environmental information booklets in crew cabins and lounges; and

— meeting with officers and crew of all departments to discuss more effective environmental protection.

Travel sagents have the opportunity to have "downstream" impacts because they can influence where and how a tourist travels. Over 40% of tourists have only a general idea of their destination and mode of travel when they first visit a travel agent. Figure 2 illustrates the percent of tourists who seek travel agents' advice according to type of travel product.

The highest percentage of tourists seek advice from travel agents about hotels. This number suggests that travel agents have the most opportunity to steer their clients towards hotels that have established good environmental practices and policies. A U. S. Travel Data Center study found that 85% of travellers indicated they would be "very likely" or "somewhat likely" to support or patronize travel companies perceived to be environmentally friendly.

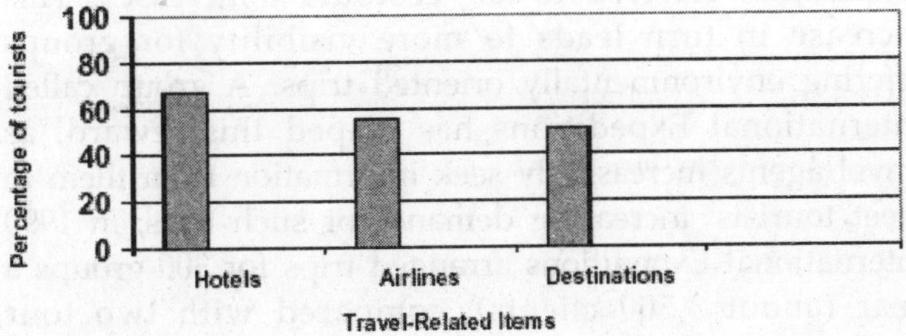

Figure 2: Percent of Tourists seeking travel agent advice based on travel product type.

Given this receptivity, it is clear that travel agents have the opportunity to influence the type of travel and the company a customer chooses. The concept of "responsible tourism" was the focus of a 1997 New Travel Expo, where over 125 travel agents discussed how they might influence tourists. The segment of tourists who actually do choose travel suppliers based on environmental principles (as opposed to stating that they would be likely to) is small now, but will most likely increase as children who have received more environmental education come of age.

Because tour operators interact with all travel suppliers, such as lodging and transportation services, they, too, have an opportunity to exert influence on suppliers. Tour operators can leverage suppliers to provide a more environmentally friendly product by fostering demand for it among their clients. An international example of a tour operator exerting leverage is the boycott of Pattaya, Thailand as a destination by German tour operators because they objected to the environmental degradation in the area.

As more tourists become aware of potential environmental degradation caused by tourism, the demand for more environmentally oriented trips (sometimes referred to as "ecotours") increases. This increase in turn leads to more visibility for groups offering environmentally oriented trips. A group called International Expeditions has reaped this reward, as travel agents increasingly seek information from them to meet tourists' increasing demand for such trips; in 1990 International Expeditions arranged trips for 300 groups a year (about 3,500 clients), compared with two tour groups in 1980.

Education of turists

The environmental impacts of the tourism industry can be partially mitigated through education of tourists and service providers. For example, efforts to educate about marine debris have targeted cruise line operators and owners. The Shipping Industry Marine Debris Education Plan, launched by the Marine Entanglement Research Programme (MERP) of the National Marine Fisheries Service, educates cruise line operators and owners by writing articles for cruise trade journals, presenting MARPOL information at cruise trade meetings, producing and distributing brochures about the problem, and presenting workshops about MARPOL compliance for members of the cruise industry.

Many educational efforts to minimize the environmental impacts of tourism are incorporated into ecotourism trips. Ecotourism attempts to minimize impact on the social, cultural, and physical environment. It can mean the development of tourism facilities in an environmentally responsible manner, recreational programmes that promote a greater awareness and appreciation of nature, and a mode of travel that is sensitive to the host community.

The Ecotourism Society calls ecotourism a nature-based form of specialty travel that is responsible, conserves the environment, and sustains the well being of local people. Eight million U.S. travellers had taken at least one ecotourism trip, and 30% (35 million) said they were planning on doing so in the next three years. Samples of ecotourism have been used internationally to guide discussions of tourism's impact on the environment. For example, the 1992 United Nations Conference on Environment and Development produced Agenda 21, a document concerning sustainable development.

In 1996 the World Travel and Tourism Council, the World Tourism Organisation, and the Earth Council developed an Agenda 21 for tourism, called "Agenda 21 for the Travel and Tourism Industry: Towards Environmentally Sustainable Development." This document advises travel and tourism companies to incorporate the sustainable development concept into tourism. Priority areas include waste minimisation, energy efficiency, fresh and wastewater management, hazardous substances, transportation, land-use planning and management, and involvement of staff, customers, and communities in environmental issues.

A potential benefit of ecotourism is the ability to raise revenues for protected areas. For example, park entrance fees can be used to support management plans and ecological studies. However, currently this idea is for the most part unrealised, as most protected areas are unable to generate enough revenues to be self-sustaining.

One successful example is Ecuador's Galapagos Islands National Park, where international visitors are charged higher fees than Ecuadorian citizens. The American Society of Travel Agents (ASTA) proposed recommending environmentally sensitive tours to their clients at a 1990 conference. They have developed guidelines for travellers to minimize their impact on the environment. These are called the "ten commandments" on ecotourism, and encourage tourists to "respect the frailty of the earth," "leave only footprints, take only photographs," and educate themselves on the local customs.

The guidelines are no more than general advice, and it is hard to determine how much they influence travellers. A perhaps more useful and pragmatic "commandment" is to ask the travel agent to identify those travel suppliers that subscribe to ASTA's Environmental Guidelines.

Tour operators also have an opportunity to influence customers through education. However, when discussing educational efforts of tour operators, it is useful to distinguish between those operators that cater to "mass tourists" and those that focus on a specific market, such as "ecotour" operators. Ecotour operators and tour operators that cater to mass tourists are both primarily economically motivated.

The critical difference is in their clientele; people who seek out ecotours are more likely to care about their impacts on the environment, so it is in the best interests of the ecotour operators to take steps to minimize a trip's impact. Tour operators catering to mass tourists are less concerned with the needs of a particular destination because environmental protection is generally not a primary concern for the mass tourist. Therefore, these operators are less likely to be concerned with the environmental impacts of tourism.

One of the ways ecotour oparators attempt to minimize impacts on the environment is by using guidelines to educate tourists. These guidelines range from specific methods to preserve and minimize impact to general platitudes that may have little effect on the tourist. Other methods used by self-identified ecotour operators include pre-trip orientations, printed information packs, videos or slide shows, lectures, discussions, and talks during the trip.

Ecotourism Issues

The numerous names and definitions make it difficult to ascertain how environmentally responsible ecotourism is. There are important distinctions among nature tourism, adventure travel, and ecotourism. Nature tourism implies enjoyment and appreciation of nature, yet it often does not include protection of the environment. Adventure travel utilizes local resources often without consideration of impacts. Ecotourism, as the above definition suggests, is concerned with the concurrent enjoyment and preservation of the natural environment.

Aside from the uncertainty and discrepancies surrounding the labels, there are also problems with the term ecotourism itself. It is possible that some travel suppliers that call themselves "eco" are only paying lip service to a marketable concept that is gaining popularity. Some travel outfitters use the label "eco" for short-term economic gain without truly abiding by environmental principles. One tour operator suggested in a survey that the label "eco-tour" should be given only to those tour operators that directly benefit the culture or environment; otherwise they should be known as "adventure travel" operators.

The development of industry standards or regulations about the definition of ecotourism would be a productive first step in differentiating these groups. The Ecotourism Society (TES) established guidelines in 1993, which are fairly comprehensive and can be used as a starting point for developing an industry standard. These guidelines include educating travellers to minimize impact, ensuring that the tour company minimizes impact by example (by offering environmentally friendly accommodations), and contributing to the economy of the region visited.

The guidelines are voluntary and are therefore not monitored or enforced. One study suggested that tour operator compliance with the TES guidelines is strongly influenced by whether or not they can gain economically from them. Therefore, emphasizing the potential for economic gain from abiding by these ecotourism guidelines would increase compliance with them. An accepted industry standard such as the TES guidelines can help identify the tour operators that conduct truly environmentally friendly tours. This identification would in turn aid travel agents in recommending qualified groups to interested tourists.

The Green Travel Network (GTN), a Washington, D.C.-based company that is partnered with Conservation International, has on-line resources for tourists interested in environmentally friendly trips. GTN attempts to ensure that ecotour operators are truly taking steps to minimize their impact on the environment by requiring that any that wish to advertise on its Web page complete a responsibility form. This form asks these operators several questions to ascertain their level of environmental responsibility, such as whether or not they have a waste management policy, and if visitation to fragile areas is monitored. GTN interviews clients of these ecotour operators to ensure that they are actually doing what they had indicated on the responsibility forms.

Ecotourism can adversely impact the environment in the same way as traditional, mass tourism. Two examples are the destruction of coral reefs in the Caribbean and the disturbance of breeding habits of birds in Antarctica. In January of 1988 an Argentine naval vessel carrying paying tourists ran aground off the coast of Antarctica, spilling 250,000 gallons of fuel, damaging rookeries of 24,000 penguins. A less dramatic type of damage is the disruption of wildlife when ecotour operators get too close to their habitat. The Virginia EcoTourism Association suggests that educating tour operators is the first step in preventing this type of damage. To that end, they are in the process of developing a guide certification system.

Technology on Travel Services

As yet, the Internet has had little impact on travel distribution methods, in part because there is not yet an easy way for customers or agents to access all the necessary information through one avenue. Therefore, the telephone still remains the preferred channel. However, the newly created Open Travel Alliance, an industry group comprising air, car, hotel, and travel agent industry representatives, is trying to change this by creating an industry-wide information standard, called the Open Travel Initiative. The goal is to create and promote electronic commerce standards that improve information exchange among travel suppliers, distributors, and consumers. The group's proposal to create a multichannel distribution system would allow customers and travel agents to differentiate among alternatives. Such a system could make it easier for travel suppliers that are more environmentally aware to promote their policies, for travel agents to sell products, and for consumers to access those suppliers directly.

Initiatives such as these signify that although the growth of the Internet has not had a significant impact on the tourism industry thus far, it has begun to change the relationships among travel agents, suppliers, and consumers, and has the potential to have an even larger effect. In fact, the president of the U.S. Tour Operators Association noted that almost all relationships among suppliers, tour operators, travel agents, and tourists in the future will be electronic.

Some industry analysts feel that the emergence of the Internet will lead to a shrinking role for intermediaries. For example, the sophistication of information technology has already begun to allow tourists to bypass the travel agent. In 1976, 40% of airline tickets issued in the United States were written by travel agents; by 1985 this amount had increased to 80%, due in part to the increased competition and more complex fare structure created by the Airline Deregulation Act of 1978. However, the rapid growth of the Internet has allowed and encouraged more prospective travellers to interact with airlines directly. An example of this is the ability of travellers to purchase tickets online ("ticketless travel"). Southwest Airlines now sells most of their tickets without the use of travel agents.

Bibliography

Altinkilinc, M., "Simulation-based layout planning of a production plant," In *Proceedings of the 2004 Winter Simulation Conference*, ed. R. G. Ingalls, 2004.

Armour, G. C. and E. S. Buffa, A heuristic algorithm and simulation approach to the relative location of facilities. *Management Science* 9(2): 249-309, 1963.

Butler, R.W., "Tourism, environment and sustainable development", *Environmental Conservation* 18 (3): 201–209, 1991.

Castillo, I. and B. A. Peters, "Unit load and materialhandling considerations in facility layout design", *International Journal of Production Research,* 40(13 Sep 10): 2955-2989, 2002.

Cater, E., "Sustainable tourism in the third world: Problem for sustainable tourism development", *Tourism Management* 14 (2): 83–93, 1993.

Eagles, P., "The travel motivations of Canadian ecotourists", *Journal Of Travel Research* 31 (2): 3–13, 1992.

Hamamoto, S., Y. Yih and G. Salvendy, "Development and validation of genetic algorithm-based facility layout- a case study in the pharmaceutical industry", *International Journal of Production Research* 37(4 Mar 10): 749-768, 1999.

Hassan, S. S., "Determinants of market competitiveness in an environmentally sustainable tourism industry", *Journal of Travel Research* 38 (3): 239–246, 2000.

Huq, F., D. A. Hensler and Z. M. Mohamed, "A simulation analysis of factors influencing the flow time and through-put performance of functional and cellular layouts" *Integrated Manufacturing Systems* 12(4): 285-295, 2001.

Lee, R. C. and J. M. Moore, "Corelap- computerized relationship layout planning", *Journal of Industrial Engineering* 18(3): 195-200, 1967.

Morris, J. S. and R. J. Tersine 1994. A simulation comparison of process and cellular layouts in a dual resource constrained environment. *Computers & Industrial Engineering* 26(4): 733-741.

Pandey, P. C., S. Janewithayapun and M. A. A. Hasin, "An integrated system for capacity planning and facility layout", *Production Planning & Control* 11(8): 742-753, 2000.

Ranky, P. G., L. C. Morales and R. J. Caudill, "Lean disassembly line layout, and network simulation models", *IEEE International Symposium on Electronics and the Environment*: 36-41, 2003.

Scarlat, C., "Developing marketing strategies for the hospitality industry", In *Research in business management*, (eds.) L. Sandovici and C., 2001.

Tompkins, J. A. and R. J. Reed, "An applied model for the facilities design problem", *International Journal of Production Research* 14(5): 583-595, 1973.

World Wildlife Fund., "Tourism certification schemes still leave much to be desired," Http://www.wwf-uk.orgnewsn_0000000132.asp., 2000.

Index